Washington, D.C.

FODOR'S TRAVEL PUBLICATIONS

are compiled, researched, and edited by an international team of travel writers, field correspondents, and editors. The series, which now almost covers the globe, was founded by Eugene Fodor in 1936.

OFFICES
New York & London

Fodor's Washington, D.C.

Editors: Andrew Beresky, Candice Gianetti
Area Editors: Betty Ross, Ralph Danford, Dorothy MacKinnon
Contributing Editors: Stephen Brewer; Ervin S. Duggan; Tom Kelly; John F. McLeod; Ben J. Wattenberg
Maps: Pictograph
Photographs: Friends of the National Zoo, John F. Kennedy Center for the Performing Arts, National Air and Space Museum, National Gallery of Art, Smithsonian Institution, U.S. Department of the Interior, Washington, D.C. Convention and Visitors Association, Washington Metropolitan Area Transit Authority, Bob Willis, Virginia State Travel Service
Illustrations: Ted Burwell, Sandra Lang
Cover Photograph: Steve Weber/UniPhoto

Cover Design: Vignelli Associates

Fodor's 89

Washington, D.C.

FODOR'S TRAVEL PUBLICATIONS, INC.
New York & London

MANUFACTURED IN THE UNITED STATES OF AMERICA
10 9 8 7 6 5 4 3 2 1

CONTENTS

FOREWORD   vii

Map of Washington, D.C. Area, viii–ix

FACTS AT YOUR FINGERTIPS

Facts and Figures, 1; Tourist Information, 1; What It Will Cost, 2; Tips for British Visitors, 2; When to Go, 3; How to Get There, 4; Hints to the Motorist, 5; Accommodations, 5; Bed and Breakfast, 7; Hostels, 7; Camping, 7; Senior Citizen and Student Discounts, 8; Tipping, 8; Business Hours and Local Time, 8; Drinking Laws, 9; Sports, 9; Hints to Disabled Travelers, 9; Security, 10; Telephones, 10; Emergency Numbers, 11; Recommended Reading, 11; Conversion Charts, 12

THE WASHINGTON SCENE

INTRODUCTION—The New Washington—and the New America   15

THE FEDERAL GOVERNMENT—How Our System Works   21

THE CEREMONIAL CITY—Washington's History   27

THE WASHINGTON WAY OF LIFE—Capital Living   40

EXPLORING WASHINGTON, D.C., AND ENVIRONS

EXPLORING WASHINGTON—Monuments, Museums, and Parks   49
     Plan of Downtown Washington, 52–53
     Orientation Map of Washington, D.C., 56–57
     Plan of the Federal Triangle—Mall—Capitol Hill Area, 61
     Plan of Georgetown, 73

A SIDE TRIP TO VIRGINIA—Arlington and Alexandria   79
     Map of Arlington, 82
     Plan of Alexandria, 86

**PRACTICAL INFORMATION FOR
THE WASHINGTON AREA**   93
   Hotels and Motels, 93
   Dining Out, 103
   How to Get Around, 124
     Map of Washington Metro Lines, 126
   Getting to Arlington and Alexandria, 127
   Tourist Information Services, 127
   Seasonal Events, 128
   Tours, 130
   Special-Interest Tours, 131
   Gardens, 132
   Children's Activities, 133
   The National Zoo, 139
   The Great Outdoors, 139
   Summer Sports, 140
   Winter Sports, 140
   Spectator Sports, 140
   Historic Sites, 141
   Architecture, 146
   Famous Libraries, 147
   Notable Churches, 147
   Museums and Galleries, 149
   Historic Homes, 156
   Movies, 159
   Music, 160
   Stage and Revues, 162
   Shopping, 163
   Nightlife and Bars, 172
   Wine Bars, 181

INDEX   183

FOREWORD

Washington, D.C. is more than a city. It is a scapegoat and an icon of hope; it is our symbol of Democracy. From its earliest years Washington has attracted critics and travelers drawn by the symbol as much as the reality. It is often maligned by those whose views differ from the political party currently in power; but those who actually visit Washington learn to separate the city from the politics and become enchanted by it.

We believe that Washington is unique among American cities. Most visitors who stay only a day or two later regret they didn't plan to spend a week or more. Once in Washington, they soon discover there is more to see than the domes, spires, parks, and tree-lined avenues they saw in their travel brochures and viewed from their airplane window.

Washington is a vibrant city that has something to offer everybody. You can visit it on a shoestring budget, eating in government cafeterias and staying in a youth hostel or an inexpensive motel. Practically none of the city's great attractions—the museums, galleries, and shrines—charge admission. And nowhere in the world is there more free entertainment. You can also visit Washington in a kingly fashion, staying in any of a wide variety of deluxe hotels, dining in the finest of restaurants, and enjoying glittering entertainment. The choice is yours.

While every care has been taken to ensure the accuracy of the information contained in this guide, the publishers cannot accept responsibility for any errors that may appear.

All prices quoted in this guide are based on those available to us at the time of writing. In a world of rapid change, however, the possibility of inaccurate or out-of-date information can never be totally eliminated. We trust, therefore, that you will take prices quoted as indicators only, and will double-check to be sure of the latest figures.

Similarly, be sure to check all opening times of museums and galleries. We have found that such times are liable to change without notice, and you could easily make a trip only to find a locked door.

When a hotel closes or a restaurant produces a disappointing meal, let us know, and we will investigate the establishment and the complaint. We are always ready to revise our entries for the following year's edition should the facts warrant it.

Send your letters to the editors of Fodor's Travel Publications, 201 E. 50th Street, New York, NY 10022, or 30–32 Bedford Square, London WC1B 3SG, England.

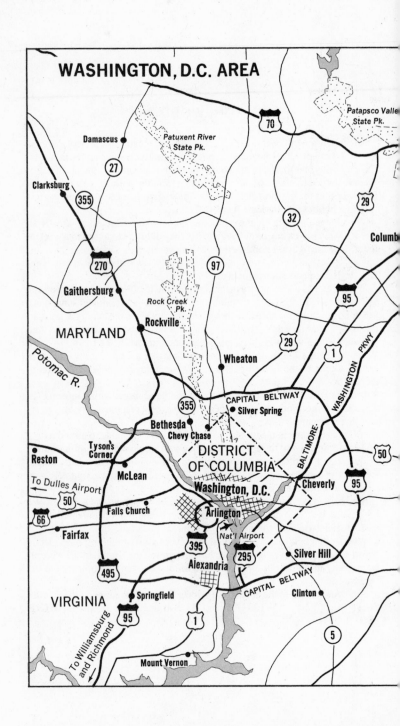

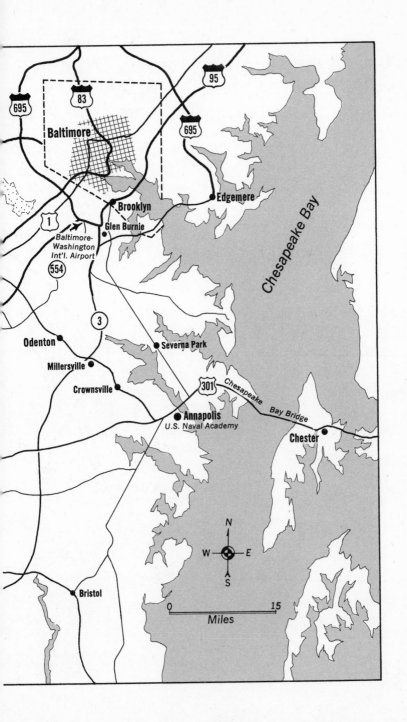

FACTS AT YOUR FINGERTIPS

FACTS AT YOUR FINGERTIPS

FACTS AND FIGURES. Washington, D.C. became the nation's capital on December 1, 1800. The name is derived from George Washington and Christopher Columbus. The District's motto: *Justicia Omnibus* (Justice to all). Although the District of Columbia was originally a square 10 miles on a side, the Congress in 1845 returned to Virginia its portion, so the present area of the District is only 69 square miles. The land is generally flat, though with a series of escarpments rising from the river level. The two best-known high spots are Jenkins Hill and Mount St. Alban, one crowned by the Capitol, the other by the National Cathedral. The population of the District of Columbia is now 626,489, down from 1970. The population of the Greater Washington area, including the suburbs in Maryland and Virginia, is 4.4 million people. The center of the city is filled largely with monumental architecture and ceremonial spaces. The chief industry is administration, the voluminous production of words—spoken, on paper, and in computers—for the governing of 243 million (1988 estimate).

The Potomac River runs from northwest to southeast through the heart of Washington, emptying into the Chesapeake Bay. Arlington and Alexandria, Virginia, lie to the west of the city, and Maryland lies to the north and east. As Washington is low-lying and between two rivers, the Potomac and the Anacostia, the climate is humid year-round, often oppressive in summer, chilly in winter. Spring is the best season, and the most popular with tourists. Fall weather is generally fine, and tourists have fewer lines to contend with.

TOURIST INFORMATION. Information on what to do and see in Washington may be obtained from the *Washington Convention and Visitors Association,* 1575 I St., N.W., Washington, DC 20005, (202) 789–7000. However, should your plans encompass an area beyond that of metropolitan Washington, write to the *Maryland Department of Economic and Community Development,* Office of Tourist Development, 45 Calvert St., Annapolis, MD 21401; (301) 269–3517. They will send you free an attractive, illustrated guide to Maryland covering the western, central, and southern parts of the state, Annapolis, Baltimore, the upper Chesapeake region, the southern Eastern Shore, and Maryland forest and park facilities. It is detailed and extremely helpful. Included with this guide is the official highway map of Maryland, as well as a guide to outdoor recreation and campgrounds and a calendar of events. Should a trip to Virginia be part of your itinerary, write to the *Virginia Division of Tourism,* 202 N. Ninth St., Suite 500, Richmond, VA 23219; (804) 786–4484. The packet of material they will send you includes pamphlets on some of the most historic and delightful places in Virginia—Williamsburg, Assateague, Chincoteague National Wildlife Refuge, Stratford Hall Plantation, Monticello, Richmond, and Virginia Beach. One pamphlet covers the historic homes in Virginia, another the sights of Richmond, including its outstanding Virginia Museum. An official highway map of Virginia will

1

be sent, as well as a book on Virginia State Parks. Other sources of information: *Alexandria Tourist Council,* 221 King St., Alexandria, VA 22314 (703) 549–0205; and *Arlington Visitors Center,* 735 18th St., S. Arlington, VA 22202 (703) 521–0772.

WHAT IT WILL COST. Costs vary greatly in the Washington area. Motels several miles from the city will obviously be much cheaper than those in downtown Washington. You can pay $50 for a double in a suburban motel and $80 for a double in a motel of the same chain in the city. In the city of Washington, moreover, you can be charged $6–$7 in your hotel for a breakfast that might cost no more than $4 in a restaurant just around the corner. For this reason the cost estimates are given within a range. Two people can travel in the D.C. region for about $140 a day (not counting gasoline or other transportation costs).

Sales tax in D.C. is 6 percent, in Maryland, 5, and in Virginia, 4.

Budget Tips. You can cut expenses by traveling off-season, when some hotel rates are lower. The budget-minded traveler can also find bargain accommodations at guest houses, tourist homes, hostels, or YMCAs and YWCAs. Some state and federal parks also provide inexpensive lodging.

There are no admission charges to the great tourist attractions—the Smithsonian Institution, the Archives, the Lincoln Memorial, or even the National Zoo (although the zoo does have pay parking). The National Capital Parks Administration has even abolished the 10-cent charge it once asked for riding the Washington Monument elevator.

After lodging, your next-biggest expense will be food, and here you can make very substantial cuts if you are willing to eat only one meal a day in a restaurant. Plan to eat simply and to picnic. The Washington area is well equipped with picnic and rest areas, often in scenic spots, such as Rock Creek Park, or at parks beside the historic Potomac River. Washingtonians themselves are great picnickers.

TIPS FOR BRITISH VISITORS. Passports. You will need a valid passport and a U.S. Visa (which can only be put in a passport of the 10-year kind). You can obtain the visa either through your travel agent, or directly from the *United States Embassy,* Visa and Immigration Department, 24 Grosvenor Sq., London W1A 2JB (01–499–3443). Note that the embassy no longer accepts visa applications made in person.

No vaccinations are required for entry into the U.S.

Customs. If you are 21 or over, you can take into the U.S. 200 cigarettes, 50 cigars or three pounds of tobacco; one U.S. quart of alcohol; duty-free gifts to a value of $100. Be careful not to try to take in meat or meat products, seeds, plants, fruits, etc. Avoid narcotics like the plague. Returning to Britain, you may bring home (1) 200 cigarettes or 100 cigarillos or 50 cigars or 250 grams of tobacco; (2) two liters of table wine and, in addition, (a) one liter of alcohol over 22% by volume (most spirits), (b) two liters of alcohol under 22% by volume (fortified or sparkling wine), or (c) two more liters of table wine; (3) 50 grams of perfume and ¼ liter of toilet water; and (4) other goods up to a value of £32.

Insurance. We heartily recommend that you insure yourself to cover health and motoring mishaps, with *Europ Assistance,* 252 High St., Croydon CRO 1NF (tel. 01–680 1234). Their excellent service is all the more valuable when you consider the possible costs of health care in the U.S.

Tour Operators. The price battle that has raged over transatlantic fares has meant that most tour operators now offer excellent holidays in the U.S. Among those who service Washington, D.C. are:

American Connection, 294 Hight St., Slough, Berks SL1 1NB (0753–692525).

North American Vacations, 3 Price St., Hebburn, Tyne and Wear NE31 1D2 (0632–836226).

Poundstretcher, Airlink House, Hazelwick Ave., Three Bridges, Sussex RH10 1YS (0293–548241).

Premier Holidays America, Westbrook, Milton Rd., Cambridgeshire CB4 1YQ (0223–355977).

Saga Holidays, Enbrook House, Sandgate Rd., Folkestone, Kent CT20 3SG (0303–47000).

Speedbird, Alta House, 152 King St., London W6 OQU (01–7418041).

Superbreaks Ltd., Grosvenor Hall, Bolnore Rd., Haywards Heath, West Sussex RH16 4BX (0444–414122).

Travellers Jetways, 93 Newman St., London W1P 3LE (01–637–5444).

Airfares. We suggest that you explore the current scene for budget flight possibilities. All the main transatlantic carriers have standby tickets, available a short time before the flight only, as well as APEX and other fares at a considerable saving over the full price. Quite frankly, only business travelers who don't have to watch the price of their tickets fly full-price these days—and find themselves sitting right beside an APEX passenger! At press time, the roundtrip APEX fare to Washington cost from £353. Check out the small ads in daily and Sunday newspapers for last minute, low-cost flights; prices are from £299.

Electricity. 110 volts. You should take along an adapter since American razor and hair-dryer sockets require flat two-pronged plugs.

WHEN TO GO. The very best season to visit Washington is autumn, after Labor Day to mid-November. The weather is generally delightful and the heavy family vacation season is over. The National Capital Parks' battalion of gardeners see that chrysanthemums and other seasonal plants replace the earlier blooms.

Washington can be very hot and humid in the summer. Indeed, according to legend, Washington was long considered a "tropical hardship post" by certain European countries, and their diplomats were paid a bonus to go there. In these days of air conditioning, however, there is little difference between Washington and most other major North American cities in the summer. Washington's many trees and parks indeed give a feel of leafy coolness to much of the city.

Winters are generally moderate. It's something of a joke to visitors from other parts of the country how the occasional light snowfall can bring traffic to a near-halt. Heavy snowfalls, however, are not unknown.

Spring finds Washington at its most beautiful, but the city is very crowded with school children on field trips, conventioneers, and camera-toting tourists. The famous cherry blossoms come into bloom in early April, preceded by tulip-tree magnolias and followed by crab apples, dogwood, azaleas, wisteria, and tulips by the thousand.

The chart below will give you an idea of what to expect temperature-wise throughout the year.

	Jan.	Feb.	Mar.	Apr.	May	June	July	Aug.	Sept.	Oct.	Nov.	Dec.
Normal High	42.6	44.4	53.0	64.2	74.9	82.8	86.8	84.4	78.4	67.5	55.1	44.8
Normal Low	27.4	28.0	35.0	44.2	54.5	63.4	68.0	66.1	59.6	48.0	37.9	29.8
Mean Temp.	35.0	36.2	44.0	54.2	64.7	73.1	77.4	75.3	69.0	57.8	46.5	37.3

Rainfall is evenly distributed throughout the year.

Washington has a rich array of seasonal events, from the Kite Flying Contest, National Cherry Blossom Festival, and White House Easter Egg Roll in the spring through the July 4th fireworks display and the Smithsonian Festival of American Folklife on the Mall, and the Pageant of Peace, which begins with the lighting of the nation's Christmas tree in mid-December on the Ellipse, near the White House. Many think the city's biggest attraction is the Congress, when it's in session. Somehow the city is less vibrant when Congress is in recess, as it is over Christmas, Easter, and other key holiday periods.

HOW TO GET THERE. By plane: Washington National Airport handles most of the city's domestic traffic and is accessible by the Metro subway. *TWA, United,* and *Eastern* are among the long-distance carriers serving the airport, and the short hops are flown by *US Air, Piedmont, Pan Am,* and *Continental.* Cab fare to downtown is approximately $8; to the Maryland suburbs, $16–18; to the Virginia suburbs, $10–15. (Be sure to get into a D.C. cab for D.C. destinations and a Virginia cab for suburban destinations; tell the driver in advance that you want a receipt. Groups pay only $1 extra per passenger no matter how many different drop-off points you request.)

Washington Dulles International Airport, 25 miles away west in Virginia, serves the wide-bodied jets for long-distance flights both domestic and international, as well as short hops flown by *Delta, Braniff,* and *Continental.* Cab fare to downtown is approximately $30. Washington is also served by Baltimore-Washington International (BWI), a $40-plus taxi ride (there is also an Amtrak station on the edge of the airport). The *Washington Flyer* (202/685–1400) offers daily continuous bus service to all three airports (20 minutes and $5 downtown from National; 35 minutes and $12 from Dulles; 45–50 minutes and $12 from BWI).

By train: Washington is well served by *Amtrak,* which is headquartered here. Amtrak's plush Metroliner from New York to Washington boasts travel times as short as two hours and 49 minutes, but is frequently late. Those on a tight schedule may wish to fly, unless the weather is poor. Trains leave from the historic and newly renovated Union Station, Massachusetts Ave. and North Capitol St., near the Capitol Building.

By bus: Washington is a major terminal for *Greyhound/Trailways.* The terminal is at First and L Sts., N.E. (3 blocks north of Union Station), tel. (301) 565–2662.

By Car: I-95 is the major access route from north or south; 270 enters the city from the northwest coming from Hagerstown and Frederick, Maryland. If you are on the eastern shore of the Chesapeake, take US 50 over the toll bridge, through Annapolis and into Washington. The Beltway, I-495, encircles the city for 60 miles. Motorists unaccustomed to

four-lane high-speed driving with exits and access roads at frequent intervals should use extreme care in negotiating this dangerous stretch of highway.

HINTS TO THE MOTORIST. Even in the nation's most densely populated areas, there are interstate highways conducive to high-speed driving.
Nevertheless, Washington, D.C.'s neighbor states of Maryland and Virginia strictly observe the 55 mph speed limit and show reduced accident
statistics to justify doing so. Both states use sophisticated speed detection
devices, including radar and aircraft. (But radar detectors are illegal in
Virginia.)

As in most East Coast metropolitan areas, traffic around Washington
is consistently, sometimes alarmingly, heavy. Moreover, the nation's capital is a city of commuters and enjoys some particularly slow-moving rush
hours. Congestion is especially common on the bridges over the Potomac—from the six-lane I-95 span to the southeast, to the downtown cluster of bridges between 14th Street and Key Bridge, all the way northwest
to the Cabin John bridge carrying eight lanes of I-495 over the river. Traffic is also heavy, day and night, on the Beltway, as the loop of six- to eight-
lane superhighway around the city is known (the eastern half is designated
I-95, the western half I-495). Major approaches to the city include I-95,
U.S. 29, Connecticut Avenue, and the Baltimore-Washington Parkway
(which feeds into New York Avenue) from the north; U.S. 50, Pennsylvania Avenue and Branch Avenue from the east and southeast; I-395 from
the south, U.S. 50, I-66 and the George Washington Memorial Parkway
from the west.

Weekday parking in town is often either difficult or expensive, but rarely
both (commercial lots start at about $6.50 for three hours in the downtown
business district and range up to more than $12 at some of the newer luxu-
ry hotels and in Georgetown). On weekends and after 6:30 P.M. weekdays,
most on-street parking regulations and meter-feeding rules are suspended
and parking becomes less of an adventure (except in Georgetown).

If you'd like to (or have to) leave your own car at home, all major car
rental agencies can be found at any of the three nearby airports as well
as in the downtown hotel/business district, at Union Station, and in such
high-density suburban communities as Bethesda, Silver Spring, College
Park, Arlington, Alexandria, and Fairfax.

ACCOMMODATIONS. Tourism is big business in Washington—the
second biggest employer, after government. An estimated 15 million people visit the capital each year, so even with 48,000 hotel and motel rooms
in the metropolitan area, and new accommodations opening every month,
it's hard to keep up with demand at certain times of the year.

The best time to find a room in downtown hotels is on the weekend,
because business travelers and conventioneers are generally out of the city
by then. In fact, many hotels and motels offer especially low weekend
rates. For example, certain deluxe hotels that charge $95 to $150 for dou-
bles midweek charge as little as $40 a night on weekends. And hotels and
transportation companies often put together attractive weekend package
holidays that include extras such as sightseeing and Sunday brunch. The
Washington Hotel Association (833–3350) publishes a yearly brochure on
such rates and package deals.

Although summer is traditionally the peak travel time for families, summer is a slow season for business travelers in Washington. Hotels are busiest in the spring and fall, and reservations are especially heavy in April, when the cherry trees are in full blossom and the summer heat has not descended.

Armed with the knowledge that hotels and motels have their heaviest occupancy rate in the spring and fall, and from Monday through Thursday, the knowledgeable traveler can do a certain amount of negotiating on rates. At the very least, when you are quoted a price for a room, assume that the reservations desk is quoting a price at the high end of the scale. Never hesitate to ask if they have anything at a lower price, or if they have weekend specials or family rates. Many hotels and motels charge reduced family rates, even midweek, and in some there is no charge for children.

It's difficult to rate some of the older hotels within the city proper, because the size and quality of the rooms vary so widely. One historic hotel, famous for its deluxe suites, has other rooms that are minuscule, and sometimes face air shafts. (Ask to see a room before you agree to take it.) For this and other reasons, including the occasional expense of parking your car (not every hotel provides free parking), many visitors, particularly those with autos, prefer to stay in the suburbs.

Of course, you can get to know a city better by staying right in it. And it is certainly worth a few extra dollars to be within a few minutes' walk of what, after all, you came to see—be it the White House, the Smithsonian, the Kennedy Center, or the National Zoo. And the city itself is where the action is for theater and a varied nightlife.

More and more hotels are being constructed and opening near the new Convention Center. The brand-new Grand Hyatt is right across the street (at 1000 H St., N.W.) and the tiny Henley Park Hotel is very close. Several other hotels are just blocks away (among them the new J.W. Marriott Hotel, Hyatt Regency, the Vista International, the Washington Plaza, the Gramercy Hotel, and the Capital Hilton).

One important question many tourists ask is: Where is it most safe to stay? A sad fact is that no city is immune to crime, though on a crimes-per-capita basis Washington is far less crime-ridden than many other major U.S. cities.

In one sense, a mid-city hotel may be safer than an outlying motel: city hotels are simply more security conscious, take more precautions, and maintain professional security staffs.

Naturally, some parts of a city are safer than others. And it is especially important to take precautions at night in some of the less savory neighborhoods. The personnel at your own hotel can warn you about which areas may be unsafe.

A new and continuing development in the Washington area is conversion of apartment houses into hotels. At least a dozen in Washington offer kitchens and living-lounge areas in addition to sleeping space. Some are bargains by any standard, others are good buys only in that they give you more space. Depending on the location, season, and day, prices may range from $40 to well over $100 a day for family occupancy.

Hotels and motels—listed later in this guide—are divided into five categories, based on price but also taking into consideration the degree of comfort you can expect to enjoy, the amount of service you can anticipate, and the atmosphere that will surround you in the establishment of your choice. Our ratings are flexible and subject to change.

We should also point out that limitations of space make it impossible to include every establishment. We have, therefore, listed those which we recommend as the best within each price range.

BED AND BREAKFAST. The bed-and-breakfast concept is relatively new to the United States although many families have opened their homes to visitors in Europe and Great Britain for decades. If you are interested in finding out about such accommodations in the Washington D.C. area, there are a number of local bed-and-breakfast services, including: *Bed & Breakfast League,* 3639 Van Ness St., N.W., Washington, DC 20008 (202–363–7767); *Bed & Breakfast Ltd.,* Box 12011, Washington, DC 20005 (202–328–3510): *Sweet Dreams & Toast Inc.,* Box 4835–0035, Washington, DC 20008 (202–483–9191) and, for homes in the Alexandria area, *E.J. Mansmann,* 819 Prince St., Alexandria, VA 22314 (703–683–2159).

HOSTELS. Because of the great size of the U.S. and the distances involved, youth hostels have not developed here the way they have in Europe and Japan. Although their members are mainly younger people, there is no age limit. You must be a member to use youth hostels; write to *American Youth Hostels, Inc.,* 1017 K St. N.W., Washington, DC 20005 (202) 783–4943. A copy of the *Hotel Guide and Handbook* will be included in your membership. Accommodations are simple, dormitories are segregated by sex, common rooms and kitchen are shared, and everyone helps with the clean-up. Lights out 11 P.M. to 7 A.M., no alcohol or illegal drugs allowed. Membership fees: $20. Hostel rates vary from $4 to $10 per person per night. In season it is wise to reserve ahead; write or phone directly to the particular hostel you plan to stay in. The *Washington International Hostel,* which opened in August 1987, is in a renovated building at 1009 11th St., N.W. (202) 737–2333. With 260 beds going for $10 each a night, it's now the largest hostel in the U.S.

CAMPING. There are no tent or trailer parking areas within the District of Columbia. The nearest, however, is in Greenbelt National Park, 12 miles northeast and just off the Baltimore-Washington Parkway, and at Cedarville, near Brandywine, 20 miles from the District off U.S. 301. In Virginia, 20 miles southwest on Va. 123, is Burke Lake, and 32 miles south, off Va. 619, is Prince William Forest Park. All are open to campers year-round. Write the state travel offices of Maryland, Virginia, and West Virginia for lists of state park facilities. There is also camping in the Shenandoah National Park from April through October.

Useful Addresses: *National Park Service,* U.S. Department of the Interior, Washington, DC 20025; *National Forest Service,* U.S. Department of Agriculture, Washington, DC 20025. For information on state parks, write *State Parks Department,* State Office Building in the capital of the state in which you are interested.

The National Campers & Hikers Assoc., Box 451, Orange, NJ 07051. Commercial camping organizations include *American Camping Assoc., Inc.,* Bradford Woods, Martinsville, IN 46151, and *Camping Council,* 17

E. 48th St., New York, NY 10017. Also *Kampgrounds of America, Inc.,*
P.O. Box 30558, Billings, MT 59114.

SENIOR CITIZEN AND STUDENT DISCOUNTS. Some attractions
throughout the city and suburbs offer considerable discounts to senior citizens and students. However, it is difficult to generalize as to who is eligible
to receive such discounts. The best bet is to carry your Senior Citizen iden-
tification card with you and be prepared to show it at the movie or theater
box office if proof of age is required. Sometimes you need only state that
you are a senior citizen; at other times you must show a driver's license
or passport. Students should carry with them at all times a high school
or college ID, an international student traveler card, or a driver's license.

TIPPING. The going rate on restaurant service is 15 percent on the
amount before taxes. Tipping at counters is not universal, but many people
leave 25 cents on anything up to $1 and 10 percent on anything over that.
For bellboys, 50 cents per bag is usual. However, if you load him down
with all manner of bags, cameras, coats, etc., you might consider giving
quite a bit extra. At the end of your stay in hotels and motels you should
leave the maid $1.25–$1.50 per day, or $7 per person per week for multiple
occupancy. If you are staying at an American Plan hostelry (meals included), $1.50 per day per person for the waiter or waitress is considered suffi-
cient and is left at the end of your stay. However, if you have been surrounded by an army of servants (one bringing relishes, another rolls, etc.),
add a few extra dollars and give the lump sum to the captain or maître
d'hôtel when you leave, asking him to allocate it.

Give 15 percent on taxi fares. Bus porters are tipped 25 cents per bag,
drivers nothing. On charters and package tours, conductors and drivers
usually get $5–$10 per day from the group as a whole, but be sure to ask
whether this has already been figured into the package cost. On short local
sightseeing runs, the driver-guide may get 25 cents per person, more if
you think he has been especially helpful or personable. Airport bus drivers,
nothing. Redcaps, 50 cents per suitcase. Tipping at curbside check-in is
unofficial, but same as above.

BUSINESS HOURS AND LOCAL TIME. The Washington, D.C. area,
like the rest of America, is on Standard Time from the last Sunday in October until the last Sunday in April. Many of the government offices have
staggered work hours in order to avoid traffic congestion, but most businesses, including the Federal Government, carry on a five-day, 40-hour
work week, with 9 A.M. to 5 P.M. the most common work hours. Lunch
hours are generally from 12 noon to 1 P.M. or 1 to 2 P.M. Most downtown
department stores are open late on Monday, Thursday, and Friday evenings. Those located in suburban shopping malls are usually open Monday
to Friday until 9:30 P.M. Few of them open before 10 A.M. Most grocery
stores are open seven days a week from 8 A.M. to 9 P.M., with shorter hours
on Sunday evening.

Holidays. Most businesses and banks will be closed the following holi-
days: New Year's Day, January 1; Washington's Birthday (observance),
February 15; Easter Sunday; Memorial Day; Independence Day; Labor
Day; Thanksgiving Day; Christmas Day.

In addition, banks and some businesses may be closed on Martin Luther King, Jr. Day, January 18; Lincoln's Birthday, February 12; Good Friday (from noon); Columbus Day; Election Day (partially) in November; Veteran's Day, November 11.

On Washington's birthday, most of the department stores as well as smaller stores have tremendous sales, which attract great enthusiasm among the ardent bargain-hunters. A great deal is made of the Cherry Blossom Festival, usually held the last week in March, with parades, dances, and the crowning of a Cherry Blossom Princess. However, much to the chagrin of the promoters, the blossoming of the cherry trees does not always coincide with the celebration of the Festival. Perhaps the best-attended annual event is the dramatic display of fireworks on the Mall on the Fourth of July. Free concerts, special Smithsonian museum events, and family picnics precede this colorful display. Every four years in January the inauguration of a new President is the excuse for days of elaborate social activities, from formal receptions to balls to the Inaugural Parade.

DRINKING LAWS. Liquor is sold in package stores 9 A.M.–9 P.M. Monday–Thursday, until 10 P.M. Friday, until midnight on Saturday, never on Sunday. In restaurants it is served 8 A.M.–2 A.M. Monday–Thursday; 8 A.M.–3 A.M., Friday and Saturday; 10 A.M.–2 A.M., Sunday. The legal drinking age is 21, but those under 21 born before Sept. 30, 1968, can buy and consume beer and wine only. Proof of age in the form of a driver's license is usually required.

SPORTS. For major league *baseball,* Washingtonians must travel to nearby Baltimore to see the Orioles. However, the nation's capital has just about every other sport, from *polo* (played on grounds near the Lincoln Memorial, most Sundays from May through July and September through October) to a *boomerang* tournament (on the Mall in early May). There are 1,000 *tennis* courts listed in the *Washington Tennis Guide* with an impressive number of courts in Rock Creek Park at 16th and Kennedy Sts., N.W. You're likely to see at least 1,000 *joggers* at any given time along the C&O Canal, Rock Creek Parkway, and in East Potomac Park. There are professional *basketball, football,* and *hockey* events. The Potomac River has been cleaned up enough (from its once polluted state) for *fishing* and *boating,* and the Chesapeake Bay, within an hour's drive to the east, is a paradise for these pursuits.

HINTS TO DISABLED TRAVELERS. Important sources of information in this field are: The *Travel Information Center,* Moss Rehabilitation Hospital, 12th St. and Tabor Rd., Philadelphia, PA 19141, and *Easter Seal Society for Crippled Children and Adults,* Director of Education and Information Service, 2023 W. Ogden Ave., Chicago, IL 60612. Many of the nation's national parks have special facilities for the handicapped. These are described in *National Park Guide for the Handicapped,* available from the U.S. Government Printing Office, Washington, DC 20402. TWA publishes a free 12-page pamphlet entitled *Consumer Information about Air Travel for the Handicapped,* which explains available arrangements and how to get them. Facilities for rail passengers are noted in *Access Amtrak,* available from Amtrak Passenger Relations, 400 North Capitol St., N.W., Washington, DC 20001. Other publications giving valuable information about facilities for the handicapped are: the book *Access to the World,* by Louise Weiss, published by Henry Holt & Co. and available by order from your local bookstore. (Holt will not accept orders from individuals.) *The Wheelchair Traveler,* by Douglass R. Annand, Ball Hill Rd., Milford, NH 03055, is no longer being annually revised, but the author will supply copies of the relevant portions if you write to him about where you will be traveling. For a copy of the *Handicapped Driver's Mobility Guide,* contact your local AAA (stock #3772). It costs about $1.

Access Tours specializes in travel arrangements for the handicapped. You can join one of their groups or, with four or more people, form your own and travel just about anywhere in the world. You can reach them at Suite 1801, 123–33 83rd Ave., Kew Gardens, NY 11415; 718–263–3835 or 800–533–5343.

The following guides have been published specifically for handicapped travelers visiting Washington:

The Deaf Person's Quick Guide to Washington. Available free from the Martin Luther King Memorial Library, 901 G St., N.W.

A Tactile and Large Print Atlas of Greater Washington, D.C. by Margaret Rockwell and Joseph Widel.

SECURITY. Washington can be a disarming city in that its noble architecture and clean streets make it appear safer and more pristine than it really is. Although there are many fine hotels northeast of Scott Circle, once past 15th Street the neighborhoods start to become a bit seamy. As in most other places in the world these days, don't leave money or valuables in your hotel room—no matter what part of town you stay in. Be sure always to lock your door—even when you are inside. For valuables, use the safe-deposit boxes offered by hotels; they are usually free.

Carry most of your funds in traveler's checks, and be sure to record the numbers in a separate, secure place. When using a charge card, make a point of returning it to your purse or wallet immediately after use. It is also wise to tear up the carbons after you sign your charge receipt. Watch your purse or wallet, especially on the 14th St. "strip" between H St. and Thomas Circle—an area heavily populated by prostitutes and pickpockets. Never leave your car unlocked, and don't keep valuable articles in plain sight in the car even when it is locked.

Women should be especially careful of their purses when dining in restaurants. Instead of slinging your purse over the back of your chair, place it in your lap or under the table between your feet.

Try to avoid walking in sparsely populated areas at night. It is wise to avoid many areas of southeast Washington—particularly the area around the Anacostia River, which is among Washington's most crime-ridden. Washington is in many ways a commuter city, so remember that some of the most bustling areas at noon time can turn into ghost towns after 6 in the evening.

It isn't hard to have a safe vacation in Washington, D.C.—but it would be a shame to spoil a pleasant stay because of a little carelessness.

TELEPHONES. The area code for the District of Columbia is 202; for Maryland, 301; and for Virginia, 703 (for the northern part of the state). Calls made within the greater metropolitan area do not necessitate using the area code before the number. For assistance from the operator on person-to-person, credit-card, and collect calls dial "0" first. Pay telephones require 25 cents in D.C., Maryland, and Virginia. For information or directory assistance, dial 411.

EMERGENCY NUMBERS. In the Washington, D.C. area, the proper emergency number for fire, police, ambulance, and paramedics is 911. Or dial "O" for Operator and ask for help in connecting you immediately with the appropriate agency. The non-emergency police service number is 727–4326. For other emergency numbers see the first page of the telephone directory.

For the Poison Control Center, dial 625–3333.

RECOMMENDED READING. There are hundreds of books, fact and fiction, written about every aspect of Washington. Here are a few we especially recommend for their usefulness both during the visit and as souvenirs:

The White House: An Historic Guide, by Margaret B. Klapthor, and *The Living White House,* by Lonnelle Aikman, both published by the White House Historical Association; *We, the People: The Story of the United States Capitol,* by Lonnelle Aikman, published by the U.S. Capitol Historical Society, and *Federal Justice Under Law: The Supreme Court in American Life,* by Mary Ann Harrell, published by the Foundation of the Federal Bar Association. All of these were produced by the National Geographic Society as a public service and are available from the Society's own bookshop, 17th and M Sts., N.W.

Washington on Foot, edited by Allan A. Hodges and Carol A. Hodges for the National Capital Area Chapter, American Planning Association, Smithsonian Institution Press.

Natural Washington: A Nature-Lover's Guide, by Bill and Phyllis Thomas, Holt, Rinehart and Winston.

Weekender's Guide, Washington-Baltimore Area, by Robert Shosteck, Potomac Books.

The Outdoor Sculpture of Washington, D.C., by James M. Goode, Smithsonian Institution Press.

Best Restaurants (& Others) Washington D.C. & Environs, by Phyllis C. Richman in cooperation with *The Washington Post,* 101 Productions.

Washington Itself, by E.J. Applewhite, Alfred A. Knopf.

Footnote Washington (Tracking the Engaging, Humorous and Surprising Bypaths of Capital History), by Bryson B. Rash, EPM Publications, Inc.

A Museum Guide to Washington, D.C. by Betty Ross, Americana Press.

CONVERTING METRIC TO U.S. MEASUREMENTS

Multiply:	by:	to find:
Length		
millimeters (mm)	.039	inches (in)
meters (m)	3.28	feet (ft)
meters	1.09	yards (yd)
kilometers (km)	.62	miles (mi)
Area		
hectares (ha)	2.47	acres
Capacity		
liters (L)	1.06	quarts (qt)
liters	.26	gallons (gal)
liters	2.11	pints (pt)
Weight		
grams (g)	.04	ounces (oz)
kilograms (kg)	2.20	pounds (lb)
metric tons (MT)	.98	tons (t)
Power		
kilowatts (kw)	1.34	horsepower (hp)
Temperature		
degrees Celsius	9/5 (then add 32)	degrees Fahrenheit

CONVERTING U.S. TO METRIC MEASUREMENTS

Multiply:	by:	to find:
Length		
inches (in)	25.40	millimeters (mm)
feet (ft)	.30	meters (m)
Length		
yards (yd)	.91	meters
miles (mi)	1.61	kilometers (km)
Area		
acres	.40	hectares (ha)
Capacity		
pints (pt)	.47	liters (L)
quarts (qt)	.95	liters
gallons (gal)	3.79	liters
Weight		
ounces (oz)	28.35	grams (g)
pounds (lb)	.45	kilograms (kg)
tons (t)	1.11	metric tons (MT)
Power		
horsepower (hp)	.75	kilowatts
Temperature		
degrees Fahrenheit	5/9 (after subtracting 32)	degrees Celsius

THE
WASHINGTON
SCENE

INTRODUCTION

The New Washington—and the New America

by
BEN J. WATTENBERG and **ERVIN S. DUGGAN**

Ben J. Wattenberg is a senior fellow at the American Enterprise Institute and co-editor of Public Opinion. *Chairman and co-founder of the Coalition for a Democratic Majority, he has hosted public television series "Ben Wattenberg at Large" and "In Search of the Real America." Author of the best-selling books* The Birth Dearth, The Good News Is the Bad News Is Wrong *and* The Real America, *he has also co-authored* This USA, Against All Enemies, *and* The Wealth Weapon. *He is a member of the Board of International Broadcasting and also writes a syndicated weekly newspaper column.*

Ervin S. Duggan, a journalist and author, is the head of a Washington consulting firm that manages editorial projects for corporate clients. A Washington resident for two decades, he co-authored Against All Enemies, *a novel of the White House.*

In one of his most famous witticisms, former President John F. Kennedy once referred to Washington as a city of "Southern efficiency and Northern charm"—thus paying tribute, in backhanded fashion, to the hybrid nature of America's capital city.

15

Washington—one of the world's few capitals deliberately founded as a showplace and a seat of government—is in fact several cities, and the alert visitor can sense, if not experience, all of them. It is, most visibly, monumental Washington: the tourists' city of temples and ceremonies. In a typical year, about 18 million visitors come to Washington. It is this monumental city, whose buildings glow like white elaborately carved moons at night, that many of these millions come to see first: Washington as the physical expression of the nation's history and ideals. One sees the tourists—pilgrims in casual clothes—lined up to tour the White House, the Capitol, the Washington Monument, the Jefferson and Lincoln Memorials. One sees them swarming slowly through the museums along the Mall, studying the artifacts of American history and culture, from Lindbergh's *Spirit of St. Louis* to the Hope Diamond to the star-spangled banner that flew over Fort McHenry. One sees them standing in silent clusters before the Tomb of the Unknowns, where solemn, heel-clicking military guards march an endless vigil in memory of America's war dead. And at the National Archives, where the lights are dim in the great Exhibit Hall to protect the ancient documents, one sees them peering down through two centuries of history to see the Declaration of Independence, the Constitution, and the Bill of Rights.

It is monumental Washington that rightly inspires hushed, patriotic awe—and that rightly preoccupies most visitors to the capital. But there are other Washingtons, and to glimpse these other sides of the city is to sense not only what the nation's capital has become, but what America has become in the climactic years of the Twentieth Century.

Headquarters of "Big America"

America has grown prodigiously since World War II—in population, in world importance, and in complexity. So has Washington—especially since the sixties, when the Federal Government began its great-growth period as dispenser of services and as regulator-in-chief to a vast, diverse populace.

As the Federal budget has grown from just over $100 billion in 1963 to over a trillion today, Washington has changed physically, too. The sleepy Southern city of mid-century has lately acquired a brisk, distinctly urban pace—complete with swooshing Metro subway trains, crowded airports, and traffic-laden freeways. The population of metropolitan Washington—the city and its surrounding suburbs in Maryland and Virginia—has grown by more than a million to its current 4.4 million since 1960.

The Congress, which once closed down for the summer, is now in session virtually the year 'round; its committees and subcommittees have multiplied and their staffs increased manyfold. The bureaucracy of Capitol Hill alone now numbers roughly 18,000. Since the early sixties, the Senate and the House have constructed three vast and expensive new office buildings—the Dirksen, Rayburn, and Hart buildings—and have filled up several nondescript annex buildings on Capitol Hill. Yet space is still short: only the nation's prisons are more crowded than staff offices on Capitol Hill.

Beyond Capitol Hill, Washington's burgeoning bureaucracies long ago overflowed the great Federal office buildings. Today, virtually every department of government leases acres of commercial office space, downtown and in the suburbs, to house its people, their computers, and their mountains of official paper.

Fortunately, however, Washington is still a city of distinctly human scale. Because a cherished law limits building heights in the city, Washington lacks the overwhelming, sky-touching structures of New York, Chicago, or even modern Baltimore. (However, no such constraints limit the height of office towers in Rosslyn, on the Virginia side of Key Bridge.) But Washington is a major city nonetheless: the nation's tenth largest. Ronald Reagan may have succeeded in his plan to cut the *growth* of the Federal budget and the Federal bureaucracy, but a lower *rate of growth* is still growth, nonetheless—not retrogression. Washington is unlikely to return to the stately pace of its past, for we are Big America now, which, like it or not, means Big Government—and a Big Washington.

The same phenomenon is apparent on the international scene. We hear talk these days that America is a diminished super power, that America is simply one nation in a newly multipolar world, that Soviet strength is growing, that there is disarray in the Western Alliance. (There is *always* talk about disarray in the Western Alliance.) But when all is said and done, the United States and the Soviet Union remain the two world super powers, we remain the leader of the free team, and the stronger the Soviets get, the more important America is to the rest of the world. And so, up and down Massachusetts Avenue, in and out of elegant embassies, top diplomats of the world can be seen climbing in and out of limousines headed for the State Department, the Defense Department, the World Bank, and all the other places where Washington stores its most precious products: power and influence.

As headquarters of Big America, Washington is increasingly a center also for Big Media. Journalism, printed and electronic, is a major Washington employer. The media are everywhere in Washington: visit a major Congressional hearing (and you can walk right in, since the law requires that all hearings must be public) and you may find your view obstructed by a forest of television cameras; peer through the wrought-iron fence near the White House West Wing in late afternoon, and you may glimpse several media stars, bathed in harsh white lights, recording their "stand-ups" for the evening news broadcasts. The White House Press Office lists about 1,800 journalists accredited to cover the Presidency alone. Although *Time, Newsweek,* and *The New York Times* have their headquarters in New York, they maintain large bureaus in Washington, as does almost every other major publication in the world. And the *Washington Post* building at 15th and M streets, N.W.—as befits a newspaper of worldwide fame and influence—is an important stop for tourists.

There is also Big Business in Washington. Not many of the nation's major corporations are headquartered in Washington, but the increasing impact of Washington on business—Washington's growing role as regulator of American business and industry—has made it necessary for industrial America to establish its outposts in Washington. Hundreds of larger corporations, from American Express to Xerox, maintain Washington offices as listening and lobbying posts. Others rely on trade associations representing whole industries. In 1970, roughly 700 national trade associations had their headquarters in Washington; today the number has more than doubled and is still growing. Today, Washington's downtown K Street, once an avenue of simple row houses, is Washington's Influence

Alley, lined with blocky office buildings where the trade-association lobby-ists roost, as well as with the expensive restaurants where they meet, trade intelligence, and plan their strategies. Their efforts are supplemented by the work of Washington's thousands of lawyers, many of whom reap large annual incomes and considerable national fame by helping their corporate clients find access to the mighty and navigate the legislative and regulatory mazes of Washington.

A Cultural Capital?

America—and Washington—have changed not just in size and com-plexity. The past generation has brought considerable cultural progress and maturity to America. Witness, in cities across the country, the bur-geoning growth of art museums and performing arts centers; the flowering of regional theater and dance companies; the exploding market for classi-cal music, live and on millions of stereo discs. And witness the emergence of America as a more highly educated nation, in which high-school gradu-ation has become the norm and college attendance the experience of a ma-jority of young citizens.

Washington, the nation's capital, reflects this trend also. Few sympho-nies are composed here, relatively few paintings are painted here, and the books that are written here tend to be works of journalism rather than of literature. But surely Washington is one of the world's leading centers of cultural display—on stage and in its incomparable cluster of museums and galleries. On the Mall alone, some of the world's greatest museums offer the visitor a dazzling collection of art and artifacts. The National Gallery of Art, with its rakish East Building designed by I. M. Pei, pres-ents the gamut of art from Old Masters to startling contemporary works. And the Smithsonian Institution, home of the Freer Gallery, the National Museum of Natural History, the National Museum of American History, and the Arts and Industries Building, has added, in the past few years, several new stars to its diadem of national museums: the Hirshhorn Muse-um and Sculpture Garden, dedicated to twentieth-century art; the Nation-al Air and Space Museum, where the visitor can see the Wright Brothers' original Kitty Hawk Flyer and the Apollo 11 moon-shot command mod-ule; Arthur M. Sackler Gallery, a new museum of Asian art; and the Na-tional Museum of African Art.

At the Kennedy Center for the Performing Arts on the banks of the Potomac, the visitor can sample, all under one capacious roof, not only opera, drama, and the National Symphony, but dance, film, and chamber music, too. And outside Washington, in the rolling Virginia countryside near Dulles International Airport, there is Wolf Trap Farm Park, the na-tion's only national park dedicated to the performing arts. Wolf Trap has been rebuilt after a 1982 fire destroyed the indoor-outdoor pavilion. Once again concertgoers enjoy picnics and music at the park.

Washington boasts some impressive home-grown cultural institutions, also—among them the Arena Stage, a regional theater company that has won a national reputation for showcasing new dramatic works; the Wash-ington Ballet, a local company with a world-class reputation; and the Phil-lips Collection, a jewel of a museum in a handsome townhouse at 1600 21st Street, N.W.

Washington has several universities that are entirely adequate and often excellent, but it boasts no Sorbonne, no Harvard. Those who point this out, supposedly as evidence that Washington lacks true standing as a cultural and intellectual capital, ignore an important and interesting fact: Washington is the home of several internationally important centers of thought and research that might accurately be called "universities that award no degrees." The Smithsonian, with its array of scholars and curators in history, anthropology, paleontology, and other disciplines is one such center. The National Institutes of Health in nearby Bethesda, the health-research arm of the Department of Health and Human Services, is another. Such political and economic think-tanks as the Brookings Institution, the American Enterprise Institute, and the Georgetown University Center for Strategic and International Studies are others. The Library of Congress is yet another.

Any city so endowed with cultural and intellectual riches, even if it were not a national political capital, would rank as a major international city. Washington has become such a city and as such, reflects the emergence of the United States as the world's leader in art, science, and the performing arts. Washington is the increasingly civilized and sophisticated capital of an increasingly civilized and sophisticated nation.

A Capital of Social Progress

The new America of the eighties, let us hasten to add, is not just bigger and a bit more cultured: it is profoundly changed in other ways as well, which the new Washington faithfully reflects.

Take race relations. Until the fifties, Washington, like many other American cities, was rigidly segregated by race, although it always has had a relatively large black population. Today, however, after a generation of social change strongly encouraged by the Federal Government, the city of Washington is led by a black mayor and a black city government. Washington could boast, though it doesn't, that it is something of a showcase of expanding opportunity for black citizens in America. For Washington has what may be the largest, most prosperous, and most influential black middle class of any American city: Here, black judges, doctors, reporters, television commentators, and bureaucrats prosper and are early evidence of the arrival of a new age in America.

To be sure, no millennium in race relations has been achieved in Washington or in the country at large. But the progress of black people in the nation's capital, as evidenced by their increasing visibility and eminence in education, politics, business, and the professions, is a forceful reminder of how far America has come over the past 30 years and of how quickly in America revolutionary change is accepted as routine.

Another American revolution in recent years has been in opportunities for women. Here, too, Washington reflects and may even lead the nation. A recent analysis in the *Washingtonian,* a local magazine, proclaimed that "D.C. Is the Best Big City for Women." According to 1987 figures of the Bureau of Labor Statistics, 43 percent of the managerial and professional workers in Washington—the job-holding elite, in other words—are women.

An Unfinished City

It is no utopia, this lavishly landscaped city on the Potomac. It does have its share of human frailty and thus its share of scandals, crime, poverty, injustice, and chicanery. But utopias, after all, exist only in books and in the imaginations of their authors. Washington, for all its faults, for all its unsolved problems, is nonetheless a fit reflection of the land it serves and represents.

This capital city remains, like America, a symbol of earnest striving toward great goals, the goals of "liberty and justice for all." And so the new Washington, like the new America, remains a worthwhile example to the world of an energetic people devoted to those ends.

THE FEDERAL GOVERNMENT

How Our System Works

by
BETTY ROSS

Betty Ross is the author of A Museum Guide to Washington, D.C. *and* How to Beat the High Cost of Travel *and has contributed scores of articles to newspapers and magazines. She has observed the Federal Government closely, both as a longtime resident of Washington, D.C., and from a vantage point inside the executive branch, as a former Voice of America official and an ex-White House staffer. A Smith College graduate, she is a member of the American Society of Journalists and Authors and the Society of American Travel Writers.*

New York may be the fashion capital of the United States and Los Angeles the center of entertainment, but government—and power—is the name of the game in Washington.

The Federal Government is a major employer, an important landlord, and a source of contracts, contacts, or conversation for Washingtonians. It is a patron of the arts and a provider for the needy. To some, pervasive government is what's wrong with Washington. To others—particularly the party in power—it's what's right.

The Federal Government occupies some of the choicest real estate in town, yet pays no taxes to the District of Columbia. On the other hand, although citizens of the District *do* pay taxes, they could not vote until some 20 years ago. This has changed; now they can help elect the President, but still they have only a non-voting delegate in Congress.

In Washington, the "separation of powers" doctrine becomes more than just a phrase in the Constitution. A visit here gives you a chance to see the legislative, executive, and judicial branches of government in action, to see how the system of checks and balances works. As Boswell put it, you have an opportunity, "instead of thinking how things may be, to see them as they are."

The Legislative Branch

In Pierre L'Enfant's eighteenth-century plan for the city of Washington, the U.S. Capitol and the White House were just far enough away from each other on Pennsylvania Avenue to emphasize the separation of powers between the legislative and executive branches. L'Enfant chose Jenkins Hill as the site for the Capitol; it is the focal point of an area now called Capitol Hill.

Guided tours of the Capitol leave from the Rotunda almost continuously from 9 A.M. to 3:30 P.M. daily throughout the year. The Senate side of the Capitol faces Constitution Avenue, while the House side is approached from Independence Avenue.

Drop by the office of your Senator or Representative to pick up passes to the Visitors' Galleries. Without a pass, you are not permitted to watch the proceedings. There are two Senate office buildings at First and Constitution Avenue, N.E., named respectively, for former Senators Everett Dirksen and Richard Russell. A third, honoring Senator Philip A. Hart, opened in November 1982 at Second and Constitution, N.E.

The House office buildings, named for former Speakers Joseph Cannon, Nicholas Longworth, and Sam Rayburn, are located in that order along Independence Avenue between First Street, S.E., and First Street, S.W. It is generally agreed by residents and visitors alike that the Rayburn Building is the least attractive and, at $75 million, one of the most expensive structures in the city.

According to the Constitution, "the Congress shall assemble at least once in every year, and such meeting shall begin at noon on the 3rd day of January, unless they shall by law appoint a different day." In the years before air conditioning, Congress usually recessed during the summer and reconvened in the fall. Today, however, with Congressional calendars more crowded and air conditioning commonplace, sessions frequently last much longer. It is not unusual for the House and/or Senate to sit through the summer and well into the fall.

Congressional sessions usually begin at noon; committee meetings are generally held in the morning. Check the *Washington Post*'s "Today in Congress" listings to find out what is going on.

Don't be surprised to see only a handful of Senators or Members of Congress on the floor during a session. Much Congressional business dealing with constituent problems is done in committees or in offices. When a vote is taken during a session, bells are rung to summon absent Members to the floor.

To save time, many Senators and Members of Congress make the brief trip between their offices and the Capitol on the Congressional subway.

Visitors may ride, too. The Senate restaurant in the Capitol—famed for its bean soup—is open to the public at all times. Cafeterias in the Rayburn, Longworth, and Dirksen office buildings are also open to visitors. Watch the hours, however. From 11:30 A.M. to 1:15 P.M. only Members of Congress and their staffs are admitted.

There are two Senators from each state, who are elected for six-year terms at an annual salary (in 1988) of $89,500 each. The 435 members of the House serve for two years and also receive $89,500 per year.

How a Bill Becomes Law

Legislation is a complicated, time-consuming process. Here, briefly, is the usual legislative procedure in the House of Representatives.

—A bill is introduced by a Member, who places it in the "hopper," a box on the Clerk's desk. It is numbered (H.R....), sent to the Government Printing Office, and made available the next morning in the House Document Room.

—It is referred to a committee.

—The committee reports on it, usually after holding a hearing, either before the full committee or a subcommittee.

—The bill is placed on the House calendar.

—Any bill that involves the Treasury is considered by the House sitting as a Committee of the Whole. In that case, the Speaker appoints a chairman who presides and there is a period of general debate, followed by a reading for amendment, with speeches limited to five minutes.

—A bill is given a second reading and consideration in the House. (Bills considered in Committee of the Whole, however, receive a second reading in committee.) Amendments may be added after the second reading.

—It is given a third reading, which is by title only. The Speaker puts the question to a vote and it may be defeated at this stage by a negative vote.

—If it passes, however, it is sent to the Senate.

—The Senate considers the bill, usually after it has been referred to a committee and reported favorably by that committee.

—If the Senate rejects the House bill, it notifies the House. Otherwise, the bill is returned to the House from the Senate, with or without amendments.

—The House considers the Senate amendments.

—Differences between House and Senate versions of a bill are resolved by a joint House-Senate conference committee.

—The bill is printed in final form or "enrolled" on parchment paper.

—It is proofread by the Enrolling Clerk, who certifies its correctness.

—Once certified, the bill is signed, first by the Speaker of the House and then by the President of the Senate.

—It is sent to the President of the United States.

—The President approves or disapproves the bill, usually after referring it to the appropriate Department for recommendations.

—If the President vetoes the bill, it is returned to the Congress. If it fails to pass by a two-thirds vote, no further action is taken.

—If the bill has either been approved by the President or passed over a veto, it is filed with the Secretary of State and then becomes law.

Such a brief summary cannot possibly convey the intrigue, the drama, and the behind-the-scenes maneuvering by Members, their staffs, and lobbyists involved in the legislative process. Often the stakes are high and the battles hard fought. If you are lucky, you may be able to watch an important debate or a newsworthy vote during your visit to Capitol Hill.

The Executive Branch

The White House is at 1600 Pennsylvania Avenue, N.W., the most prestigious address in the country. However, its first occupant, Abigail Adams, was disappointed in the damp, drafty "President's Palace." She complained that it had "not a single apartment finished" and "not the least fence, yard, or other convenience without." On the other hand, Thomas Jefferson found the house "big enough for two emperors, one Pope, and the grand lama"—and still unfinished.

When Franklin Delano Roosevelt became President in 1932, the entire White House staff consisted of fewer than 50 people. Today, approximately 1,800 people work for the Executive Office of the President. They are crammed into offices in the East and West Wings of the White House and in the ornate Executive Office Building (formerly the State, War and Navy Building), adjacent to the White House to the west on Pennsylvania Avenue.

The President's annual salary is $200,000; the Vice President receives $115,000. They are elected for a four-year term. If the President dies or becomes incapacitated, the Vice President is next in line of succession. He is followed, in order, by the Speaker of the House of Representatives, the President pro tempore of the Senate, the Secretaries of State, Treasury, and Defense, the Attorney General, the Postmaster General, and the Secretaries of the Interior, Agriculture, Commerce, Labor, Health and Human Services, Housing and Urban Development, Transportation, Energy, and Education.

The Judicial Branch

Traditionally, the opening session of the Supreme Court, on the first Monday in October, marks the beginning of Washington's social season, and the quadrennial Inaugural festivities add to the excitement. The Inaugural week in January usually includes a star-studded gala, as well as receptions honoring the new President, Vice President, and their wives.

The Supreme Court meets from October through June in a Corinthian-columned white-marble building at First and Maryland Avenue, N.E. Until 1935, the Justices used various rooms in the Capitol. For a while, in the nineteenth century, they met in taverns, boardinghouses, and at the home of the Clerk of the Court, Elias Boudinot Caldwell, at Second and A streets, S.E. You can see the Old Supreme Court Chamber on the ground floor of the Capitol.

Approximately 5,000 cases are submitted for appeal each year and the Justices choose about 3 percent—roughly 160 cases in all—those which raise Constitutional questions or affect the life or liberty of citizens.

Justice Felix Frankfurter said, "The words of the Constitution are so unrestricted by their intrinsic meaning or by their history or by tradition or by prior decisions that they leave the individual Justice free, if indeed they do not compel him, to gather meaning not from reading the Constitution but from reading life."

In the courtroom, the nine black-robed Justices are seated in high-backed black leather chairs in front of heavy red velvet draperies. Lawyers for each side present their oral arguments, with the Justices often interjecting questions or comments. Generally, the Court sits for two weeks and then recesses for two weeks to do research and write opinions.

They are on the bench Monday, Tuesday, and Wednesday from 10 A.M. to noon and from 1 to 3 P.M. from October through April and they usually hear about four cases a day. During this first part of the term, the Justices meet privately every Wednesday afternoon and all day Friday to discuss the cases they have heard that week and to take a preliminary vote on decisions.

The Chief Justice assigns different members to write the opinions. If he is on the minority side in a particular case, however, the senior Justice in the majority assigns the opinion. Any Justice may write his or her own opinion, agreeing or disagreeing with the majority. During the remainder of the term, in May and June, the Justices usually meet every Thursday to decide on releasing their opinions.

Monday is "Decision Day," probably the most interesting time to visit the Supreme Court. That is when the Justices announce their decisions and read their opinions.

Throughout the year, in the courtroom, staff members give a brief lecture about the Court Monday through Friday, every half-hour from 9:30 A.M. to 4:30 P.M. Lectures are not given on holidays or when the Justices are on the bench hearing cases. In addition to exhibits about the Supreme Court and its Justices, the Court boasts one of the best government cafeterias in town—second only to those at the National Gallery of Art. It is open to the public.

Supreme Court Justices are appointed by the President with the advice and consent of the Senate. They serve for life or, as the Constitution says, "during good behavior."

Associate Justices receive $110,000 per year; the Chief Justice's salary is $115,000. After ten years of service, they may resign or retire with full pay.

Veteran Court-watcher Anthony Lewis called the Supreme Court a "symbol of continuity, instrument of change," and added that "no more remarkable institution of government exists than the Supreme Court of the United States."

Lobbyists

Virtually every special-interest group in the country, as well as a sprinkling of foreign governments, is represented by someone who "lobbies" for its cause in Washington. Lobbyists frequently conduct their business over luncheons, cocktails, and dinners, as well as on the golf courses or tennis courts of suburban country clubs. Power is the magnet that draws them to the nation's capital.

Lobbyists' backgrounds are as diverse as the causes they represent. They are usually lawyers, public relations executives, or former Congressional staff members. Many were once Members of Congress or high government officials from all over the U.S. who have developed "Potomac fever," that is, they do not return home but find being a Washington representative the ideal way to continue to influence public policy.

Sometimes, it appears that every group is well represented here except the average citizen. Under those circumstances, if you have a pet project, discuss it with your Senator or Member of Congress—he or she is your lobbyist. In doing so—like Washington's highly skilled and well-paid lobbyists—you would simply be exercising your First Amendment rights to express your beliefs and influence your government.

THE CEREMONIAL CITY

Washington's History

by
TOM KELLY and **STEPHEN BREWER**

Tom Kelly is a native Washingtonian and freelance writer. His long list of journalistic credits includes contributions to the Washington Post, *the* Washington Star, The New York Times, The Reporter, The Nation, The Nation's Business, *and* Washingtonian *magazine. He is the author of* The Imperial Post—The Meyers, The Grahams and The Newspaper That Runs Washington.

Stephen Brewer is a former Washingtonian who has since made his home in New York City.

Washington, the city of diplomats, politicians, and lobbyists, owes its very existence to compromise, and that is just how the capital city came to be. A "Federal City" was first proposed during the Continental Congress in 1785, two years before the Constitution was framed and the 13 original colonies were bound together as the United States of America. When Congress met for the first time—the session was held in 1789 in New York, the temporary capital—the debate between Southerners and Northerners as to where to put the nation's capital became a hot issue. Until a solution could be reached, the capital was placed in Philadelphia, and there it remained for the next 10 years. So, first President George Washington never held office in the city that now bears his name.

The debate ended when the two great political leaders of the time, Alexander Hamilton, a New York Federalist and fiscal conservative, and Thomas Jefferson, a Virginia agrarian liberal, reached a compromise. Jefferson's Southerners agreed to support Hamilton's proposal that the Federal government assume the war debts of the 13 original states *if,* in return, Hamilton's Northerners supported the plan to move the capital city to the banks of the Potomac River. At the time this agreement was reached—it was the first of many times when conversation and persuasion would fail in Washington and compromise succeed—most of the rich land along the river's banks was laid out in manors of a thousand acres or more.

George Washington, himself a surveyor, selected the exact site of the capital. It was to be within easy reach of his own estate at Mount Vernon, below the Great Falls of the Potomac River. (The English had first called the river St. Gabriel's, then the Elizabeth. Washington and his neighbors called it by its Indian name, Potomac.)

Pierre L'Enfant, a French-born engineer who had served in the American Revolutionary Army, volunteered his services as designer of the Federal City. He had already established a substantial reputation in New York, where he had designed Federal Hall. He had also designed medals, including the Order of the Purple Heart. L'Enfant wanted to create a city "magnificent enough to grace a great nation."

L'Enfant's Grand Plan—A Shaky Start

In 1791, Washington and L'Enfant met with Daniel Carroll, owner of the huge estate of Duddington Manor, and other great landowners at Suter's Tavern in George Town to present their development plan. The landowners agreed to sell sites for public buildings to the government for $66.66 an acre and to turn over the land needed for streets and highways without charge. They intended to make their big profits from the public sale of the rest of the land to the builders of homes, hostelries, taverns, shops, and small factories. Proceeds would be divided evenly between the owners and the government, and the government would use its share of the profits to pay for the construction of public buildings.

It appeared to be a perfect scheme—until L'Enfant presented his detailed design. L'Enfant envisioned a ceremonial city with streets 100 to 110 feet wide. One avenue was to be 400 feet wide from curb to curb. The streets were to be laid out in grid blocks with diagonal avenues linking the city's major hills. Streets running from east to west would be lettered alphabetically, those running from north to south would be numbered, and diagonal avenues would be given the names of states. L'Enfant proposed that Jenkins Hill be the site of the Capitol building. The President's Palace, later known as the Executive Mansion and now more familiarly called the White House, would be built on another hill half a mile away, then a fruit orchard. In deference to the state housing the temporary capital, the grand avenue linking these two important hills would be called Pennsylvania Avenue.

The landowners, who would have to donate far more land than they had intended, were justifiably upset with the plan. But Washington backed L'Enfant, and for the moment, the engineer prevailed.

L'Enfant was so zealous that he brooked no interference or delay in transforming his dream into reality. Before work began, Daniel Carroll of Duddington started to build a new manor house where L'Enfant had planned a vista. The designer ordered the landowner to tear it down. When he refused, L'Enfant had it demolished anyway. Unfortunately for L'Enfant, Carroll was the nephew of another Daniel Carroll, one of the three commissioners overseeing the construction of the city (Thomas Jefferson was another). The commissioners fired L'Enfant and offered him a building lot near the White House, along with $2,500 in severance pay. L'Enfant refused both offers.

L'Enfant had written that he planned "on such a scale as to leave room for that aggrandizement and embellishment which the increase in the wealth of the nation will permit it to pursue at any period, however remote. . . . " Those who followed L'Enfant did not have the same vision. In fact, the city grew so slowly that in 1845, Congress ceded back to the state of Virginia its portion of the original 10 square miles.

Two years after L'Enfant's dismissal, President George Washington laid the cornerstone of the Capitol building and the first lots were offered for sale. However, aside from the few lots Washington bought, there were very few takers. But, a few days after the lots went on the block, a young man named James Greenleaf, a friend of Vice President Adams, offered to buy 3,000 parcels at $66.50 apiece. He planned to spread payment over seven years and to take title as he made the payments. The Commissioners were willing to go along with the scheme, but two months later Greenleaf came back with another plan and a partner, Robert Morris of Philadelphia. They would buy 6,000 lots for $80 each, payable as the lots were sold to other buyers. They would take full title immediately. Once more, the commissioners agreed. It seemed to be a good way for the landowners to sell land and an ideal way for the speculators to make money.

It was neither. Greenleaf and Morris, taking advantage of the fact that they had a near-monopoly on the land, asked prohibitive prices and made very few sales. By the time the proceeds were split between the original landowners and the government, the shares were negligible. The Commissioners were forced to borrow $100,000 from the State of Maryland to construct public buildings. Congress appropriated another $100,000, and by the end of 1798, the exterior of the President's Palace and the Senate wing of the Capitol were completed.

Settling in the New City

Soon after Washington died in December 1799, Congress voted to name the new city after him. Six months later, the Senators and Representatives and their 126 employees moved from Philadelphia to Washington. On arriving there they found just 372 houses, most of them built of wood. The city's population was just 3,000 then. Most of the Federal employees found lodging in boarding houses on Jenkins Hill, near the unfinished Capitol building. Work quarters were cramped. When the Justices of the Supreme Court came to town in 1801, they were given the small office of the Senate clerk. In 1860, with the completion of the Capitol's Senate wing, the Justices moved to the old Senate chamber but didn't get their own building until 1935!

Upon his arrival, Secretary of the Treasury Wolcott assessed the new city: "There are few houses in any one place and most of them small, miserable huts, which present an awful contrast with the public buildings. The people are poor, and as far as I can judge, they live like fishes, by eating one another."

The public buildings did promise to be grand, though. In many ways, the majesty of the government buildings' architecture bears the stamp of Thomas Jefferson, the nation's third President. An architect and scientist, as well as philosopher and statesman, Jefferson served as minister to France in the early days of the Republic. He traveled widely throughout Europe, where he was particularly influenced by Roman architecture and its contemporary Palladian revival. The design of many of Washington's buildings reflects his taste.

Likewise, it was Jefferson who, in 1803, planted the first rows of poplars along Pennsylvania Avenue. Many varieties have been added over the years, including the Japanese cherry trees that bloom so beautifully each spring around the Tidal Basin and the Jefferson Memorial.

On March 4, 1801, Jefferson walked from his boarding house to his inauguration at the Capitol. He then walked back to his boarding house, where he stayed for another two weeks while workmen prepared the President's Palace.

Construction of the new city progressed slowly. By the time the south wing of the Capitol was ready for occupancy in 1807, the speculators had gone bankrupt. The city was still a dream when President James Madison took office, but he and his wife Dolley were a great social success. Mrs. Madison's drawing room was filled with "gallants immaculate in sheer ruffles and small clothes" and "dainty belles in frills, flounces, and furbelows."

In 1812, the war hawks in Congress persuaded their colleagues to go to war with Great Britain over America's rights to the sea. Two years later, a British force under Admiral Cockburn and General Ross defeated a hastily assembled militia at Bladensburg, Maryland, and marched into Washington. They burned the President's Palace, the Capitol, and other public buildings and withdrew the next day.

The Madisons took up temporary residence at the Octagon House, owned by their friend Colonel Tayloe, and Congress met for the time being in the one public building left untouched by the British, the combined Post and Patent Office at Seventh and F streets. Many of the Senators and Representatives wanted to move the city to a less vulnerable location after the attack. But, in the midst of the enthusiasm aroused by Andrew Jackson's victory over the British in New Orleans, Congress voted to rebuild the capital on its present site. The White House, according to legend, got its name when the fire-blackened walls were covered with heavy white paint. (At Teddy Roosevelt's urging, Congress officially changed the name of the Executive Mansion to the White House in 1900.) The Capitol was rebuilt in time for President James Monroe to take his oath of office on its new "elevated portico" in 1817.

The Monroes were no less "highbrow" than the Madisons had been. In her "Court Circles of the Republic," Mrs. Ellet wrote with approval that "elegance of dress was absolutely required and on one occasion Mr. Monroe refused admission to a near relative who happened not to have a suit of small-clothes and silk hose in which to present himself at a public reception."

Washington grew slowly as the Federal establishment expanded, and L'Enfant's grandiose plans were long forgotten. In 1820, the government ordered farmers to stop planting near the streets, which were littered with stumps, wood piles, and bricks. Walking was difficult by day and downright dangerous by night.

On July 4, 1828, President John Quincy Adams turned the first spadeful of dirt for the Chesapeake and Ohio Canal, which was to link Washington's tidewater port of George Town—and the Chesapeake Bay—with the Western wilderness, just as the recently completed Erie canal had linked Upstate New York with the Great Lakes. The business leaders of Alexandria, Virginia, were so convinced that their city would become a great trading center when the canal began operating—and so determined that they would be less hampered if they were once again part of the State of Virginia—that they petitioned the government to secede from the District of Columbia. Congress rather absent-mindedly agreed to return all of the District south of the Potomac to Virginia. The businessmen of George Town, the terminus of the canal, tried to have their portion of the District returned to Maryland, but the state wasn't interested in having them back.

Much to the disappointment of the merchants, the canal never became an important waterway nor did Washington develop as a great commercial center. What the planners of the canal hadn't taken into account was the fact that the Potomac River, the canal's artery to the Chesapeake Bay, is virtually an unnavigable river.

The Unrefined Capital

On his inauguration day, Andrew Jackson, the "brawler from Tennessee," rode down Pennsylvania Avenue with a retinue of "country men, farmers, gentlemen, mounted and dismounted, boys, women and children, black and white, carriages, wagons, and carts." Jackson was a determined democrat. He quickly sprang to the defense of Peggy O'Neale Timberlake, the new bride of his Secretary of War. Led by Mrs. Calhoun, the wife of the Vice President, the grandes dames of Washington snubbed the beautiful Mrs. Timberlake. A fierce feud developed between Jackson and Calhoun, and as a result, Calhoun quit the Democratic Party. As his next Vice President, Jackson chose Martin Van Buren, who was himself elected President in 1836.

Washington, meanwhile, remained undeveloped and unimpressive. It was more of a rugged frontier town than a world capital. In those days, the White House was never locked and anyone could stroll on the grounds. Once, when Van Buren was President, a drunk wandered into the White House and spent the night on a sofa!

Harriet Martineau, an English woman who visited Washington in 1835, described the city in her diary as: "Straggling out hither and thither, with a small house or two a quarter of a mile from any other . . . we had to cross ditches and stiles and walk alternately on grass and pavement and strike across a field to reach a street . . . grave judges, saucy travellers, pert newspaper reporters, melancholy Indian chiefs, and timid New England ladies, trembling on the verge of the vortex . . . all these mixed up together in daily intercourse with the higher circles of a little village. . . . "

A few years later Charles Dickens would describe the city as "spacious avenues that begin in nothing and lead nowhere; streets a mile long that only want houses, roads, and inhabitants; public buildings that need but a public to be complete and ornaments of great thoroughfares which need only great thoroughfares to ornament."

Dickens predicted, confidently, that Washington would never improve. But, the city grew, and it soon began to mushroom. In 1850—the same year Congress passed a law making it legal to own slaves in the District of Columbia but illegal to buy and sell them—Washington had a population of 51,687. By 1860, on the eve of the Civil War, it had a population of 75,000. And, when the war began, the population sky-rocketed.

The Union Nerve Center

Located on the front between the Union and Confederate armies, Washington became the nerve center of the Northern war effort. More than 500 new residents poured into the city every day, and the streets swarmed with politicians, soldiers, camp followers, and fugitives. Businessmen, speculators, and even such writers as Walt Whitman and Harriet Beecher Stowe made their way to Washington. The city still lacked charm, but it would never be a small town again. Mary Clemmer Ames described Washington as it looked in the middle of the war: "Forts bristled above every hilltop. Soldiers were entrenched at every gateway. Shed hospitals covered acres on acres in every suburb. Churches, art-halls, and private mansions were filled with the wounded and dying. . . . The endless roll of the Army wagon was never still."

Camps, hospitals, and supply depots sprang up all over the city. Troops were housed wherever space could be found, even in the East Room of the White House and the basement of the Capitol building. Thousands of Union horses were corralled in Foggy Bottom. Whereas Washington had had just one large hospital when the war began, soon there were 36. Among the thousands of women who came to Washington to nurse the wounded were Clara Barton and Louisa May Alcott.

The war also brought wealth and improvements to Washington. The city's four theaters flourished, and the newly invented game of baseball was played with fervor on the South Lawn of the White House. A new water project was built to bring water to the rapidly growing city from Great Falls on the Potomac River. Work on the still uncompleted Capitol continued, too. On December 2, 1863, the Statue of Freedom was installed on top of the rotunda's new cast-iron dome.

Growth brought with it many problems. Slums grew up as wooden shacks were hastily built along alleys. The crime rate soared. Heavy traffic rumbled over the broken pavement of the city's streets. Rain turned all of Washington into a muddy sea. Tiber Creek—now covered by Constitution Avenue—became an open sewer, and from it diseases spread throughout the city. Thousands, including President Lincoln's young son, died during a typhoid epidemic.

Washington was threatened repeatedly with direct assault and encirclement. In fact, from the White House, President Lincoln could see the Confederate flag flying over Alexandria, just across the river. At one point, when mobs outside Baltimore burned the railway tracks, Washington's only link to the rest of the Union, panic ensued and thousands fled the city. But calm was soon restored when troops rebuilt the lines.

In 1864, General Jubal Early and a force of 19,000 Confederate soldiers approached the city from the north and drove to Fort Stevens, now well within the city limits. The Confederates were repulsed as President Lincoln watched from a parapet.

On April 14, 1865, a few days after General Robert E. Lee offered the surrender of the Confederacy, Lincoln was shot by actor John Wilkes Booth at Ford's Theatre on 10th Street. Booth jumped onto a horse in an alley at the back of the theater, rode east on Pennsylvania Avenue through southeast Washington, and crossed the 11th Street Bridge to southern Maryland. He was killed in Virginia a few days later while resisting capture by Union troops. Four other conspirators—among them the first woman hanged in the United States—were executed in the yard of the old District Penitentiary. Ford's Theatre, barely saved from a mob that wanted to burn it to the ground, was closed. Except for a brief stint as an office building in 1893, it was not used again until it was completely restored in the early 1970s.

Washington led the way in the emancipation movement, banning slavery six months before the Emancipation Proclamation became law. Washington was also the first place to abolish the Black's Code of Law, which was designed to keep blacks in inferior positions. And, it was in Washington that the first blacks were recruited into the U.S. Army.

Washington's Gilded Age

In the period immediately after the war, Washington's commerce hovered near collapse as army supply traffic dwindled. A huge and needy ex-slave population put enormous demands on the city, which was already hard-pressed to supply the non-taxpaying government buildings with water, light, sewers, and other services.

But, the situation soon changed. In fact, under President Grant, Washington entered a Gilded Age, marked most notably by corruption in Congress. But, as the Federal government became more important, Washington's prestige grew. A new, affluent population—made up partially of the *nouveau riche* who could not break into the social circles of more established cities—came to Washington, which, with a population of some 170,000 by 1870, was becoming a sizable city. Washington began to look like a great world capital. The Capitol building was finally completed, more public buildings went up, the wide avenues were paved. Real estate, which 100 years earlier could hardly be given away, suddenly became valuable.

Entertainment and social life became more sophisticated. Other world powers built the handsome embassies that still grace the city and sent some of their most distinguished citizens as ambassadors.

In 1871, Congress appointed Alexander Robey Shepherd, a contractor who by somewhat dubious means had made a fortune in D.C. real estate after the war, to serve as Vice President of the Board of Public Works. Shepherd, who was later promoted to Governor of the District, soon convinced Congress to spend $6 million to improve the city. Over the next three years he literally transformed what had been a pesthole into a handsome, modern capital. He paved 80 miles of streets, sodded parks, built sewers, covered pestilent Tiber Creek, planted trees, laid sidewalks—and spent $22 million in doing so. Once again, Washington was broke. Worse, Congress decided that the city was incapable of ruling itself, and in 1874 ruled that from then on the District would be run by three congressionally appointed commissioners. Citizens would still pay taxes, of course, but they could not vote. So, Washingtonians were faced with the same situation that had stirred the colonists into battle against the British—taxation without representation. Shepherd moved to New Mexico.

Electric lights came to Washington in 1881, the Washington Monument was completed in 1884, and electric streetcars began clanging down Pennsylvania Avenue in 1888. Still more buildings, including the Library of Congress, went up. Washington's wealth continued to soar, and with the new prosperity property values increased. The Chevy Chase farm, just over the Maryland line, was subdivided for building lots and Washington had its first suburb. Alexander Graham Bell founded the National Geographic Society, one of Washington's most venerable institutions, in 1888.

Presidents came and went without leaving their mark on the city. On July 2, 1881, Charles J. Guiteau assassinated President James Garfield at the old Baltimore and Potomac railroad station at Sixth and B streets. Guiteau believed he was doing the Republican Party a great favor by his dreadful act and that he would be amply rewarded. The hapless Guiteau was tried, convicted, and hanged at the Washington jail.

President Grover Cleveland, still a bachelor when he was elected, was the first President ever to be married in the White House. During his term, in 1894, a band of some 300 ragged unemployed workers, called "Coxey's Army," marched all the way to Washington from Massillon, Ohio, to petition the government for jobs. Coxey, the group leader, was arrested while making a speech from the Capitol steps and the dispirited army broke up.

In 1901, President William McKinley was assassinated during a visit to Buffalo, New York. He was succeeded by Theodore Roosevelt, the hero of the Spanish-American War Battle of San Juan Hill. In the words of his daughter Alice, Teddy Roosevelt "wanted to be the bride at every wedding and the corpse at every funeral." Teddy filled the White House with all sorts of interesting people, including, in the words of William Allen White, " . . . Western bullwackers, city prize-fighters, explorers, rich men, poor men, an occasional black man, editors, writers . . . men whose faces had never been seen in the White House before." One of Roosevelt's favorite activities was taking fat military men on long walks through Rock Creek Park.

The automobile made its appearance in Washington in a centennial celebration in 1900. As the United States entered the Twentieth Century, it had 75 million inhabitants and was the richest nation on earth. Washington would soon share some of this wealth, when in 1902 Congress approved an ambitious beautification plan for the city. The unsightly railroad tracks between the Capitol and the Washington Monument were taken up and replaced with the beautifully landscaped Mall. A new railroad station, Union Station, was built just north of the Capitol, and more buildings were constructed to house the increasing numbers of government workers. But even the energetic Roosevelt couldn't persuade Congress to appropriate money for slum clearance. Congress' reluctance on this account can be attributed to the fact that embittered Southern Senators and Representatives saw no need to aid the city's black population, which by 1910 was the largest in the country.

World War I and Hard Times

Woodrow Wilson was in the White House when the United States entered World War I in 1917. This war changed the city as much as the Civil War had half a century before. Tens of thousands of government war workers descended on the city. They worked in the temporary office buildings that had been constructed in the city parks. Among the people flooding into Washington were some of the most capable men of the day: Bernard Baruch, whom Wilson enlisted to mobilize industry; law professor Felix Frankfurter, who tackled labor issues; Herbert Hoover, who was assigned the task of providing war-ravaged Europe with food.

Wilson suffered a stroke in September 1919, but his strong-willed wife was determined that he serve out his term. The President remained isolated in the White House, and for a full year and a half the nation lacked an effective chief executive. The White House had no relationship with Congress, or with prominent Washingtonians, or with the official community. Many of the routine functions of Washington came to a halt.

Edward G. Lowry described the atmosphere of the city as one of "bleak and chilly austerity suffused and envenomed by hatred of a sick chief magistrate." Nor was this dismal situation alleviated by Attorney General Mitchell Palmer, who fearing that the Russian Revolution had spawned similar revolutionary sentiment in the United States, launched a campaign against radicals. In the short-lived but often violent burst of hysteria that followed, many innocent foreigners were beaten by mobs or jailed and deported.

During the 1920s, construction began on the massive, Romanesque headquarters of the departments of Commerce, Labor, and Justice, as well as the Post Office and National Archives. These buildings were constructed in what has come to be known as "Federal Triangle" between Pennsylvania Avenue and the Mall. In 1921, the Tomb of the Unknown Soldier, honoring those who lost their lives in the World War, was dedicated just across the Potomac on the grounds of the Robert E. Lee Plantation, now known as Arlington National Cemetery. That same year, Congress authorized funds to build a new bridge to span the Potomac just behind the Lincoln Memorial.

The year 1926 saw a low ebb in racial relations in this increasingly black city when the Supreme Court ruled that blacks, Jews, and other minorities could be barred from buying and renting homes. Racism even crept into the city's newspapers.

Warren Harding succeeded Wilson. Although he surrounded himself with a few good men, such as Charles Evans Hughes, his Secretary of State, and Herbert Hoover, his Secretary of Commerce, Harding had more than his share of scoundrels in his Cabinet. Some of his colleagues went to prison for stealing government lands and assets. Harding, who many historians believe was an honest man, died suddenly in San Francisco in August 1923, just before Teapot Dome and other scandals broke.

Calvin Coolidge took office next, followed by Herbert Hoover and the great Depression. The Depression changed the appearance and the significance of Washington—the appearance, because Federal building continued during these hard times, although it did nothing to alleviate Washington's unemployment; the significance, because America looked to Washington for help, although all too often Washington looked the other way.

A 1931 Hunger March to Washington produced no results. The next year—when Hoover was near the end of his term *and* his rope—tens of thousands of Bonus Marchers, veterans of World War I who wanted their promised bonuses ahead of schedule, came to Washington and camped on the flat land near the Anacostia River. They were finally dispersed and their village of shacks, called "Hooverville," was burned to the ground by an Army contingent led by General Douglas MacArthur.

Boom Time and More Problems

Franklin Delano Roosevelt was elected in a landslide in 1932. Though he and his wife, Eleanor, were clearly aristocrats, they gave Washington society its greatest down-to-earth push since the days of Andrew Jackson. Once more, as in Teddy Roosevelt's day, the White House was filled with interesting people—labor leaders and laborers, artists and philosophical anarchists, people of all races and religions, newspaper people like Walter Winchell and Walter Lippmann, movie actors, and Harvard professors. The relationship between the White House and Congress, which had withered in the Wilson years, been casually chummy under Harding, at arm's length with Coolidge, and bitter with Hoover, was, in the beginning at least, wonderfully harmonious under Roosevelt. He brought the New Deal, the Brain Trust, and the National Recovery Act to Washington and the nation. Congress passed new programs, such as Social Security. Together, the White House and the Hill made sweeping changes in the American way of life. Roosevelt also brought, via the New Deal, hundreds of thousands of new government employees to Washington. In fact, the number of government jobs jumped from 63,000 to 93,000 the first year the New Deal was in effect.

The face of the city changed, too. The Supreme Court, a magnificent example of classical Greek architecture, and the Folger Shakespeare Library, an equally magnificent example of the neoclassical style, went up on Capitol Hill. Perhaps the most imposing building of them all was the National Gallery of Art, which was built on the Mall at the foot of Capitol Hill. The Thomas Jefferson Memorial, a glistening domed rotunda, was erected across the Tidal Basin from the Washington Monument and the Lincoln Memorial.

The bombing of Pearl Harbor by the Japanese on December 7, 1941, brought to Washington the greatest frenzy of activity in its history. The city was to become the paramount world capital. New government offices were organized and the workers poured in—the city and its environs grew by an average of 75,000 people a year throughout the war and the next two decades. An estimated 40,000 people flowed through Union Station every day. Among them were businessmen on their way to the Hill to negotiate price codes; union chiefs in town to argue wages; war correspondents; thousands of armed-forces personnel; blacks fleeing poverty in the South; European Jews escaping Hitler. The Pentagon, the huge, five-sided headquarters of the armed services, was built across the river in Virginia, and the new State Department Building, almost as large, went up several blocks from the White House between Virginia and Constitution avenues.

Roads and other public works were built to accommodate the waves of new residents. Even Georgetown, the city's oldest neighborhood, changed as young professionals whom the New Deal brought to town discovered its dilapidated but charming row houses and began to renovate them. So effective were their efforts that today Georgetown is one of Washington's choicest and most expensive neighborhoods.

The new people in Washington lived in whatever quarters they could find, rode streetcars to work, ate in government cafeterias, and went to crowded movie houses for entertainment. All was not well in this boomtown environment, though. A 1936 ruling that relief payments could not be made to families in which there was an employable father at home encouraged many men to desert their families, forcing mothers to go to work and sending children into the streets, where they often took up crime. Funds from the Community Chest, organized in 1928 to bring blacks and whites together in a joint effort to help the needy, went largely to nations overseas, and Washington's needy blacks, for whom it was intended, received only a fraction of the proceeds. In 1939, black opera singer Marian Anderson was barred from performing at Constitution Hall. But with the intervention of Secretary of the Interior Harold Ickes, she performed anyway—in a dramatic setting in front of the Lincoln Memorial.

Wartime Washington had many other problems, too. There was a severe shortage of housing, and the bigger the bureaucracy became, the harder it was to handle.

When the smoke of World War II cleared away, Washington was the only functioning major world capital. Washington officials had the world's problems on their hands: the awesome responsibility of nuclear weaponry, the gruesome effects of which were demonstrated when the United States dropped the A-bomb on Hiroshima; the rebuilding and economic recovery of practically all of Europe; the pursuit of NATO and other treaties that would ensure that another world war would not happen again.

As Russia strained at her borders to bring neighboring nations under the influence of Communism, the cold war era—and along with it a new age of diplomacy—began. Much of the activity in Washington at this time was centered around the shiny new State Department headquarters in Foggy Bottom.

Senator Joe McCarthy of Wisconsin set Washington—and the nation—on its ear when he began to look for Communist infiltrators. His accusations led to the demise of many an official and public personality and culminated in a full-scale investigation of Communism before a Congressional subcommittee.

The Activists' City

Washington's real building boom began at war's end. Between 1950 and 1970, the Washington area's population increased from 1.5 million to 3 million—making it the fastest-growing metropolitan area in the United States. New multi-lane highways were built to all points of the compass, and the nearby farms of northern Virginia and southern Maryland quickly became suburbs—bedroom communities in Arlington and Fairfax counties in Virginia and Montgomery and Prince Georges counties in Maryland.

These suburbs became the headquarters for businesses and industries. Meanwhile, as industry boomed in the United States during the 1950s, big business, big labor, and big journalism took over in Washington. Civil rights took a leap forward under President Eisenhower, and in 1954 public schools were integrated under the *Brown* vs. *Board of Education* ruling in the Supreme Court. Washington became the center for civil rights activities. In one of the biggest such demonstrations ever staged in the United States, hundreds of thousands of blacks and whites gathered in front of the Lincoln Memorial in 1963.

The 1960s began with the brief, happy administration of John F. Kennedy, who lavished more attention on Washington than had any President since Thomas Jefferson. His beautiful wife, Jacqueline, completely refurbished the White House with period furnishings. Lafayette Square, across the street from the White House, was restored, along with the houses facing it. Architect Eero Saarinen designed an exquisite terminal for the new Dulles International Airport. Many people consider it to be the finest such building ever built. In the southwest section of the city, row after row of rat-infested slum housing was cleared to make way for new apartments and public buildings.

The mood of Washington changed abruptly with Kennedy's assassination. Turmoil rolled across the country. In Washington, the great explosion came in the spring of 1968, after civil rights leader and Nobel Peace Prize-winner Martin Luther King was shot to death in Memphis. In the predominantly black sections of Washington along Seventh Street N.W. and H Street N.E., blocks of stores were looted and burned. Elaborate plans for rebuilding were soon announced, but the scars were still evident a decade later.

With the unpopular war in Vietnam came hundreds of thousands of peace marchers who demanded that Richard Nixon end U.S. involvement there. In 1972, not long after the war ended, the Watergate scandal broke, shocking the nation and shaking its faith in the Presidency and those who serve in Washington. Yet through these difficult years and the problems and tensions that came with them, the city continued to change, to become more like the magnificent city that L'Enfant envisioned. In the mid-'60s President Lyndon Johnson's wife, Lady Bird, planted flowers and shrubs that brought color to parks that had been somber green for years and the country's bicentennial was lavishly celebrated in 1976. Since 1964, Washingtonians have been able to vote in presidential elections. In 1973, Congress once again gave Washingtonians the right to vote for local government.

In the west end of the city, the Kennedy Center was built on a site overlooking the Potomac. It attracts the world's greatest dramatic and musical companies and elevates Washington to a first-class theater and music town. The Mall has gained new splendors: the Hirshhorn Museum, the East Wing of the National Gallery of Art, the Air and Space Museum, the Arthur M. Sackler Gallery, and the National Museum of African Art.

A splendid subway system, Metro, has been built under the city's streets, linking downtown Washington—where a massive rebuilding project is taking place—to the suburbs.

L'Enfant's Dream Continues

Now, the city has never looked grander. New buildings rise among the trees and flowers, but much of the past remains. The Capitol stands solid, its interior walls still showing the scorch marks of the fires of 1814. Names like Jenkins Hill, Duddington, and Timberlake are preserved—at least for the moment—in the names of smart restaurants on Capitol Hill. Fort Stevens, where President Lincoln stood under fire, has been lovingly restored. Bronze statues of Civil War heroes grace Thomas Circle, Logan Circle, Scott Circle, Sheridan Circle, and many of the city's other parks. In these same parks, where thousands of soldiers camped during the Civil War, you can still find the names and initials that men carved into trees more than a century ago.

Even the pugnacious L'Enfant would be pleased if he saw Washington today.

THE WASHINGTON
WAY OF LIFE

Capital Living

by
TOM KELLY

Washingtonians—the 4.4 million people who live in the city and its four adjacent counties in Maryland and Virginia—are usually friendly people and pleasant to strangers; perhaps not as patient and polite as folks in, say, Charleston, South Carolina, but more so than those in New York City. Washingtonians honestly feel that they are the hosts and hostesses of the nation, and that the capital city, its monuments, and its historic places belong to those who don't live there as well as those who do.

The life-styles of Washingtonians—the way they live, dress, eat, drink, relax, and entertain themselves and others—are influenced by a consciousness of the ceremonial city in which they live. In other words, in a city of flags, trumpet flourishes, and State of the Union messages, people tend to be formal. To a considerable degree Washingtonians, male and female, live up to the stereotypical image of government bureaucrats wearing conservative three piece suits and carrying attache cases. But Washingtonians are somewhat like chameleons and the degree of formality depends upon who is President. For example, Washingtonians felt younger and more dashing but still properly preppy when John F. Kennedy was in charge. Although Jimmy Carter's down-home style never really did catch on, some ambitious hostesses tried serving peanut soup to their guests when he first arrived. When Ronald and Nancy Reagan were in town, the accent was on elegance at dinner parties the like of which had not been seen since the Madisons and Monroes were in the White House. In fact, the sale of women's white gloves jumped sharply.

High Society

Washington society, led by the highest level of elected officials, changes significantly every four or eight years. Politics notwithstanding, high society maintains an anchor through a somewhat mystical branch of permanent VIPs called the Cave Dwellers. The locals chide that these aristocratic families have been around Georgetown so long that their more remote ancestors supposedly lived in caves! In their purest form, the Bealls, Clagetts, Bowies, Blairs, and other Cave Dwellers actually have been in place longer than the White House. In recent decades, the term has been broadened to include bluebloods who seem to have been around forever but who were actually born somewhere else.

Most Washingtonians, however, are neither high-born nor natives; two-thirds arrived here as adults, some decades ago, some just the other day. They're proud of it and they tend to keep their home state links alive. Fifty active State societies operating in Washington specialize in casual picnics and occasional formal dances in downtown hotels. Each state is represented in the spring Cherry Blossom Festival by a Princess, very often the daughter of a Senator, a Member of Congress, or a high member of the current administration. Teas and other festivities also abound. The best of the State gatherings is unquestionably Louisiana's annual Mardi Gras Ball, held on a weekend after Fat Tuesday. It sparkles with marvelous food and music, ladies in colorful gowns, some gents in white tie and tails, dozens of beauty queens from all over the State and thousands of "throws"—the small favors traditionally tossed from floats at Carnival parades in New Orleans.

Working Washington

The Federal Government is no longer the area's biggest single employer. Nearly one-fourth of the local population works for Uncle Sam, and the rest work in hundreds of other enterprises. In addition to those who work for the government directly, however, there are a great many employed by the government indirectly as lawyers, consultants or contractors. Some folks on the outskirts of the D.C. area actually farm or raise horses. The Washington area has the highest percentages of lawyers and psychiatrists in the country—though this does not mean the inhabitants are either more litigious or crazier than other people. Most of the lawyers work in or out of government writing or interpreting laws or lobbying to change legislation. A great many of the psychiatrists are engaged in research.

Basically, Washington life-styles, like life-styles everywhere, reflect fundamentals such as income, education level, birth place, and cultural and religious backgrounds—but other influences have crept in, too. One of the most enduring semi-social units among government workers is the office car pool. Working for the Federal Government is like working for big brother—government offices provide newcomers with basic car pool information—who lives near where they live—and soon they become absorbed into the often small, benevolent, and protective societies within the impersonal whole. Pool members tip each other off about job openings and job threats and trade information about office politics.

Who Lives Where

The Washington area includes the city itself, which has something less than a third of the population, and the Maryland and Virginia suburbs, which divide equally the rest of the population. Although each section has a separate government and a distinct style, the distinctions are not readily apparent to the visitor. As one drives out Connecticut Avenue, Chevy Chase, D.C., becomes Chevy Chase, Maryland, without changing in appearance or substance; high-rise Rosslyn in Virginia is conveniently across the river from the classic homes of Georgetown and hundreds of thousands of people move back and forth across the State lines each day in autos or aboard the clean, modish subway cars of the Metro system.

Washington bulges with people in the daytime and much of it remains lively at night. Some sections, such as Southwest, which was rebuilt in the 1950s and 1960s, have huge government office buildings that pretty much empty out after 5 P.M. However, Georgetown and the main commercial and social avenues, Connecticut, Wisconsin, and the part of Pennsylvania east of the Capitol, are heavily populated until the bars and night spots close their doors.

The differences between the people in one section of the Washington area and another are not dramatic but they exist. The Virginia suburbs have a much higher level of military families, reflecting the presence of the Pentagon and other military installations located there. People who have moved to the area from the deeper South seem to feel more at home settled in Virginia. Virginians themselves are likely to be from "WASP" families and give the impression, at least, of that sedateness associated with Southerners. The Maryland suburbs on the other hand have more cultural and ethnic variety—more Catholics and Jews, more delicatessens, more Irish music pubs, and more church-sponsored Greek and Italian food festivals. Both suburban areas abound in bowling alleys, fast-food outlets, and shopping malls.

Most people inside the city and around it are solidly set in the middle class. Two of the counties, Fairfax in Virginia and Montgomery in Maryland, are often cited as having the highest average family incomes in the country. Average incomes in the District and the other two counties (Arlington County, Virginia, and Prince Georges County, Maryland) are also impressively high. This prosperity is based to a great degree on families with two income producers, both earning good and often very good salaries. Combined annual family incomes of between $35,000 and $50,000 are common, and many families take in between $60,000 and $90,000. Nevertheless, clear economic boundaries exist with subtle and not so subtle shadings. The very rich people live in all three jurisdictions: in the District in Georgetown, along Foxhall Road, and in Spring Valley; in Potomac, Maryland; and in Middleburg and Warrenton, Virginia. People who are not considered rich but who are very well off may be found in Cleveland Park and on Capitol Hill in town, in Chevy Chase, Bethesda, and Kensington, Maryland, and in Fairfax and McLean, Virginia.

There are also poor people in the city, many of whom live between Seventh and 14th streets, N.W., in sections of Anacostia in the southeast section of the city, and in rural pockets of poverty in all the counties.

Washington itself is split into quadrants. The Capitol is the center point. The Northwest quadrant, by far the biggest, includes most of the government buildings and monuments, the major business sections and office buildings. It contains some of Washington's most beautiful areas, such as Georgetown and Rock Creek Park, as well as some of the worst slums. The Southwest quadrant was the site of a massive urban renewal project in the 1950s and 1960s, and has developed into a largely residential area for government workers who inhabit the modern apartments and condominiums there. Southeast and Northeast Washington are also pretty much residential areas.

About 65 percent of the people who live in the city itself and nearly 28 percent of those who live in the general area are black. Brookland in Northeast Washington—a large neighborhood of quiet streets and trim lawns—has had a large number of middle-class black families for decades (former Massachusetts Senator Ed Brooke grew up there), and the concentration has grown in recent years. The greatest number of high-income black families live along 16th Street, N.W., a stretch of large, handsome houses extending from downtown Washington across the Maryland line, bordering Rock Creek Park and usually referred to as the Gold Coast. The poorest blacks, who compose the largest bloc of poor people in the city, live between North Capitol and 14th Streets in Northwest and in sections of Southeast across the eastern branch of the Potomac from the rest of the city. The city west of Rock Creek Park and in the Capitol Hill section closest to the Capitol is heavily populated by whites. The most thoroughly integrated section of the city is in the high-rise and town-house residential section of the new Southwest.

Prince Georges County, Maryland, claims the heaviest concentration of blacks in the suburbs, where they make up about 30 percent of the population. The next highest black population is in Alexandria, Virginia. The other counties, Montgomery in Maryland and Arlington and Fairfax in Virginia, have far fewer.

Few other ethnic divisions exist in the city and its surroundings. Unlike Boston and New York, Washington was never an immigrant town although clusters of immigrants did arrive here in the early years of the century. The Irish settled in the section north of the Capitol called Swampoodle, Italians stayed in the areas south and east of Union Station, where many worked as stone masons and tile setters, and Germans congregated on the eastern edge of town on Bladensburg Road. Their descendants have long since dispersed themselves throughout the area. Among the newer immigrants, the concentration of Cubans and other Hispanic groups in Adams Morgan, the area around 18th Street and Columbia Road, has given the neighborhood a lively and exotic stamp. Many Koreans and Vietnamese immigrants live in Arlington County in Virginia.

People of all income levels are constantly concerned with schools no matter where they live in Washington. The public schools in Montgomery and Fairfax counties are considered very good, those in Prince Georges and Arlington judged average or better and, sadly, those in the District have been pronounced bad. Yet, there is hope for the District schools, for they are well-funded, test scores have improved recently, and some individual schools are now quite impressive. However, many families who can afford it tend to send their offspring to private schools. The city abounds with these schools, most with high tuitions and many of which are very good.

The area residents themselves have a high level of education. More holders of graduate degrees live here than in any comparable area, and about half of Washington's middle level bureaucrats are taking graduate degrees at Georgetown, George Washington, or American universities. The area abounds in fine institutions of higher education, but, surprisingly, they do not greatly influence the scene, either intellectually or socially.

Entertainment—The Great Capital Pastime

Life-styles are different of course for the single person living in D.C. Most young and affluent singles live in Georgetown, Foggy Bottom, Adams Morgan, or Capitol Hill. The more adventuresome reside amid nighttime Washington around Dupont Circle, where Connecticut, the avenue of smart shops, chic restaurants, and art-movie houses, intersects Massachusetts, the avenue of embassies and well-preserved nineteenth-century mansions that now serve as clubs, national societies, associations, and political think-tanks. Single Washingtonians support a wide variety of drinking and meeting places.

Washingtonians, married and single, spend a lot of time and money entertaining themselves and each other. Although the thousands of lobbyists, lawyers, and consultants keep hundreds of downtown expense-account restaurants afloat, most entertainment takes place at home, from casual backyard barbecues in Annandale to very formal dinners in Georgetown. The importance of the latter, where White House aides, newspaper publishers, editors, columnists, Cabinet members and diplomats exchange toasts and information, has perhaps been exaggerated, but entertaining in Washington is often serious business.

Gossip—the transfer of inside information or what passes for inside information—is serious business too. The city's premier professional gossip, Diana McLellan, whose column formerly appeared in the local papers, now writes on a variety of subjects for *Washingtonian* magazine. The town bubbles with talented amateurs as well, and Washington gossip is seldom idle. It has been said that in Washington sound travels faster than light and a whisper in a Congressional cloak room can be picked up instantly in a Georgetown salon. Much of the gossip has commercial value for lobbyists, lawyers, and other persons strategically situated—like who is resigning or being fired, who is being appointed, which Senators have decided not to run again and why, who is particularly friendly with whom, and who has just made some important person's hate list. The proper word in the proper ear can make or blight a career—so can invitations given or received.

Who entertains whom is grist for the gossip mill. Career Army and Navy officers (and all upper-echelon career officers come to Washington sooner or later) entertain appropriate Congressmen and defense contractors; lawyers entertain clients, judges, agency heads, and other lawyers;

television and newspaper people entertain political movers and shakers; and Presidential aspirants entertain selectively on all levels, from county party chairmen to archbishops. The same rituals occur on less glamorous levels. Division directors in government offices entertain their bosses and well-placed staffers from the Hill; research scientists from the National Institutes of Health entertain foundation officials, and so on down the line. All the upwardly mobile, in and out of government, entertain key Congressional committee chairmen every time they get the chance.

Washingtonians also engage in activities for sheer pleasure and their cultural life reflects their education level and prevailing affluence. Residents and tourists alike patronize the several first-rank legitimate theatres, led by the Eisenhower at the Kennedy Center, the art galleries, topped by the National Gallery, and the concert halls.

Washington is a mixed sports town, where football is king. The Redskins sell out every game, year after year—and it is prudent for the ambitious to be seen at the game with the right people. On the other hand, big league baseball left town years ago for lack of support and the Bullets of the NBA draw indifferent support. Attempts to draw fans to big league soccer and hockey games have lost investors lots of money.

No matter what the sport season, a central fact in Washington life— some would say *the* central fact—is the weather. Washington has two lovely seasons. Spring, beginning in late March and lasting half-way through June, is clean, fresh, and flowery. Summer, particularly the weeks from mid-July to mid-September, is almost always awful—very hot, very humid. Fall is as nice or nicer than spring and with a little luck, the crisp clear air and colorful foliage last into December. The winter is often as miserable as summer, having more rain than snow.

Washingtonians often go on picnics in the warm months—family picnics, romantic tête-à-tête picnics, church picnics, state society picnics, and volley-ball team picnics. The weather is ideal for picnics in the spring and fall, and even in the dog days of summer it is possible to eat and enjoy under the huge old trees of Rock Creek Park. Parks and picnic tables appear in abundance, and an endless supply of wine and cheese shops provide ample opportunity for spontaneous dining.

While you're in Washington, sample the Washington life-style. Pick up a sandwich and soda or one of the exotic temptations offered on a local vending cart, sit yourself down in Lafayette Park, and enjoy the view of the White House as you lunch among the area denizens—but remember to keep your eyes and ears open, for you never know what bit of gossip you may learn to pass on.

EXPLORING
WASHINGTON, D.C.,
AND ENVIRONS

EXPLORING WASHINGTON

Monuments, Museums, and Parks

by
JOHN F. McLEOD

John F. McLeod, a founder and past president of the Society of American Travel Writers, is a distinguished travel writer, formerly the travel editor of the Washington Daily News.

Before you start out, make sure you have familiarized yourself with Washington's layout, because it can seem pretty confusing at first. Washington is divided into four sections—northwest, northeast, southeast, and southwest—directions that relate to the Capitol Building. In line with its major axis are North and South Capitol streets, dividing the city into east and west with regard to street numbers, which increase in size as you walk away from the Capitol. West of the Capitol the dividing line is the center of the Mall; to the east, East Capitol Street. Alphabetical streets, beginning with "A," progress from it. The alphabetical streets for some reason skip "J" (one theory holds that this is so because infamous traitor Benedict Arnold belonged to J company in the Army) and end with "W." Perhaps because it might otherwise be confused with 1st Street, I Street is often spelled Eye Street. Beyond the first alphabet is a second sequence of two-syllable streets (Adams, Belmont, Clifton); then the three-syllable letter-

49

of-the alphabet names (Allison, Buchanan); and, still farther out, a fourth alphabetical sequence of streets named for trees (beginning with Aspen). It's well for the first-time visitor finding his way around the city to ignore, as best he can, the many diagonal avenues which shoot across the city, linking Washington's many circles and parks, although once you get used to their pattern they are great time-savers, particularly for motorists.

A Starting Point

Start a Washington walking tour—and leisurely walking is by far the best way to explore this city—from Lafayette Square directly in front of the White House. Lafayette Square was named, of course, for the Marquis de Lafayette, the gallant young French nobleman who served at the side of General Washington. Yet the square is dominated by an equestrian stat-ue (sometimes called the "hobby horse") of Andrew Jackson. It's an exact duplicate of one facing St. Louis Cathedral in Jackson Square in New Orle-ans. The statue, cast in 1853, is the first equestrian statue cast in America. The horse's hindquarters are of solid bronze made from melted cannon. Lafayette's statue, in the southeast corner, is just one of four standing on each corner of the square. Circling the square clockwise you find the stat-ues of three other Revolutionary War heroes: Rochambeau, commander of all French troops, particularly recognized for his help at the decisive last battle of Yorktown; Baron von Steuben, the Prussian drillmaster; and Thaddeus Kosciuszko, the dashing Polish nobleman who gained fame at the crucial Battle of Saratoga. No one is quite sure why Lafayette's statue wasn't placed in the center of the park, or why, since the imposing figure of Andrew Jackson dominates it, the park wasn't named for the great Democrat and hero of the War of 1812. The short street on the west side of the park, however, is named Jackson Place. (The one on the east is Mad-ison Place.) Whatever the speculations about the name, it's a most pleasant little park, one on which National Capital Parks' gardeners lavish much attention. It's pleasant to sit on one of the many benches in the park and watch the pigeons and squirrels and the people going by while you study your map and guidebook. Bernard Baruch, advisor to presidents, used a Lafayette Park bench as a sort of outdoor office.

While the official geographic name is Lafayette Square, and is so indicat-ed on most maps, this 8.2-acre square is also sometimes called Lafayette Park and it is indeed part of the National Park system. As custodian of the park, the National Park Service is also responsible for its wildlife, which included at last count some 140 gray squirrels, said to be the largest concentration of this type of squirrel ever reported in scientific literature.

There's an old Washington saying: "The squirrels are in Lafayette Park, but the nuts are across the street." The White House, of course, is just across Pennsylvania Avenue.

Three major Metro stops of Washington's subway system are only a block or so from Lafayette Square. They are the Farragut North and Far-ragut West stations, a bit north and west of Lafayette and Farragut Squares at Connecticut Avenue and K Street and 17th and I streets, and McPherson Square on I Street between 14th and Vermont Avenue. Metro can help your sightseeing around town, if your time is short or your feet give out. There are good large maps and directions at each of the Metro stations.

You can get a map and helpful local literature from the Washington Convention and Visitors Association, quite close to the park, at 1575 I Street, N.W., Washington 20005 or you can write in advance. Anyone interested in very detailed maps and travel literature should call in person at that traveler's mecca, the Washington headquarters of the National Geographic Society, located a few blocks away in a complex of buildings on M Street, from 16th to 17th streets. There, at 1145 17th Street, N.W., is the society's Explorers Hall, a permanent exhibition that tells the story of 100 years of adventure and discovery by more than 200 pioneering expeditions in many fields and many lands. Explorers Hall also contains the world's largest free-standing globe. The society's building is the work of Edward Durell Stone, who also is the designer of the Kennedy Center for the Performing Arts. His building for the National Geographic Society is considered by many to be one of the more handsome non-government structures built in Washington in recent years. To reach it from the park, a pleasant stroll up 16th Street takes you first to St. John's Church, called the "Church of the Presidents" because every president, starting with Madison, has attended it. It's a beautiful little church, erected in 1816 from a design by Benjamin Latrobe, and now almost dwarfed by the big buildings around it. To the east is the monolithic structure, so typical of bureaucracy, of the Veterans Administration. To the north is the more attractive but equally overwhelming headquarters of the AFL-CIO. Across the street is one of Washington's more gracious small hotels, the Hay-Adams, occupying the site where once lived Henry Adams, historian son and grandson of two presidents, and John Hay, biographer of Lincoln and secretary of state at the turn of the century.

Heading up 16th Street past the Sheraton-Carlton and Capitol Hilton hotels, you see the embassy that attracts the most attention, that of the Soviet Union at 1119 16th Street. It is in a palatial mansion built in the Taft era by the widow of George M. Pullman, the railway sleeping-car king. Beyond it are the University Club and buildings housing the American Chemical Society and National Education Association.

In your strolls, it won't take you long to discover that much of the city is torn up by construction projects. Currently the biggest is the Pennsylvania Avenue Redevelopment Project. The Metro subway, which has been ballyhooed as "the biggest public works project ever undertaken by man," is now largely completed in the downtown area. It eventually will be an 87-station, 103-mile system, if built as planned. Target date for completion: 1993. Completed portions already criss-cross the city, reaching into suburban Virginia and Maryland. Tourists now put a Washington Metro ride high on their "must" list of things to do. The basic fare is 80¢, although it may be more, depending upon the distance covered and time of day. For more information, write or call Washington Metropolitan Area Transit Authority, 600 Fifth Street, N.W., Washington, D.C.; (202) 637–7000.

Welcome to the White House

Probably the first of the great Washington attractions in which you will wish to spend considerable time is the White House, just south of Lafayette Park. Construction began on the White House in 1792—only in those days it was called the President's Palace—after the basic design, submitted by

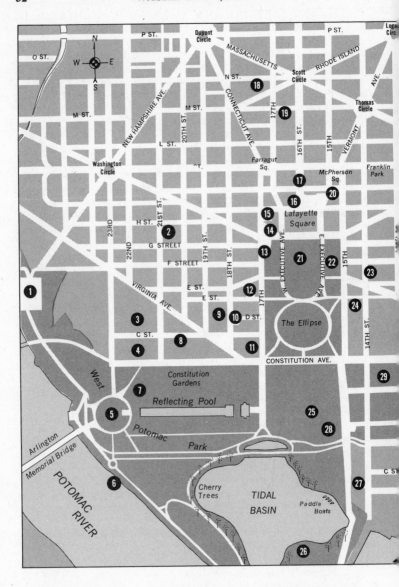

Points of Interest

Blair House **14**
Botanical Gardens **45**
Bureau of Printing and
  Engraving **27**
Capitol **47**
China Friendship Archway **54**
Constitution Hall **10**
Corcoran Art Gallery **12**
Commerce Dept. Building
  (Aquarium & Visitor's
  Center) **24**
Dept. of Energy **52**

Dept. of Interior **9**
Dept. of Justice **36**
Dept. of State **3**
Executive Office Building
  (former) **13**
FBI (J.E. Hoover Building) **35**
Federal Reserve Board **8**
Ford's Theater **34**
Freer Gallery of Art **40**
George Washington Univ. **2**
Government Printing Office **53**
Hirshhorn Museum &
  Sculpture Garden **41**

House Office Buildings **46**
Jefferson Memorial **26**
John F. Kennedy Center **1**
Library of Congress **48**
Lincoln Memorial **5**
Metro Center **31**
National Academy of
  Sciences **4**
National Air & Space
  Museum **42**

Cherry-blossom time at the Tidal Basin, with the Washington Monument in the

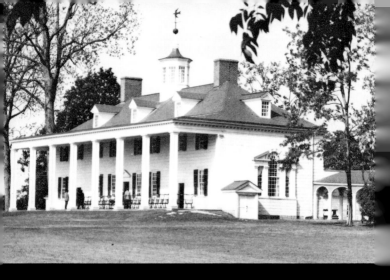

Mount Vernon, plantation home and final resting place of George Washington, overlooks the Potomac River in Virginia (top). One of Washington's most popul

The Lincoln Memorial is an inspiring tribute to the Great Emancipator — and a popular tourist attraction (top). A statue of Andrew Jackson stands in the center of Lafayette Square, which is opposite the White House (bottom).

The Old Smithsonian Institution "Castle" dates back to 1846 (top). The Jefferson Memorial is considered by many to be the most beautiful structure in the nation's capital (bottom).

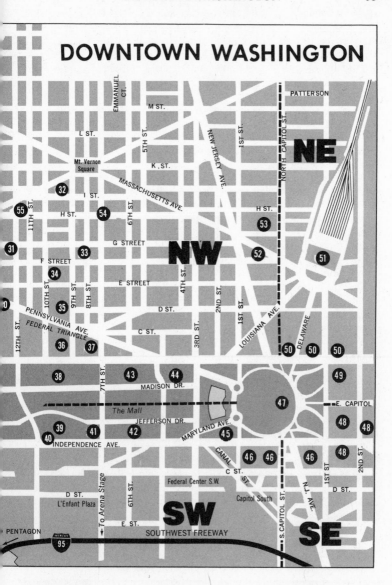

DOWNTOWN WASHINGTON

National Archives **37**
National Gallery of Art
(East Building) **44**
National Gallery of Art
(West Building) **43**
National Geographic Society **19**
National Museum of
American Art & Portrait
Gallery **33**
National Museum of
American History **29**
National Museum of Women
in the Arts **55**

National Natural History
Museum **38**
National Theater **23**
Org. of American States **11**
Pavilion at the Old P.O. **30**
Potomac Boat Tour Dock **6**
Renwick Gallery **15**
St. John's Church **16**
St. Matthew's Cathedral **18**
Senate Office Buildings **50**
Smithsonian Institution **39**
Supreme Court **49**
Sylvan Theater **28**

Treasury Dept. **22**
Union Station **51**
Veterans' Administration **20**
Vietnam Veterans Memorial **7**
Washington Convention &
Visitors Assn. **17**
Washington D.C. Convention
Center **32**
Washington Monument **25**
White House **21**

James Hoban of Charleston, South Carolina, was selected in a competition. Contrary to what you might think, George Washington never slept there. In fact, the White House remained largely unfinished until Andrew Jackson strode in and took over as president in March 1829.

The White House is open to the public Tuesday through Saturday from 10 A.M. to 12 noon. Entering near the East Gate on East Executive Avenue, you may visit all of the rooms on the State floor. When the tour is over, you leave through the Main Portico, facing Pennsylvania Avenue.

Beginning at 8 A.M., from Memorial Day to Labor Day, you may obtain tickets with specific times of admission at a booth on the Ellipse, south of the White House. At other times of the year, however, you must stand in line outside the East Gate. Lines are generally not very long in late fall or winter. No matter how long the line is though, you will get in if you join it before noon, unless an official function results in shortened hours.

Guided tours of the Executive Mansion for VIPs are scheduled early in the morning, before the building opens to the general public. Ask your Senator or Member of Congress to arrange this for you, but allow plenty of lead time, particularly during the spring and summer months. Constituents, in groups of 50 or 60, usually see various rooms on the ground floor, in addition to those included in the public tour.

On rare occasions visitors get a glimpse of the President or some of his family and distinguished guests. Tourists see only the ground-floor public rooms—not the offices, the kitchens, press room, the presidential living quarters on the second and third floors, and so on.

What you do see are the most famous rooms. The East Room, the largest of all, is a lofty, dignified salon of white and gold with touches of blue. It is associated with splendid and solemn events: weddings and funerals, receptions and small concerts or recitals. President John Adams' wife, Abigail, hung her laundry in it. Today, it is mainly the public audience chamber, one of the most beautiful rooms in the world since Harry Truman had the White House gutted, strengthened and completely restored in 1948-52 (the balcony and South Portico were also added then).

The Green Room, named for the wall coverings of moss-green watered silk, is done in a graceful and delicate American Federal style. It's a fashionable parlor such as Adams or Jefferson might have known. Furniture includes a particularly striking New England sofa, originally the property of Daniel Webster. Paintings include portraits of Benjamin Franklin, President John Quincy Adams and Mrs. Adams.

The oval-shaped Blue Room was designed as the most elegant room of the president's house. The White House's first wedding took place here when President Grover Cleveland married Frances Folsom in 1886. This is where portraits of the first seven presidents hang.

The Red Room, called the "President's Ante-Chamber" in the original plans, is hung in cerise silk with gold scroll borders and is furnished as an Empire parlor of the early Nineteenth Century. One touch many visitors like is a little music stand near the fireplace which holds a copy of a lively air, "President Jackson's Grand March." The music stand dates from the room's architectural era.

The State Dining Room, second largest room in the White House, is used for official luncheons and dinners. Much of the design is English Regency. In Theodore Roosevelt's day a stuffed moose head commanded the room from atop a mantel decorated with carved buffalo heads. The mantel remains, but the moose head is long gone.

The Diplomatic Reception Room is especially notable for its superb wallpaper, *Scenic America,* made in Europe in 1834 and painstakingly transferred from a rural Maryland house in 1961. The wallpaper, based on earlier European engravings, shows American natural wonders that were particularly admired by Europeans: Niagara Falls, the Natural Bridge of Virginia, and so forth. This was the room Franklin D. Roosevelt used for his famous radio "fireside chats."

The Library, one of the newer rooms, didn't exist until this century. Its walls are a distinctive pale yellow, and furnishings include original Duncan Phyfe pieces. The book collection includes 2,700 volumes selected in 1962 by a special committee as representative of American thought and tradition.

Occupants of the White House may, of course, change the furnishings as they see fit; the tastes of a couple from, say, California may not be the same as those of a couple from Georgia. Changes of décor are inevitable.

World's Tallest Masonry Structure

Another favorite tourist spot where you are likely to stand in line is the Washington Monument. You may no longer walk up the 898 steps and you now need a special permit to walk down them. The 555-foot shaft of the Washington Monument, believed to be the tallest masonry structure in the world, is the dominant landmark in the city. It stands straight and clean against the skyline and can be seen from almost any direction. It's almost due south of the White House, from which it can be reached by a pleasant few minutes' stroll around the Ellipse and across Constitution Avenue. It's open 8 A.M. to midnight, April 1 through Labor Day, 9 A.M.–5 P.M. the rest of the year.

In 1783, even before the Continental Congress had selected the site of a permanent capital city, it approved erection of a monument honoring George Washington. Pierre L'Enfant designated the site, which was approved by Washington himself. It wasn't until 1833, however, that a National Monument Society was organized to sponsor a designer and to appeal for construction funds. In 1848 the cornerstone was laid and construction on the obelisk began. In 1855 construction funds were exhausted and building stopped until after the Civil War. Work was not resumed until 1878. The monument finally opened to the public in 1888—over 100 years after its construction was approved.

The monument grounds are a particularly splendid sight on a bright, breezy day when the 50 "star-spangled banners" surrounding it spank briskly in the wind. The big view is from the top of the monument, but there are also splendid vistas of the city from the knoll on which it stands. Few tourists complain of the wait. The elevator ride up takes only a minute, during which the National Park Service gives you a capsule lecture about the monument. You are told, for instance, to note the sharp change in the shade of the stone about a third of the way up the shaft showing where the long interruption in building occurred when the money ran out amid religious controversy whipped up by the anti-papist Know-Nothing Party in 1855.

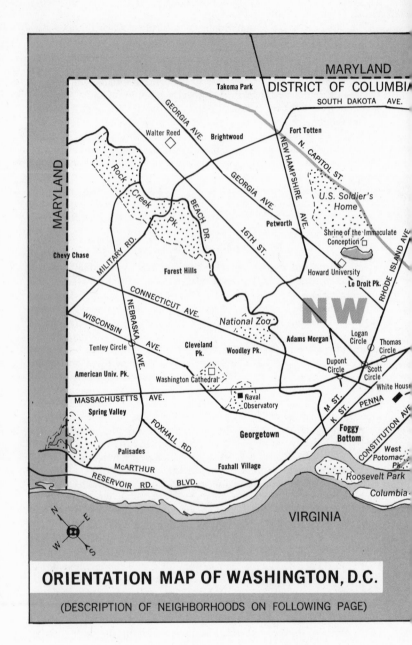

ORIENTATION MAP OF WASHINGTON, D.C.

(DESCRIPTION OF NEIGHBORHOODS ON FOLLOWING PAGE)

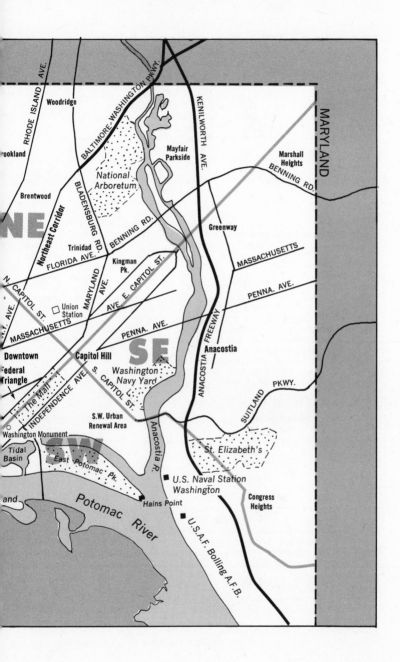

DESCRIPTION OF NEIGHBORHOODS
(map on preceding pages)

NORTHWEST

This is Washington's largest quadrant and holds nearly all of the city's sightseeing attractions, nightlife, shopping, business, and its most swank neighborhoods as well as some of its most depressed areas. The Northwest has the highest density of white residents in a city that is about 65% black. Along 16th St., nicknamed The Gold Coast, are many beautiful large houses owned by many of the city's affluent black families, as well as scores of embassies, churches, and temples. The area west of 16th St. and Rock Creek Park has retained its identity as a collection of comfortable neighborhoods from the Federalist and Victorian houses of **Georgetown** to the luxurious **Foxhall Road** estates to the comfortable turn-of-the-century **Cleveland Park** houses and the newer homes of **Chevy Chase.** East of 16th St. are more residential neighborhoods, including many newly-rehabilitated homes. One of the poorest areas of the city is the area between 7th and 14th Sts., N.W. **Adams Morgan** is an ethnically mixed area with a fairly young population. Its commercial area is a vibrant mix of ethnic goods, general merchandise and restaurants. **Dupont Circle** is one of the city's most desirable locations and a center of activity at night. Branching off Dupont Circle is Massachusetts Ave., known locally as Embassy Row. Also near Dupont Circle is the Connecticut Ave./K St. area known as the 19th St. Corridor, an area full of life by day and night. This area is also the center of Washington's "new" business district. Nearby **Georgetown** is the oldest part of the city and contains renowned Georgetown University, elegant residences as well as some of the finest restaurants, most chic shops and colorful street and nightlife in the city. Farther up Wisconsin Ave., the **Tenley Circle** area is active at night with the college and young professional crowd. **Foggy Bottom** is the location of large government offices, George Washington University, the Kennedy Center and expensive apartment complexes such as the Watergate. **Downtown** Washington's traditional business district is undergoing a face lift and revitalization, sparked by construction of a new Convention Center. It has some life at night in the form of Ford's Theater. The adjacent **Federal Triangle** area refers to a collection of federal buildings there. Washington has a small Chinatown section around G and H streets between 6th and 8th Sts., not far from the Convention Center.

SOUTHWEST

The **Southwest Urban Renewal** area was the first such project in the country back in the '50s and '60s. Today it is a section of increasingly integrated neighborhoods as well as a center for government offices. The area is also distinguished by the Arena Stage, L'Enfant Plaza and the southwest waterfront. **The Mall** area, active by day, abuts the city's major museums and some of its leading attractions.

SOUTHEAST

The Capitol sits at the center of the four quadrants but the **Capitol Hill** area spreads more to the southeast and southwest. This area has been renovated and is very popular with the young professionals and government workers who frequent the mix of bars, restaurants, and specialty stores that contribute to the area's vitality. Farther south and east, the neighborhoods become more rundown and less safe as the population dips below the poverty level in areas like **Anacostia.** There are large tracts of public land in the Southeast such as Bolling Air Force Base and St. Elizabeth's Hospital.

NORTHEAST

The southern and northern portions of the Northeast are characterized by comfortable, stable residential neighborhoods, such as **Brookland.** The principal sights in the area are the Shrine of the Immaculate Conception, the largest church in the U.S., the Franciscan Monastery with its reproductions of early Christian art, catacombs and replicas of Christian shrines, and the National Arboretum, more than 40 acres of flowering plants, trees and shrubs.

Many of the blocks of stone in the monument were contributed by states, foreign governments, or organizations. (You may read the inscription on the inside faces of the stones if you walk down the stairs.)

On summer evenings, free concerts are presented in the Sylvan Theater, under National Park Service sponsorship, on the south slope of the monument grounds. The schedule varies, so check the local newspapers for details.

The most spectacular time to be around the monument grounds is on the Fourth of July. There is generally music and other entertainment through the afternoon and early evening. After dark comes one of the country's most spectacular displays of fireworks. A crowd of some 100,000 people is usually on hand to watch it. When July 4 falls on a weekend or becomes part of a long weekend, the celebration is often extended for several days, with the Mall becoming a sort of midway for a music and crafts festival.

The Washington Monument is the centerpiece of Washington's grandest vista, the axis of its grand design. To the east is the great green corridor of the Mall, sweeping to the Capitol. To the west, across the Reflecting Pool that bears the shimmering image of the monument's soaring shaft, is the Doric Parthenon of the Lincoln Memorial. We suggest you walk along the south side of the reflecting pool, perhaps stopping to see the statue of John Paul Jones, the Revolutionary War naval hero, and the District of Columbia World War Memorial.

Constitution Gardens and The Vietnam Veterans Memorial

Added to the Mall as a Bicentennial project and extending west of the Washington Monument between Constitution Avenue and the Lincoln Memorial Reflecting Pool is Constitution Gardens, a 42-acre park with flowering trees, natural plantings of flowers, a six-acre lake, and refreshment and information kiosks.

The Vietnam Veterans Memorial, which was dedicated in November 1982, is in Constitution Gardens, at 23rd Street and Constitution Avenue. The V-shaped black granite memorial, designed by Maya Lin, lists the names of 58,156 Americans who died or were lost in Vietnam. In a relatively short time, it has become one of the capital's major attractions.

Lincoln and Jefferson

A pilgrimage to the Lincoln Memorial is to many the greatest emotional experience of visiting the city. It was brilliantly conceived, built, and located. Neither a tomb nor a shrine in the religious sense, it is considered by many to be the most eloquently moving memorial erected in memory of any man.

Perhaps the most physically humble and awkward of all U.S. presidents, Abraham Lincoln to many was the greatest because he bore his heavy burdens with dignity and humility.

In the massive statue by Daniel Chester French, he is seated looking out over the city's great Mall, past the spire of the Washington Monument and the long reflecting pools to the Capitol Building, two miles away.

Roger Angell wrote of the "tired, infinitely distant eyes" of Lincoln and of the "great hands" and of "soft light falling through the marble ceiling."

The best time to visit the Lincoln Memorial, many agree, is late on a rainy night when you are likely to be alone with your thoughts.

On his last night in Washington as president, Richard Nixon quietly paid a midnight visit to the Memorial. Whenever it is open you will find visitors, from many lands and of many ages, reading the words of two of his greatest speeches—the Gettysburg Address and the Second Inaugural—carved on the walls of the chamber.

Inscribed above the statue itself are the words:

"In this temple, as in the hearts of the people for whom he saved the Union, the memory of Abraham Lincoln is enshrined forever."

Washingtonians also urge visitors to go to the Memorial by daylight. As at the Washington Monument, you have a magnificent view—in one direction back across the Reflecting Pool and the Mall; in the other, the fabled Potomac River and the Arlington Memorial Bridge. In a direct line is another memorable specimen of the Doric-columned Arlington House, also called the Custis-Lee Mansion, home of Robert E. Lee. It sits high on a hill in Arlington National Cemetery, directly overlooking the grave of President Kennedy.

From the Lincoln Memorial it's another brief, relaxing stroll across West Potomac Park to the Tidal Basin, famed for its flowering Japanese cherry trees. Among the trees is a Japanese stone lantern, which is lighted each spring by a woman from the Japanese Embassy to begin the week-long Cherry Blossom Festival, which takes place in early April. Around the basin to the east, swan boats may be rented. On the south shore of the basin stands the Jefferson Memorial erected on land that was reclaimed from what had been a swampy edge of the Potomac. The exterior and the setting of this John Russell Pope classic is superlative, but most visitors agree that the giant statue of Jefferson within it is something of a letdown.

The Memorial was built in the Pantheon form that Jefferson favored in designing his own Monticello and the University of Virginia rotunda. Its rounded form accents the spire of the Washington Monument to the north and the rectangular perfection of the Lincoln Memorial, which forms the other apex of the triangle of monuments to the west.

One of the most pleasant get-away-from-it-all sites in Washington is Hains Point in East Potomac Park, which projects like a ship's prow into the broad expanse of the tidal Potomac, where it is joined by the Anacostia River. Here, even when not a leaf moves in the rest of the city, there is always a breeze. There is a golf course, swimming pool, and indoor and outdoor tennis courts. Most of the thousands of people who visit the point on a summer day, however, just go to enjoy the breeze, and perhaps bring a picnic lunch and watch the boats on the rivers. The side of East Potomac Park facing the Potomac is lined with double-blossom cherry trees, which are a bit showier and later-blooming than the variety around the Tidal Basin. On the east side of the park are giant weeping willow trees.

If you've done all of this by foot, we suggest you call a taxi and return to your hotel. You've had a good day of it, and you'll be tired.

Around Jackson Place

A tour for another day, again beginning at Lafayette Square, takes you down one side of the Mall to the Capitol and brings you back along the other side. This covers a lot of ground, and if you have small children

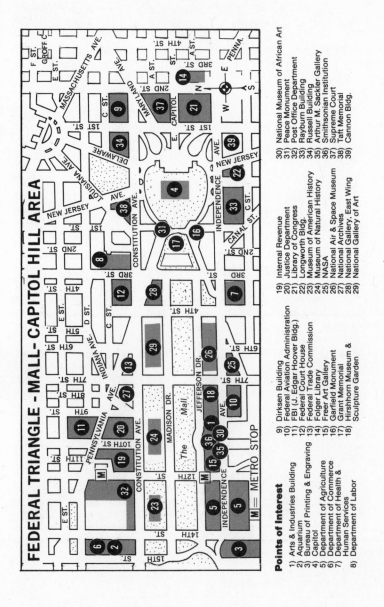

FEDERAL TRIANGLE – MALL– CAPITOL HILL AREA

Points of Interest

1) Arts & Industries Building
2) Aquarium
3) Bureau of Printing & Engraving
4) Capitol
5) Department of Agriculture
6) Department of Commerce
7) Department of Health & Human Services
8) Department of Labor

9) Dirksen Building
10) Federal Aviation Administration
11) FBI (J. Edgar Hoover Bldg.)
12) Federal Court House
13) Federal Trade Commission
14) Folger Library
15) Freer Art Gallery
16) Garfield Monument
17) Grant Memorial
18) Hirshhorn Museum & Sculpture Garden

19) Internal Revenue
20) Justice Department
21) Library of Congress
22) Longworth Bldg.
23) Museum of American History
24) Museum of Natural History
25) NASA
26) National Air & Space Museum
27) National Archives
28) National Gallery, East Wing
29) National Gallery of Art

30) National Museum of African Art
31) Peace Monument
32) Post Office Department
33) Rayburn Building
34) Russell Building
35) Arthur M. Sackler Gallery
36) Smithsonian Institution
37) Supreme Court
38) Taft Memorial
39) Cannon Bldg.

along you may wish to divide this tour in two, perhaps one down along the south side of the Mall, another returning. Before you start on the long walk, you might just take a look across Jackson Place at one of the original homes still facing Lafayette Square. It's Decatur House, once occupied by the naval hero, Commodore Stephen Decatur, who originated the toast, "Our country! In her intercourse with foreign nations, may she always be in the right; but our country, right or wrong." The house was designed by Benjamin Latrobe. Henry Clay and Martin Van Buren, later the eighth president, also lived there. The house is now a museum, operated by the National Trust for Historic Preservation.

A bit west of the square and facing Pennsylvania Avenue is Blair House, originally owned by Francis P. Blair, confidant of presidents from Jackson to Lincoln. It now fittingly serves as the presidential guest house. President Harry S. Truman lived here during the White House renovation. He was in Blair House when Puerto Rico nationalists attempted to carry out an assassination plot. Next door is the Renwick Gallery, the Smithsonian's showcase of American decorative arts and design. The U.S. Chamber of Commerce headquarters building, also facing the square, is situated where once stood a mansion occupied by Daniel Webster when he was secretary of state.

The Treasury Ruins the Plan

Heading toward the Capitol from the White House area, you come first to the Treasury Building, built in 1842 and the oldest of the government department buildings. When Andrew Jackson designated its site next to the White House (he liked to keep his eye on those handling the cash), he threw into the ashcan for the time being the L'Enfant plan, which provided that Pennsylvania Avenue, the city's main ceremonial street, should lead directly from the Capitol to the White House. Legend has it that Jackson became so enraged over the long debate about where to build the Treasury that he threw his walking stick down on the ground and said the building would stand where the stick fell. As a result, inaugural and other parades must dogleg around the Treasury Building. On either side of the building are statues of two famous early secretaries of the treasury. Alexander Hamilton, the first, is on the south side; Albert Gallatin on the north. The history of the Treasury and its functions is told through exhibits inside the building.

From the Treasury, walk south on 15th Street past the Hotel Washington (which has an excellent rooftop dining room and cocktail lounge) to the Commerce Department Building. When constructed, this was the world's largest government office building. It reputedly has five miles of corridors and 5,000 windows. Of particular interest are the aquarium in the basement and Visitors Center in the lobby.

The Federal Triangle

Commerce is the first of a complex of buildings called the Federal Triangle, between Pennsylvania and Constitution avenues. The others, east along Pennsylvania Avenue, are the District Building, housing District of Columbia municipal offices; the classic, semi-cylindrical "new" Post Office Department Building and the "old" Romanesque one with the tower, site of the Pavilion at the Old Post Office, an eclectic collection of shops and restaurants (the U.S. Postal Service now is actually located in L'Enfant Plaza S.W.); Labor Department; Internal Revenue Service; Department of Justice; the National Archives; and the Federal Trade Commission. Across the street from the Justice Department is an FBI structure named for J. Edgar Hoover. The popular FBI tour is given here every 15 minutes, weekdays from 9 A.M. to 4:15 P.M.

The National Archives, a handsome building modeled after the Pantheon, houses America's most precious documents, including the Declaration of Independence and the Constitution. It's open from 10 A.M. to 5:30 P.M. daily except Christmas. There are special facilities for students and researchers, but most visitors make only a brief stop to see the documents, protected by one of the world's most elaborate burglar-alarm systems. Sealed in glass containers filled with inert gas, they also are protected against deterioration.

The Mall Museums

On the south side of Constitution Avenue, opposite the Federal Triangle on one side and facing the green expanse of the Mall (an ugly mass of railroad tracks and switching yards up until the early part of this century) on the other, are—heading east—the Smithsonian's Museum of American History, formerly the Museum of History and Technology; the venerable Museum of Natural History, formerly called the National Museum; and the handsome National Gallery of Art. There are Metro stops at both the Federal Triangle and the Smithsonian.

Near the top of everyone's must-visit list, the Museum of American History displays in striking fashion some of the Smithsonian's most popular collections, including the famous display of first ladies' inaugural gowns and the original American flag Francis Scott Key so proudly hailed as it flew from Fort McHenry during the War of 1812. The old National Museum is famed mostly for its display of the biggest elephant of record, 13 feet high, killed in Africa in 1955. It also houses the 45½-carat Hope Diamond, largest blue diamond in the world, and a fabled 330-carat sapphire, plus the gold nugget found by James Marshall, which launched the 1848 California gold rush. The National Museum of American Art, formerly the National Collection of Fine Arts and once housed here, has been moved to the fine old Patent Office Building at Eighth and G streets, N.W., also housing the National Portrait Gallery.

The finest collection of art in Washington—and one of the very best in the world—is in the National Gallery of Art. The beautiful rose-white marble building and one of the collections within it was the gift of Andrew Mellon, the Pittsburgh financier who was Secretary of the Treasury under Hoover. It also houses the at least equally famous collections of Chester Dale, Samuel H. Kress, Joseph Widener, and Lessing Rosenwald. The building was designed by John Russell Pope, architect of the Jefferson Memorial, and is especially renowned for its great rotunda. Corridors from it lead to some 100 exhibit halls. Sightseers often plan their tours so as to have lunch in the Garden Cafe here or in the East Building's self-service Buffet, Cascade Cafe or Terrace Cafe. A favorite time for Washingtonians is Sunday evening, when visitors may also enjoy the free concerts of the National Gallery Orchestra. Probably the most famous single painting in the gallery is Leonardo da Vinci's *Ginevra de Benci,* but it also contains great works from almost all the major European schools and is strong in French Impressionists as a result of the Chester Dale bequest. Across from the gallery on Constitution Avenue splashes one of the simplest but loveliest of Washington's many fountains, a memorial to Andrew Mellon, who gave Washington its richest gift.

Just east of the Gallery is the $94.4-million annex designed by I. M. Pei. Opened in 1978, it includes contemporary works of art, one of the more interesting being the Alexander Calder mobile inside the great central courtyard. It also houses changing exhibitions of wide-ranging diversity from many eras.

The Capitol—Monument on a Pedestal

Heading east along Constitution Avenue you'll almost have reached Capitol Hill. At the very foot of the hill, at the eastern end of the Mall, is one of the biggest statuary groupings in the city, the Grant Memorial. The bronze of General Grant is said to be the second-largest equestrian statue in the world, topped only by the one of Victor Emmanuel in Rome, and that by only half an inch.

Also at the western foot of the hill are statues of President Garfield and Chief Justice John Marshall. At Constitution Avenue and First Street stands the relatively new memorial to Senator Robert A. Taft, a 100-foot-high bell tower with a solitary bronze figure of Taft at its base.

Capitol Hill itself encompasses not only the 131 acres of the Capitol grounds, but in general terms also includes the three Senate office buildings to the north of it, the three House office buildings to the south, the Library of Congress and Supreme Court buildings to the east, plus the surrounding residential and business area, which includes a half-dozen hotels. At the northernmost edge is the monumental Union Station, which formerly housed a National Visitors Center, in addition to serving as a railroad station. The Visitors Center site is now being converted into a shopping center and a 1,300-car garage for both buses and private cars. Nearby is an entrance to Washington's Metro subway system, serving the north, or Senate, side of the Capitol Hill area. There's another Metro station on the south side near the House office buildings.

L'Enfant selected what was then called Jenkins' Hill as the Capitol site, calling it "a pedestal waiting for a monument." Today, it holds the country's most majestic and important buildings, covering 3½ acres. The 535 Members of Congress who convene in its two houses are served by more than 7,500 staff employees. The building is a complicated labyrinth and few indeed are the native Washingtonians who can find their way about easily. Historical tours of the building leave from the Rotunda from 9 A.M. to 3:45 P.M. daily except Thanksgiving, Christmas, and New Year's Day and include the Rotunda, Statuary Hall, the original part of the Capitol and the crypt area. If you prefer to wander on your own, don't miss the old Supreme Court Chamber and the old Senate Chamber.

The style of the Capitol building is the result of a design competition conducted by Thomas Jefferson who wanted a classical Greek design. The contest was won by Dr. William Thornton who received a prize of $500 for his basic design, which later was improved upon by other noted architects such as Benjamin Latrobe. The Capitol building's architecture also set the style for state capital buildings for the next 150 years. Today the Capitol building is 751 feet long, 350 feet wide, and from the base to the top of the Statue of Freedom on the dome it is 287 feet high. That 19-foot-high statue itself looks roughly like Pocahontas, but the sculptor, Thomas Crawford, who did his work in Rome, said he had a freed Roman slave in mind. Before the statue was placed on the dome in the mid-1850s, the sculptor was forced to substitute a feather headress atop Freedom's head. The original cap the statue wore, modeled after those worn by Roman slaves, was rejected by Southern Senators, led by Mississippi's Jefferson Davis, on the grounds that it was a deliberate provocation of the South during a time when the issue of slavery was being hotly debated within the Capitol. The cast-iron dome on which she stands weighs 4,455 tons, and engineers say it expands and contracts according to outside temperatures as much as four inches a day.

The most impressive room in the Capitol is the Rotunda, under the great dome. The official tours start from here. (Here is where the flag-draped caskets of presidents John F. Kennedy, Dwight Eisenhower, and Lyndon B. Johnson lay in state.) The dome rises to 180 feet above the Rotunda's floor.

The 10-ton bronze "Columbus Doors" leading to the Rotunda are masterworks portraying the story of Columbus' discovery. On the high walls hang eight immense oil paintings telling the story of America in scenes showing "The Baptism of Pocahontas" and the surrenders of General Burgoyne and Lord Cornwallis, among others. Atop the dome is a giant allegorical painting done by Italian artist Constantino Brumidi (who worked as Michelangelo did in the Sistine Chapel, lying on his back, applying paint with utmost speed to fresh plaster). Figures were painted as much as 15 feet tall so as to appear in natural scale from below. "My one ambition," Brumidi wrote, "is that I may live long enough to make beautiful the Capitol of the one country on earth in which there is liberty." He was able to complete only a third of his painting, however, when he died after a fall from the scaffold. A pupil, Filippo Costaggini, took eight years to complete eight other sketches left by Brumidi. The final gap in the 300-foot-long circular frieze wasn't completed, however, until 1953. The frieze depicts scenes from American history. Brumidi fell as he was painting Penn's treaty with the Indians. The last scene painted was the Wright Brothers' first powered flight in 1903.

From the Rotunda, the next stop is what many consider the most interesting single room of the Capitol. Now called Statuary Hall, it originally was the legislative chamber of the House of Representatives. It is renowned for its reverberating acoustics. A slight whisper uttered in one part of the hall may be heard distinctly across it, a phenomenon which delights modern tourists much more than it did the legislators. When Statuary Hall was set up, each state was invited to contribute two statues of native sons or daughters they considered sufficiently worthy of the honor. The weight of statues, however, strained the beams supporting the floor, and now there's a limitation of one favorite son per state. Other statues have been placed in the Hall of Columns or elsewhere in the building. Just outside Statuary Hall is a statue of Will Rogers, the humorist who gained fame making jokes at Congress' expense.

To watch Congress in session, from either the House or Senate gallery, it's necessary to get a pass from a senator or member of Congress. This is no problem. If you're a constituent, you can bet you will receive a warm welcome. While getting the passes you might also obtain permission to lunch in one of the Capitol restaurants, where the bean soup has been a popular specialty for years. It's made and served every day by special order of Congress! A must for every young visitor to the Capitol is to ride on one of the miniature subways connecting the Capitol with the Senate and House office buildings on either side. If you wish to watch a Congressional committee meeting—and, incidentally, they are often more interesting and livelier than what transpires in the actual legislative sessions—watch the daily newspapers' "Today in Congress" listing of the meetings, specifying which are public.

Taxpayers who have a penchant for snorting in righteous indignation particularly like to look over the Sam Rayburn House Office Building, which cost about $75 million, as compared with a total of $12 million spent for the first two Congressional office buildings.

The Library of Congress and Supreme Court

You'll hear less indignation about another expanding institution on the Hill, the Library of Congress, which has recently opened a third building to house its ever-expanding collection. It all began with a $5,000 appropriation in the early 1800s to stock one room in the Capitol. Now, the library is generally believed to be the largest and most important in the world, with over 83 million items. It offers both permanent and special exhibitions of manuscripts and documents. A unique feature is the Coolidge Auditorium endowed concert series. Some of these concerts are played on the library's collection of rare Stradivarius instruments. The library's musicology section also has one of the world's finest collections of folk-music recordings. The original building is of ornate Italian Renaissance design, with an interesting copper dome and Neptune Fountain outside. The annex is of severe, functional modern design. A handsome building just around the corner at 201 E. Capitol Street, S.E., is the Folger Shakespeare Library, containing the largest Shakespearean collection in the world. It also has a model of the Globe Theater, in which many of Shakespeare's plays were first performed in seventeenth-century London, plus a large exhibition gallery with a wide assortment of Elizabethan-era relics.

Just north of the Library of Congress on First Street is the Supreme Court Building. It is unlike any other building on Capitol Hill. Designed by Cass Gilbert and constructed of the whitest of white marble, its rows of Corinthian pillars and sculptured pediment look much as the proudest temples of Rome must have appeared when Rome was in her glory. The Court meeting inside is equally impressive in a way even the Senate could never be. Check the local newspapers for schedules and try to visit when the Court is in session, arriving early enough for the opening ceremonials at 10 A.M. to hear the ancient call of the bailiff crying: "Oyez, oyez, oyez . . . " and, as the black-robed figures of the Supreme Court justices file in one by one, intoning, "God save the United States and this Honorable Court." The most exciting time to visit the Supreme Court is Monday, which is "Decision Day."

When you go to the Supreme Court, you will find two lines for visitors— one for a three-minute "look-see" and another one for those who want to hear the oral arguments, which usually last about an hour. If you are in that second line, after checking your coat, camera, etc., at the entrance, you may stay as long as you like.

From the Supreme Court, retrace your route back on First Street, S.E., to Independence Avenue, turn left and stroll down past the three House Office Buildings, and just beyond First Street S.W., see the U.S. Botanic Gardens, the favorite spot on the Hill for all who take their gardening seriously.

The Botanic Gardens are especially noted for their orchids, which bloom continously, but there's also a different display of plants throughout the year, from azaleas in early spring to poinsettias at Christmastime.

Just across from the gardens on Independence Avenue is the graceful bronze Bartholdi Fountain, a creation of F. Auguste Bartholdi, sculptor of the Statue of Liberty.

Strolling west on the south side of Independence Avenue, you pass what is still called the H.E.W. Building (formerly for the Health, Education and Welfare Department). It now houses many offices of the Health and Human Services Department. The Education Department, which now has its own Secretary, is housed in other office buildings nearby. H.E.W. is a modern building without much character, but inside, on its second floor, is one of the most vital operations in Washington, the Voice of America of the U.S. Information Agency. The Voice of America broadcasts over 1,200 hours a week in 44 languages over a network of 112 transmitters. You can get an excellent idea of its operation in a 30-minute free tour given at 8:40 A.M., 9:40 A.M., 10:40 A.M., 1:40 P.M. and 2:40 P.M., Monday through Friday, except holidays. Beyond VOA, heading west, are the new space-age buildings of the National Aeronautics and Space Administration and of the Department of Transportation. They are part of an extensive southwest complex of buildings resulting from redevelopment.

James Smithson's Legacy

Washington's current number-one tourist attraction is the National Air and Space Museum, one of the Smithsonian museums, on the north side of Independence Avenue at Seventh Street. Its opening, on July 1, 1976, was a major event of the Bicentennial celebration. The two exhibits most visitors wish to see are the Wright Brothers' 1903 Flyer (later nicknamed the *Kitty Hawk*), first heavier-than-air machine to fly; and Charles Lindbergh's *Spirit of St. Louis,* the little monoplane which made that historic New York-to-Paris nonstop flight. There are also spacecraft, a moon rock, and films which dramatize flight and space travel. The films are especially popular. It's wise to buy your tickets early for a specific performance, tour the museum or go sightseeing and then plan to return in time to watch the movie. Tickets are $2 for adults and $1 for children, students, and senior citizens.

Just west on Independence Avenue is the Joseph H. Hirshhorn Museum and Sculpture Garden, which houses what has been called one of the world's finest collections of modern art, some 6,000 works by such artists as Alexander Calder, Joan Miro, Henry Moore, and Pablo Picasso. The controversial cylindrical building has been dubbed "The Doughnut" by nearby office workers.

Walk another block west and you'll see the towers and turrets of Washington's most interesting architectural curiosity and one of its most cherished treasures, the main building of the Smithsonian Institution. Affectionately known as "the Castle," it was built in 1852 with funds willed by that curious English scientist, James Smithson, who had never even seen America but bequeathed it a half million dollars when he died in 1829. The institution now administers numerous divisions, ranging from the adjacent Freer Gallery of Art to the National Zoological Park (Washington Zoo, 3001 Connecticut Avenue, N.W.). In the main hall of the Smithsonian are exhibits showing the great scope of the institution's work. The Smithsonian has been called "the nation's attic," and it contains, at last count, something over 30 million catalogued items. After a brief look-in, you'll probably want to come back and spend hours exploring the galleries.

Adjacent to the main administration building is the Victorian-styled Arts and Industries Building currently housing an exhibit of goods and machinery that were originally shown at the Philadelphia Centennial Exposition in 1876. Nearby is the Smithsonian's new Arthur M. Sackler Gallery and the National Museum of African Art.

On the far western side of the Smithsonian Mall complex is the small but elegant Freer Gallery, famed for two quite contrasting collections. In one section are art treasures from the Near and Far East—Japanese screen paintings, sculptures in ivory, jades, and bronzes, as well as rare Greek, Aramaic and Armenian Biblical manuscripts. The other collection is of paintings by Americans, and it includes probably the world's finest collection of the works of James McNeill Whistler, who was a draftsman in Washington for the U.S. Coast and Geodetic Survey before moving on to London and Paris, where he achieved fame as an artist. Perhaps the most fascinating thing in the gallery is the Peacock Room, moved bodily from London where Whistler had designed it for a shipowner. The gallery and most of the collections in it were a gift of Charles Freer, a Detroit industrialist.

Remember that the Smithsonian's museum shops, as well as those at the National Gallery of Art and the Corcoran Art Gallery, offer unusual gifts and souvenirs of your visit to the nation's capital.

L'Enfant Plaza

Just south of Independence Avenue, where 10th Street would normally be, you may make an interesting diversion via L'Enfant Promenade. You begin by walking under the Forrestal Building, which houses the Department of Energy. This modern building straddles the promenade on concrete stilts. You cross the main line of railroads headed for their Potomac River crossing, scarcely noting them. Then you're at the edge of L'Enfant Plaza, a handsome quadrangle of buildings fronting a large square and lively fountain. Here are offices of such quasi-governmental outfits as Comsat, the satellite communications firm, and the U.S. Postal Service. (Its Philatelic Sales Center is on the ground floor of the west building.) The bottom two floors and top three of the east building are occupied by one of Washington's newer hotels, Loew's L'Enfant Plaza. You can stroll to the edge of the promenade overlooking the Potomac River and then on down to the riverfront, where a handsome array of new restaurants is finally open for business to replace the much-beloved (but smelly) waterfront markets and restaurants of an earlier era. After refreshment, say at

Hogate's or Phillips Flagship Restaurant, continue your stroll back up to Independence Avenue.

It's been said that only a born bureaucrat could love the Department of Agriculture buildings, which span Independence Avenue between 12th and 14th streets, N.W. The "Bridges of Sighs" over the avenue, however, are rather interesting to see, and there are generally agricultural exhibits in the patio of the administration building.

Of more interest is the structure just across 14th Street, S.W. This is the Bureau of Engraving and Printing, where the government designs, engraves, and prints paper money, bonds, and stamps. It is said that the face value of money printed here averages some $40 million a day. You can actually see the money being printed from the visitors gallery.

If you've done this tour-around-the-Mall in one day (and a lot of people do), you probably will want to soak your feet in hot water rather than go out on the town that night. You'll still, however, have seen only a part of Washington.

Heading Northwest

Back on your bench in Lafayette Square the next morning, map yourself a tour to Foggy Bottom and Georgetown in the morning and wind up with a tour of "Embassy Row" in the afternoon.

From the square, walk west on Pennsylvania Avenue, then turn left on 17th Street past what is now called the Executive Office Building. This was originally called the War, Navy and State Building, and all three of these important departments were housed here until the Pentagon was built. Patterned after the Louvre in Paris, construction began in 1871 and by the time it was completed in 1888, it was the world's largest office building. Purists now regard it as one of Washington's worst architectural monstrosities. Perversely, however, longtime Washingtonians love it, as they cherish the curious Smithsonian and old Post Office buildings. Those who work in it like it even more because of the high ceilings and general feeling of spaciousness. The building houses a presidential "hideaway" suite and offices of the Vice President, assistants of the president, and Presidential commissions. It is open for tours by appointment Saturday mornings. (Write the Preservation Office or call 202–395–5895 between 9 A.M. and noon weekdays for reservations.)

Just south and across the street is the Corcoran Gallery of Art, built by and named for a Washington banker who endowed it in 1897 in the hopes of encouraging American artists. Its largest collection is of American sculpture, paintings, and other works from the 18th century to the 20th. However, there are also some excellent works by French Impressionists. Admission is free daily because of a grant from the Armand Hammer Foundation, and on Thursday evenings, thanks to a grant from Mobil. There is an admission fee for special exhibitions.

The Corcoran hosts frequent performances by musicians, dancers, and other artists, plus post-performance receptions where those attending may meet and talk with the artists. There are also introductory tours, weekly lectures, studio sessions, and workshops. An affiliated Corcoran School of Art offers a full-time degree program and part-time courses in many fields of the fine arts, including photography.

Walking south on 17th Street you'll find the headquarters of the American Red Cross in an appropriately gleaming white building. In the courtyard is the statue of a nurse, in memory of nurses who were killed serving in World War I. Three magnificent stained-glass windows on the second floor are the largest original Tiffany windows in the U.S. outside of a church. Commissioned in 1917, they portray the ministry to the sick and wounded through sacrifice.

Another block south is the national headquarters of the Daughters of the American Revolution, whose annual convention is a Washington feature each spring. Memorial Continental Hall faces 17th Street between C and D streets, N.W. Connected to it, but facing 18th Street, is Constitution Hall, seating almost 4,000, where most of Washington's major concerts were held before construction of the Kennedy Center. Continental Hall contains one of the largest genealogical libraries in the world, where you can look up your own family tree—for a fee. There are also an historical museum and 32 period rooms representing various states. The Hall is open from 9 A.M. to 4 P.M. Monday through Friday, and 1 to 5 P.M. Sundays.

To the tourist, one of the most important of the buildings along 17th Street is the House of the Americas (formerly the Pan American Union Building), which also faces Constitution Avenue. This is the headquarters of the Organization of American States, the oldest international organization in the world. The building's interior patio is covered in winter by a sliding glass roof, which maintains a year-round tropical atmosphere. There are lush trees and plants from the OAS's 32 member states and in the center is a lovely fountain in pre-Columbian style. In the rear of the building is still another garden, centering around a statue of the Aztec god of flowers, Xochipili. There is also a beautiful Hall of the Americas and the Hall of Flags and Heroes, containing busts of the founders of the American republics and other heroes. You may also take a look at the impressive Liberator Simón Bolívar council meeting room and there is usually an interesting art exhibit in the Museum of Modern Art of Latin America, 201 18th Street, N.W., directly behind the main building.

Rawlins Square

From Constitution Avenue, you turn north again on 18th Street. In a small triangular park on your left is a handsome statue of Simón Bolívar, liberator of many South American republics. North of this is the Interior Department Building, which covers two blocks between 18th and 19th, C and E streets. Besides a museum explaining the work of the department, the building contains a most interesting craft shop displaying and selling works of American Indians—pottery, jewelry, rugs, etc. Just north of the building is Rawlins Square, which is one of Washington's loveliest jewel-like parks, especially beautiful when its tulip-tree magnolias are in bloom, generally in late March. The center of the pool is filled with water lilies.

Facing Rawlins Square to the northeast is Octagon House, which served as the temporary White House in 1814–15 for President James Madison and his wife Dolley, after the British burned the White House. Surprisingly the building does not have eight sides, as its name implies, but six! It and an adjoining new office building are the national headquarters of the American Institute of Architects, which has interesting exhibits on the development of architecture. The Octagon is open from 10 A.M. to 4 P.M. Tuesday through Friday and from 1 to 4 P.M. Saturday and Sunday, with walk-in tours available whenever the house is open.

Going east from Rawlins Square along E Street, you cross Virginia Avenue and enter what was once strictly a workingman's section of the city, quaintly called Foggy Bottom because the mists from the nearby Potomac River mingled with fumes from a gas works and brewery. Here, at 2201 C Street, now stands the second-largest office building belonging to the U.S. government, the State Department Building. This great structure is worth visiting if only to see the impressive lobby and exhibit hall, which tells the story of the department's operations. Foreign policy briefings are sometimes scheduled; you can obtain information about these and other public programs by calling 202–647–1645. The quaint old name Foggy Bottom still clings to the area around the State Department, it has been suggested, because many of the pronouncements issued by recent Secretaries of State are not noted for their clarity and precision.

From the State Department walk north on either 21st or 23rd Street to the campus of George Washington University, where the Lisner Auditorium is a popular small concert hall. Just north of the campus is Washington Circle. From it turn left onto Pennsylvania Avenue. When you cross Rock Creek you are in Georgetown, a beautiful section of the city that was once a separate town. The section pre-dates Washington. The nearest Metro station to Georgetown is the Foggy Bottom-George Washington University stop on 23rd Street, N.W., near George Washington University Hospital.

Georgetown

Georgetown was a flourishing small tobacco port long before the District of Columbia was formed. A distinct community within the District, it prides itself on narrow streets, some with cobblestones, far different from the broad avenues in other parts of the city.

Georgetown has no government buildings of note, nor any memorials, but to many it is the most charming part of the city. To your left from Pennsylvania Avenue as you enter the section is the old Chesapeake and Ohio (C&O) Canal. North of Pennsylvania Avenue and M Street, with which it merges, is one of Washington's finest residential sections. It's a pleasure to walk along any of the brick sidewalks under the bower of trees covering its narrow streets, looking at the beautiful Federal-period homes.

Some street signs in Old Georgetown bear both the usual alphabetical and numbered names and their pre-D.C. designations, such as Water Street. Strict zoning ordinances maintain the character of the community—prohibiting construction of apartment houses and requiring all remodeling or new construction to conform to the architectural style of the neighborhood, which is, as you would expect, Georgian. Georgetown's equivalents to "Main Street" are M Street, on which are most of the restaurants and nightclubs and several galleries, and Wisconsin Avenue, which intersects M at the heart of the section. Along Wisconsin Avenue are many of the fine and unusual shops for which Georgetown is noted. We particularly recommend, for someone with an hour's browsing time, Little Caledonia, at 1419 Wisconsin Avenue, N.W.

Georgetown has been called Washington's Greenwich Village, but actually there are few similarities. A more apt comparison would be with London's Chelsea. Like Chelsea, Georgetown is close to the river, and there is as much that is genuine as is contrived. It is the "artsy-craftsy" part of the city with the highest proportion of art galleries and bookstores and quaint shops. It also has fine restaurants, jazz clubs, boutiques, and a large number of fine, old mansions on quiet, tree-lined streets, with beautiful, small secluded gardens behind tall brick walls.

John F. Kennedy and his wife Jackie lived in one such Georgetown house before he was elected president, and many other prosperous Washingtonians have chosen to live in Georgetown. *Washingtonian* magazine occasionally features an article, complete with map, on "Where Washington's VIPs Live." A good many are in Georgetown. Most of the fine Georgetown homes, of course, are closed to the public, but many are open as are the embassies, for special charity tours. Most tourists don't see Georgetown at all, but a good guide on an individually escorted tour certainly will take you there and point out homes of some very prominent people.

Two fine old homes tourists can and should visit are Dumbarton House, 2715 Q Street, N.W., headquarters of the Society of Colonial Dames of America; and Dumbarton Oaks, 3101 R Street, N.W., which also contains a notable museum of Byzantine art and is the property of Harvard University.

An especially delightful adjunct of Georgetown is the old C&O Canal, which parallels the river through much of the community and far into suburban and exurban Maryland. It is maintained by the National Park Service and is much as it was more than 100 years ago. You may hike or bike it, or rent a canoe and paddle along it, or even navigate it by mule-hauled barge. In mid-winter you can often ice skate along it.

You could profitably spend a whole day in Georgetown, particularly if you have a leisurely lunch in one of the many fine restaurants and spend much time in the shops. However, if you have only a few days in Washington, you can confine this Georgetown "tasting" to an hour or two and push on to a more internationally oriented part of the city. Georgetown is particularly worth a repeat visit at night for a taste of the nightlife at places like Blues Alley and the Bayou.

Here is a recommended two-hour daytime sightseeing stroll through Georgetown:

If you've entered Georgetown via Pennsylvania Avenue, continue west past its juncture with M Street to the Old Stone House at 3051 M, believed to be the oldest building standing in the District of Columbia, dating to 1766. It's a National Park Service property and there are guided tours. The garden, with seasonal plantings, is a delightful place to sit and watch the passing throngs.

Around the corner, at 1221 31st Street, is the original Custom House, built in 1858 to serve the then thriving port. It's now the Georgetown branch of the U.S. Postal Service and you may wish to mail your scenic post cards from here.

Turn right again at the next corner onto N Street and you'll see three of the section's most desirable houses. At 3038 is the Federal-period (1816) home of the late statesman W. Averell Harriman; at 3017, the elegant eighteenth-century house bought by Jackie Kennedy and occupied by her for

GEORGETOWN

1) Cox Row
2) Custom House
3) Dumbarton House
4) Dumbarton Oaks
5) Evermay
6) The Foundry
7) National Zoo
8) Old Stone House
9) Prospect House
10) Quality Hill
11) Renwick Chapel
12) St. John's Episcopal Church
13) Scott-Grant House
14) Vice Presidential Mansion
15) Washington Cathedral
16) Watergate

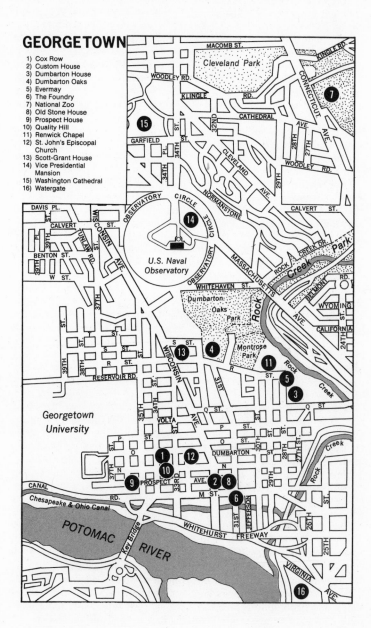

a short time after her husband's assassination; at 3014, a house built in 1799 and for a time the house of Robert Todd Lincoln, the President's son.

Turn right again on 30th Street past what is simply known as the Row of Four Houses, dating from 1790, at the corner of M Street. Cross M and walk down to the C&O Canal and Towpath. Here, on the south side of the Canal, is The Foundry, one of several somewhat controversial structures in this area adapting and somewhat preserving historic buildings. It contains a restaurant and expensive shops and is the center of much canal-side activity on spring, summer, and fall weekends. Other similar commercial adaptations just to the west are Canal Square and Dodge Center. Also alongside the canal, and much more charming, is Towpath Row, tiny houses that are as delightful to see as they are expensive to buy or rent.

Turn north from the Canal and then left on M Street. In that block, with its entrance at 3222 M Street, is Georgetown Park, probably the city's top urban shopping center, with more than 90 shops and parking for 500 cars. Built galleria-style, it has been described as a neo-Victorian extravaganza.

From M Street, turn north on Potomac and stroll up to St. John's Episcopal Church at the corner of O. Attributed to William Thornton, original architect of the Capitol, this is the home of the District's oldest (1794) church. Its current Victorian façade, however, was obviously constructed much later.

Backtrack on Potomac Street to N and turn right. At 3307 N is the house in which then-Senator John F. Kennedy and his family lived before moving to the White House. Farther east, at 3327 through 3339 N, are five houses collectively called Cox Row, particularly handsome specimens of the Federal period (1817) and named for the builder, John Cox. Across the street at 3322 is Bodisco House, which once served as the Russian Embassy.

At 34th Street, turn right and walk one block to Prospect. At 3425 Prospect, is Quality Hill, a patrician house built in 1798 and long occupied by Senator Claiborne Pell (D., R.I.). In the next block, at 3508, is Prospect House, built in 1788, once the home of the first Secretary of Defense, James Forrestal, and later serving as presidential guest house while the Trumans were living in Blair House during a White House renovation.

Still farther along Prospect, at 3600, is a house mostly known because of the steep flight of cement steps leading from it. It was the setting for a dramatic scene in the movie *The Exorcist.*

Prospect Street leads right to the campus of Georgetown University. The oldest (1789) Jesuit school in the U.S., it dominates the eastern embankment of the Potomac River. From the river below, the university's Gothic spires give Georgetown an exotic, almost medieval look.

The university's main gate is at 37th and O streets. Head east on O to bustling Wisconsin Avenue, where you can sample some of the many shops, and stroll up to R Street. At 3304–3310 R is a row of houses that were converted into a single luxurious home, "Friendship," where for many years Evelyn Walsh McLean, owner of the Hope Diamond, entertained the owners of the city's most famous names.

Backtracking on R Street, cross Wisconsin Avenue. At 3228 R is the Scott-Grant House, once occupied by President Grant as a summer White

House. Turn north on 31st Street and there is one of Washington's greatest treasures, the 16-acre estate of Dumbarton Oaks. For scholars it's famed for its Byzantine studies library and collection of pre-Columbian art. But what attracts most visitors are the surrounding gardens, perhaps the most beautiful in the city, especially from early April to late June. The buildings, administered by Harvard University, and the formal gardens surrounding them are only open from 2 to 5 P.M. Tuesday through Sunday, but the more extensive informal gardens, best entered via "Lovers' Lane" off R Street between 31st and Avon Place, may be visited daily, 8 A.M. to sunset, April 1 through October 31.

Continue along R Street east to 29th and there is the exquisite Renwick Chapel of Oak Hill Cemetery, designed and built in 1850 by the same architect responsible for the fanciful, original Smithsonian Museum.

Continue east on R Street and turn south on 28th, and you'll see Evermay, one of the true Georgetown showplaces, a manor house behind iron gates topped with gold. This was built in 1801 by Samuel Davidson, who sold the land on which the White House was built. It is open to the public on garden tours and is generally the star attraction of any tour.

Go south on 28th to Q and turn right. At 2715 you'll find Dumbarton House, not to be confused with Dumbarton Oaks. The House is one of Georgetown's oldest (1747) and stateliest. Its classic good looks stem from a remodeling (1805) by Benjamin Latrobe, who also designed Decatur House and St. John's Church on Lafayette Square.

There's a lot more to see and do in Georgetown, but that's about as much as two hours will allow.

Embassy Row

A good way to circle from Georgetown into "Embassy Row" along Massachusetts Avenue, N.W., is to cross Rock Creek Park on the unusual, curving Buffalo Bridge at Q Street. (It's so named because of the life-size buffalo sculptures at either end. There are Indian-head friezes below, which you see as you drive along the Rock Creek Parkway.) After crossing this delightful bridge, turn left on 23rd Street and you are right in the middle of the biggest concentration of Washington's embassies. On your left is that of Turkey. Across the street is Romania's. Then you're at Sheridan Circle, around which are the embassies of Ireland, Greece, Kenya, and Korea. Between Sheridan Circle and the Naval Observatory to the west are a score of embassies, among the most notable being the great mansion of the British government and the charming Japanese Chancery, with its garden and cherry trees. In the center of this array, serving the embassies of the Moslem countries, is the striking Mosque and Islamic Center, with a 162-foot-high minaret.

Just off Massachusetts Avenue, a block north on 21st Street, is the gallery that strikes many Washington visitors as their greatest delight, their own "personal" discovery. This is the Phillips Collection in the former home of Duncan Phillips. It's a small but truly great collection including Renoir's *The Luncheon of the Boating Party* and two *Repentant Peter*s, one by El Greco and the other by Goya.

Phillips opened his home and his collection to the public in 1918. Although he collected a few old masters and some of the best work of the French Impressionists, Phillips believed also in modern artists. In fact, his collection has been called the nation's first museum of modern art, with rooms filled with work by such painters as Mark Rothko, Paul Klee, and John Marin. A modern annex houses some of the collection. The museum is open daily, except Mondays and some holidays. Donations are encouraged. There are concerts most Sundays at 5 P.M. from September through May.

A few blocks east of the Phillips Collection on P Street is a cluster of commercial galleries, some specializing in the works of Washington artists, and just beyond them is Dupont Circle, a handsome small park with a splashing fountain in the center. It's also a lively social center for the somewhat bohemian crowd who live hereabout, as well as for older people who just like to sit in the sun and feed the squirrels. A Metro stop reached by one of the world's longest escalators is at Dupont Circle.

Almost everyone who likes to stroll will find this part of Washington interesting and fun.

If you head south on Connecticut Avenue to Rhode Island Avenue and then walk a half-block east, you will find St. Matthew's Cathedral, the impressive setting for President John F. Kennedy's funeral.

The Watergate Area

Winding through this section of the city is another of Washington's greatest treasures, Rock Creek Park. This park, which snakes through the whole length of the city alongside the stream for which it is named, offers an escape from the city within minutes.

Stroll along Rock Creek Park to where the stream flows into the Potomac River and you will arrive at two of Washington's newer major tourist attractions—the Watergate Complex and the Kennedy Center. Even before the famous break-in and bugging of the Democratic National Committee headquarters here, the Watergate was worth a visit because of the unusual architecture of the round apartment houses, office buildings, and hotel. It was a haunt of celebrity hunters because cabinet members and other VIPs lived here. Now tourists like to stop to take a picture of their group against one of the Watergate signs. A popular souvenir from a store in the complex is a bottle of its own Watergate brand of whisky.

The John F. Kennedy Center for Performing Arts is just to the south, also facing the river. Here is a building on a grand scale, 630 feet long and 300 feet wide. Guides will tell you the Washington Monument could be laid in the Grand Foyer, which runs the length of the building, with 75 feet to spare. The total area is big enough for four football fields. Inside are an opera house, concert hall, and three theaters—for drama, films, and chamber music—plus three restaurants ranging from a cafeteria to the deluxe Roof Terrace Restaurant. You can take a guided tour of the building from 10 A.M. to 1 P.M. daily, but the best way to enjoy it is to go for dinner and see one of the many presentations. Between acts you'll enjoy a stroll on the riverfront terrace. An evening here can be the climax of a Washington visit.

The Convention Center and Up-and-Coming Attractions

The ever-expanding Metro subway system has brought the city's neighborhoods closer together. For example, a Congressional employee now thinks nothing of hopping on the subway to go clear across the city or even to Virginia for lunch. The location of Metro Center, the hub of the subway system, in the heart of the old shopping section at 11th and F streets, N.W., has stimulated a rebirth of activity in that formerly declining area.

A major change of development patterns and growth is being stimulated not only by Metro but by the Washington, D.C. Convention Center, which has long been sought by the city's tourist industry leaders. Although Washington has always been a major convention city, it has never had a facility big enough to handle the truly giant conventions—like the American Medical Association or Rotary International.

The Washington, D.C. Convention Center is on an almost 10-acre site about midway between the White House and Capitol, between 9th and 11th streets, N.W., and extending from New York Avenue to H Street. It offers 40 meeting rooms ranging in capacity from 100 to 3,500 people and four halls totalling 381,000 square feet of exhibit and meeting space. Opened in 1983, the Center also contains the Cornerstone lounge. The Convention Center has sparked a downtown hotel boom, accounting for a large share of the 38,000 hotel rooms now in the Washington metropolitan area. Incidentally, every Washington visitor who stays in a hotel within the District of Columbia is directly contributing to the operation of the Convention Center through payment of a $1-per-day special room tax. Not far from the Convention Center is an eight-block area of Chinese restaurants, souvenir shops, and grocery stores. A million-dollar, 75-foot-wide red-and-gold People's Friendship Archway, funded jointly by the city and the People's Republic of China, marks the 7th and H streets entrance to Chinatown. This is a community traditionally bounded by G, I, 5th, and 8th streets, N.W., where land values are skyrocketing and run-down nineteenth-century houses stand side by side with upscale restaurants and "Chinese modern" office buildings.

One major reconstruction project, which has moved slowly with fits and starts, has been the effort to make Pennsylvania Avenue, historically the route of inauguration and other major parades, the truly "Grand Avenue" envisioned by L'Enfant. The Kennedy administration got the ball rolling in 1962 with the establishment of a President's Council on Pennsylvania Avenue. This in turn led to the formation of a Pennsylvania Avenue Development Corporation, which has made a number of studies and floated a lot of trial balloons (many of which were promptly shot down). Accomplishments to date include the rebuilding of Pershing Square and the adjoining Freedom Plaza, where Pennsylvania Avenue begins its dogleg around the Treasury Building, as well as the new J. W. Marriott Hotel and National Place, an office and retail complex on 14th Street between F Street and Pennsylvania Avenue. In addition, the old Willard Hotel has been restored to its former grandeur.

For years, the avenue development was symbolized by the (generally conceded) atrocious architecture of the J. Edgar Hoover Building, which was built on Pennsylvania Avenue as the first step of the aggrandizement program.

One administration's failures, however, can often be a challenge to the administration that follows. And, after much debate and planning, the north side of the avenue, facing the handsome Federal Triangle to the south, is finally being improved. The classic triangle, too, only came into being after decades of inaction and discussion. It replaced a section called "Murder Bay," which had been notorious since the Civil War.

Washington is a city that could easily adopt the French adage: The more things change, the more they are the same. Yet physically the Washington of today is not that of yesterday and no doubt that of tomorrow will be far different, too.

A SIDE TRIP TO VIRGINIA

Arlington and Alexandria

by
RALPH DANFORD

Ralph Danford has been a travel writer for more than three decades. A long-time resident of Virginia, he chose that state as his home after living in various places all over the world. He has been a member of the Society of American Travel Writers for over twenty years.

The nation's capital can be said to be embraced by Maryland, as it is on three sides, but it needs Virginia, which it faces to the southwest, to round out its entity. George Washington was not only the father of his country—he was largely responsible for the federal city, later named for him, being located so close to his home of Mount Vernon and his home town of Alexandria.

As a matter of fact, the original plans called for inclusion into the District of some 30 square miles of what is now Arlington County and part of the city of Alexandria. It was ceded back to the commonwealth in 1845 as unneeded. But, like residents of suburban Maryland, suburban Virginians consider themselves to be "Washingtonians" too. It's ironic that Washington's suburbs now have a far greater population than the city. Arlington, Alexandria, and adjoining Fairfax County are all very much part of the tourist's Washington.

The most stunning entrance to Washington certainly is via Virginia. Using Dulles International Airport, 25 miles to the west, you arrive at the Eero Saarinen terminal, designed in 1962, which many believe to be the most impressive as well as functional airport terminal in the world. Architecture critic Wolf Von Eckardt commented, "I think L'Enfant and Jefferson would approve of it."

From Dulles you are whisked through the green fields of Virginia on a road largely limited to airport traffic. A new toll road has been built immediately adjacent to the Dulles Access Road for handling the commuter traffic to the growing suburbs.

En route to the city, you pass the thriving planned "new city" of Reston and the turnoff for Wolf Trap Farm Park for the Performing Arts. Wolf Trap is the best thing that's happened to Washington summers since the invention of air conditioning. It attracts some 6,500 people per performance; 3,500 seated under shelter, the rest sprawled on the grassy slopes above.

Performances range from the Metropolitan Opera and the National Symphony to New Orleans jazz and bluegrass. A big share of the audience brings along a picnic meal, some complete with champagne and candelabra. Parking is free and ticket prices vary widely according to the event, although some of those are free too.

The Dulles Access Road now feeds, through a new link called the Dulles Connector, directly to I–66 for fast entry into Washington from Rosslyn over the Theodore Roosevelt Bridge.

For a slightly slower but more picturesque entry, take the Capital Beltway, I–495, north for a few miles and then transfer to the George Washington Memorial Parkway, which (provided you're not traveling at a traffic peak) is one of the most enjoyable scenic drives in the eastern U.S.

The Parkway, also known below Alexandria as the Mount Vernon Memorial Highway, extends 23 miles from the Beltway to Mount Vernon, paralleling the Potomac River for the most part.

The first turn-off from the Parkway is into Turkey Run Park, a wooded retreat with hiking trails, and a picnic area. The next turn-off from the Parkway is to the Central Intelligence Agency. Not so long ago the only sign around mysteriously designated the turn-off as the exit for a highway research center, but there are now clear signs designating the CIA.

Incidentally, despite what you may have heard from other sources, the Central Intelligence Agency does not—repeat not—offer public tours of its headquarters building at Langley.

For miles as you drive along you see little but the river and woods. There's little indication you're in the heart of a metropolitan area with a population of about three million. One of the first indications you are nearing the city proper is the appearance, across the river and above the trees, of the Gothic spires of Georgetown University. Then the parkway dips down to Rosslyn and its concentration of hotels and office buildings at the approach to Key Bridge (named for the "Star-Spangled Banner" composer) leading to Georgetown. Top-floor views from the hi-rises of Rosslyn (some with restaurants) provide a panorama of Washington's major monuments, museums, and government centers, as well as the Potomac River and Arlington Cemetery.

The Parkway continues past Theodore Roosevelt Island, an 88 acre wilderness preserved in the Potomac as a memorial to our conservationist

President. An impressive 17-foot bronze statue, surrounded by a moat and four granite shafts inscribed with TR's philosophy, is located at the northern end of the island. A footbridge connects the island to the Virginia shore where there is a parking area accessible from the northbound lanes of the Parkway. Continuing along the South side of the Potomac, the Parkway sweeps under the Theodore Roosevelt and Arlington Memorial bridge approaches, and onto Columbia Island, now known as Lady Bird Johnson Park.

On your right as you pass Memorial Bridge is the entrance to Arlington National Cemetery, then a maze of roads leading to the Pentagon and its many parking lots.

Still another president, Lyndon B. Johnson, is memorialized in the island park named for his wife. His memorial is a grove in which is centered a monolithic shaft of red, rough-hewn Texas granite. This is at the south end of the island. Although the administration of the 36th president was a controversial one, no one doubted his dedication—and, even more so, that of Ladybird Johnson—to beautification and conservation projects. Some 2,700 dogwoods and a million daffodils have been planted on the 150-acre island. At the very southern tip of the island is the Navy and Marine Memorial, one of the area's loveliest, of gulls in flight.

The Tidal Basin and Jefferson Memorial are across the river and to your left as you drive under approaches to the twin George Mason and Rochambeau Memorial bridges, named respectively for the author of the Virginia Declaration of Rights and the French commander at the Revolutionary War's final, decisive battle at Yorktown. Most Washingtonians simply refer to the bridge complex as the "14th Street Bridge."

Past the bridges, the Parkway skirts Washington National Airport, where planes roar in for their landings disturbingly close to cars on the roadway. Few regular drivers, however, pay much heed, nor do the hundreds of wildfowl who feed and wade in the Roaches Run Sanctuary just north of the airstrips. Louis J. Halle Jr., in his classic book *Spring in Washington,* wrote: "Ducks and gulls and herons have remained faithful to it, despite low-roaring airplanes. . . . The government pays conscience money here, posting the lagoon as sanctuary and scattering grain like Ceres. . . . " Visible to the right, as you pass the airport, is the modern complex of Crystal City—hotels, offices, apartments, restaurants, and an underground mall of shops have been developed here for quick access to downtown Washington and the National Airport.

South of the airport the Parkway runs between the river and Potomac Yards, one of the East's busiest freight railyards, and through the old town of Alexandria, past the Confederate Monument, right in the middle of the street and reminding you that this is Robert E. Lee's hometown, as well as Washington's. Off to the west, about a mile away, is the towering (333 feet) George Washington Masonic Memorial.

Incidentally, although the Masonic Memorial is modeled after the Pharos Lighthouse—one of the seven wonders of the ancient world—in Alexandria, Egypt, the origin of the city's name is quite different. It was named for John Alexander, a Scotsman, who settled here in 1669. In fact, Scottish merchants built the warehouses and set up the tobacco trade that nourished the port, and Alexandria now frequently celebrates its Scottish heritage with a pipe and drum corps parading at the slightest opportunity.

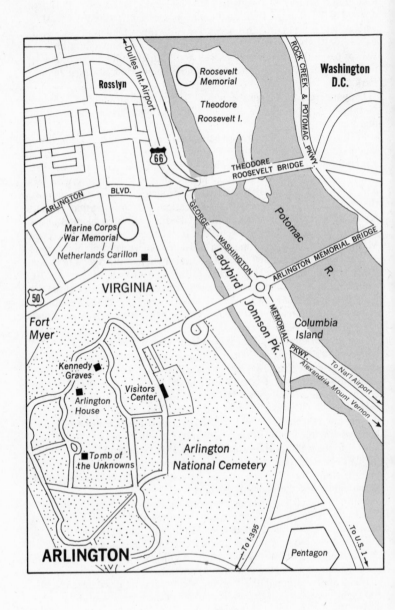

At the southern edge of Alexandria you swing over the southern loop of the Capital Beltway and its approach to Woodrow Wilson Bridge, a handsome span over the Potomac. You cross Hunting Creek and you're back on the parkway again. Halle describes it: "Below Alexandria for 12 miles the George Washington Memorial Highway follows the river to Mount Vernon through a setting of forest, river marshes, and open uplands . . . fresh earth and fresh sky. Look up when you reach Washington's home at Mount Vernon and, like it or not, you will see one or several eagles soaring against the blue. They do duty for bronze eagles over Washington's tomb."

Driving south along this section there are several scenic wayside stops and one major picnic ground and recreation area at Fort Hunt, where you also can see remnants of one of the Civil War-era fortifications that ringed Washington.

Mount Vernon

Far more than any place in the city named for him, George Washington's beloved Mount Vernon is where you can really feel the presence and the personality of the man. His home of the stately, pillared portico is far from spacious. In fact, a visiting member of the British royal family reportedly called it "a cozy place." There's a wonderful view of the river over wide, sweeping lawns, however, and the grounds are a delight. The towering trees include some planted by Washington himself, and members of the Mount Vernon Ladies Association continue to plant trees from the cuttings or seeds of the original. In fact, you can buy a tiny boxwood or other plant nurtured at Mount Vernon as a memento. The Mount Vernon Ladies Association is a pioneering example of historic preservation, having purchased the estate in 1858 from Washington heirs.

Washington's conscientious journal of his daily routine as a farmer—though a gentleman, he was no "gentleman farmer"—has enabled the staff to keep up a kitchen garden with vegetables, herbs, and espaliered fruit trees as he cultivated them. This was his home from 1754 until his death here in 1799, except for his absences for Army and presidential duties. The house and museum contain the bed in which he died, clothing, and other articles belonging to both himself and Martha Custis Washington, the widow whom he married. Visitors are fascinated by his substantial case of traveling wine bottles ("no teetotaler, he"), and what is reputed to be the key to the Bastille presented him by the Marquis de Lafayette.

Mount Vernon is one of the most visited of America's shrines, drawing a million visitors a year. Tours of the sprawling grounds are self-guided. Inside the house, small groups are ushered from room to room, each of which is staffed by a guide who describes the furnishings and answers questions. It's best to visit it on a weekday, when crowds aren't quite so heavy. It's open every day of the year, 9 A.M.–5 P.M. from March 1—October 31, 9 A.M.–4 P.M. the rest of the year; 703–780-2000. If you don't wish to drive, there are regularly scheduled tours from the city via Gray Line and other operators. An especially pleasant trip is down the Potomac River, aboard the *Spirit of Mt. Vernon,* twice daily, 9 A.M. and 2 P.M., from mid March to mid October and then on weekends to the end of the month. Boats leave from Pier 4, Sixth and Water streets, S.W., in Washington; 202–554-8000. There also is a Mount Vernon Bike Trail along the river, paralleling the

George Washington Memorial Parkway, some 16 miles between Arlington Memorial Bridge and Mount Vernon.

Also in the Mount Vernon area are two mansions worth a visit. They are Woodlawn Plantation, a gift of George Washington to his ward, Eleanor Parke Custis, and his nephew, Maj. Lawrence Lewis, after their wedding in 1799, and Gunston Hall, completed in 1758, the home of George Mason, author of the Virginia Declaration of Rights, which inspired our treasured Bill of Rights, and in recent times the United Nations Declaration of Human Rights.

The Woodlawn mansion was designed by Dr. William Thornton, first architect of the U.S. Capitol. Also on the grounds is the Pope-Leighey House, designed by Frank Lloyd Wright in the 1940s and moved to the grounds in 1965. Woodlawn is open daily except on Thanksgiving, Christmas, and New Year's Day, 9:30 A.M.–4:30 P.M.; the Pope-Leighey House open daily, March through October. Nearby is the George Washington Grist Mill, accessible year-round, via Va. 235 connecting Mount Vernon to U.S. 1.

Driving to Gunston Hall, you can look in at Pohick Church. Built in 1774, both George Washington and George Mason were vestrymen of the church. It is open 8 A.M.–4 P.M. daily; 703–550–9449. Gunston Hall is known particularly for its gardens and boxwood, some of it now 12 feet high. One well-traveled British visitor, Lord Balfour, said Gunston's boxwood was even superior to that of the Vatican, which had been considered the world's finest. Perhaps because it's so close to the Mason Neck National Wildlife refuge, Gunston is a mecca for birdlife. Those eagles, which occasionally hover over Mount Vernon and are also seen here, nest in the refuge, where they are closely protected. Gunston Hall is open daily except Christmas, 9:30 A.M.–5 P.M.

There are self-guided tours of Woodlawn Plantation and guided tours of the Gunston Hall mansion. Gunston Hall, 703–550–9220; Woodlawn, 703–780–4000.

Alexandria

Alexandria, called "the Cradle of History," is an old tobacco port founded in 1749. A walking tour is by far the best way to see the old part of Alexandria; so it might be well to start at the Alexandria Convention & Visitors Bureau.

The bureau is located in the Ramsay House, 221 King Street. It was the home of William Ramsay, the town's first postmaster and lord mayor, and is believed to be the oldest house in Alexandria. Mr. Ramsay was a Scotsman, as a swath of his tartan on the door proclaims. Open 9 A.M.–5 P.M. daily except Thanksgiving, Christmas, and New Year's Day. For information call 703–838–4200. Out-of-towners are given a 72-hour courtesy parking permit that allows them to park free at any metered spot.

Your next stop, around the corner at 121 N. Fairfax Street, is Carlyle House, the grandest of the older houses, completed in 1753 by John Carlyle, also a Scot. This was General Braddock's headquarters and the place where he met with five Royal Governors in 1755 to plan the strategy and funding of the early campaigns of the French and Indian War. Open 10–5, Tuesday through Saturday; noon-5, Sunday. For more information call 703–549–2997.

Across the street is handsome Market Square where fountains play in the heart of the old city. One block west is Gadsby's Tavern museum and restaurant, 134-8 N. Royal St., named for John Gadsby, an Englishman who was well regarded in Alexandria and Washington for his successful tavern operation. George Washington attended birthday balls here as well as meetings with his fellow gentry on matters of business, politics, and the social life. Today, Gadsby's, housed in two buildings, is part museum and part restaurant. The museum is a recreation of a typical 18th-Century tavern with its taproom, game room, assembly room, ballroom and communal bedrooms. The museum is open 10 A.M.–5 P.M., Tuesday–Saturday, 1–5 P.M., Sunday. For museum information, call 703–838–4242. The restaurant is open daily for lunch and dinner and serves 18th-Century-style meals; 703–548–1288.

From the tavern, walk north on Royal Street to Cameron, turn left and you can see a replica of Gen. Washington's small town house at No. 508. Unfortunately, it is not open to the public. Across the street and in the next block are the elegant Lord Fairfax house at 607 Cameron and, at 611, the home of Light Horse Harry Lee, a Revolutionary War general and father of Robert E. Lee. Both are privately owned and not open to visitors.

At the corner of Cameron and Washington streets is Christ Church, built in 1773, where both Washington and Lee were pewholders. Washington paid 36 pounds and 10 shillings, a lot of money in those days, for Pew 60.

In this area, along or just off N. Washington Street, you'll find a trio of houses with which the Lee family was connected. Some are open to the public—like Lloyd House at 220 N. Washington Street, a fine example of Georgian architecture built in 1797. It now contains a collection of historic books and documents relating to Alexandria and Virginia. Operated as a part of the Alexandria library, it is open to the public Monday–Friday, 9 A.M.–5 P.M. and Saturday, 9 A.M.–1 P.M. Two blocks farther north, the corner of Washington and Oronoco is known as the Lee Corner because a Lee-owned house was on each of the four corners at one time. Two survive: the Lee-Fendall House, open Tuesday–Saturday, 10 A.M.–4 P.M., and Sunday noon–4 P.M.; and the boyhood home of Robert E. Lee, open Monday–Saturday 10 A.M.–4 P.M. and Sunday, noon–4 P.M. Closed Dec. 15–Feb. 1.

It's only a few blocks to the riverfront from anywhere in what is known as Old Town. In the blocks near the river especially you'll see a lot of reconstruction. There has been an influx of good restaurants and shops, with former factories and warehouses converted to other uses.

At the foot of King Street is the Torpedo Factory (yes, naval torpedoes were actually manufactured there). It now provides studios and galleries for some 175 professional artists in such skills as jewelry, leatherworking, pottery, and stained glass. It is also the location of the Alexandria Archaeology Program with a city-operated research facility.

As in colonial days, Alexandria still functions as a port city with a customs office, Federal court, and its own tall ship, the schooner *Alexandria* which participates in tall ship events. In home port the ship provides a sail training program for young people, and it is also available for parties, receptions, and special events including the annual Waterfront Festival sponsored by the Alexandria Red Cross. As a port, the city also hosts the occasional foreign naval ship on a diplomatic visit. Interesting, too: many

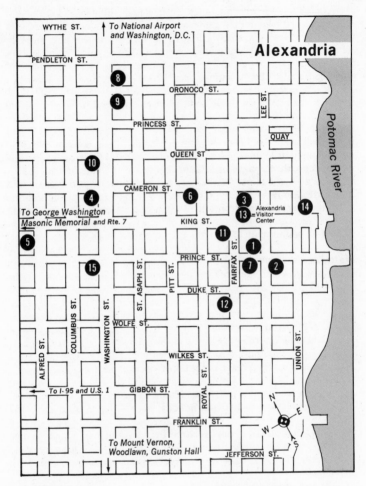

Points of Interest

1) Athenaeum
2) Captain's Row
3) Carlyle House
4) Christ Church
5) Friendship Fire Company
6) Gadsby's Tavern Museum
7) Gentry Row
8) Lee's Boyhood Home
9) Lee Fendall House
10) Lloyd House
11) Stabler Leadbeater Apothecary Shop
12) Old Presbyterian Meeting House
13) William Ramsay House
14) Torpedo Factory
15) Lyceum

of the imported items in local shops arrive on small freighters through the local port.

Returning from the waterfront you might walk up the cobblestones of the 100 block of Prince Street, also known as Captain's Row because of the homes built here by sea captains. The cobblestones, according to legend, were laid by Hessian prisoners of war. (There's one other area—the 600 block of Princess Street—that is also laid with cobblestones.) The next block is known as Gentry's Row because of other fine houses. Among them is the Athenaeum, 201 Prince Street, an example of Greek Revival architecture and built as a bank in 1850. It now houses exhibits of the Northern Virginia Fine Arts Association. Open September to July 12, 10 A.M.–4 P.M., Tuesday–Saturday; Sunday 1–4 P.M. Also open for special exhibits. For further information call 703–548–0035.

Walk down S. Lee Street to Duke Street and you will see two of the curious small houses called "flounders" at 321 S. Lee and 202 Duke. With flat, windowless walls, really a half-house, some thought they looked like the flat flounder fish. A high tax on glass may have had something to do with the lack of windows. It is thought, also, that the structures may have been intended as a future wing on a larger residence, to be built as the owner's fortune and family increased. Both are privately owned and closed to visitors.

Continue on Duke to S. Fairfax Street and there's the Old Presbyterian Meeting House. Funeral sermons for George Washington were delivered here on December 29, 1799. The Tomb of the Unknown Soldier of the American Revolution is in a corner of the churchyard.

At 105–7 S. Fairfax is the Stabler-Leadbeater Apothecary Shop, second oldest in the country and patronized by both Washington and the Lee family. The shop has one of the finest collections of apothecary bottles (800–900) in the country. Here, on October 17, 1859, Lt. Col. Robert E. Lee received orders, delivered by Lt. J. E. B. Stuart, to move to Harpers Ferry to suppress John Brown's insurrection. The shop is open 10 A.M.–4:30 P.M., Tuesday–Saturday. Call 703–836–3713. Scheduled renovation may close the shop late 1988–Spring, 1989.

From Fairfax St. walk west on Duke to St. Asaph. There's another "flounder" at 317. Up the street a bit is the attractive home at 301 S. St. Asaph now known as the Lafayette House because the good Marquis stayed there for a time in 1824 during his return as the nation's honored guest. Across the street at 601 Duke, the Dulany House with a higher set of front steps is chronicled in history because Lafayette addressed the cheering throng from it. Both are privately owned and not open to visitors.

Nearing the end of the tour, walk three blocks west to 107 S. Alfred, then a little more than a block north to the Friendship Fire Company. George Washington was a founder of the volunteer outfit and its honorary captain. On display is a replica of the $400 fire engine, then the finest obtainable, that he bought. Irregular operating hours.

Walk two blocks east to The Lyceum, built in 1839, at 201 S. Washington Street. It's the interpretive center for Alexandria's history. There's an audio-visual show, museum, gift shop and limited travel information for the entire state. The Lyceum is open daily, 10 A.M.–5 P.M., except for Thanksgiving, Christmas and New Year's Day. For information call 703–838–4994.

A little far to walk but well worth visiting is the George Washington Masonic National Memorial on Callahan Drive at King Street, a mile west of the center of the city. Its spire dominates all surroundings. Among other things, it contains furnishings of the first Masonic lodge in Alexandria, in which George Washington was Worshipful Master at the same time he served as President. There are free guided tours of the building and observation deck from 9:10 A.M. to 4 P.M. Open daily, 9 A.M.–5 P.M., except Thanskgiving, Christmas, and New Year's Day. 703–683–2007.

Arlington House, Arlington Cemetery, Pentagon

In Virginia, its northern part particularly, the heritage of George Washington and Robert E. Lee are linked and ever-present. Arlington National Cemetery, for example, was carved out of the estate of Mary Anna Randolph Custis, wife of Robert E. Lee, who had inherited the property in 1857 from her father George Washington Parke Custis who in turn had obtained the land from his foster father, John Parke Custis. Lee, who was married here in 1831 after graduation from West Point, considered the estate his home for some 30 years prior to leaving to fight in the Civil War.

Arlington House, the Robert E. Lee Memorial, is the mansion you see high on the hill directly ahead as you enter the cemetery over Memorial Bridge. After the outbreak of the Civil War and Lee's departure to assume command of the Army and Navy of Virginia—he was never to return here—Union forces occupied the house because of its strategic position commanding the approaches to the capital city. They then began burying their dead on the slopes below the mansion. In 1864, the government formally confiscated the property for nonpayment of taxes. Only after years of litigation did the courts decide that the government had confiscated the property illegally and returned it to Lee's eldest son, George Washington Custis Lee, who then sold it to the U.S. government for $150,000.

Almost any day you can witness one or more military funerals in the National Cemetery. Formerly any active or former military person, from private to commander-in-chief, could be buried in Arlington. Since 1967, requirements have become more strict and the cemetery may well become full by the year 2021 unless more land is added.

Among the famous buried here are Generals John J. Pershing and George C. Marshall, Major Walter Reed, Admirals Richard E. Byrd and Robert E. Peary, Pierre L'Enfant, Presidents William Howard Taft and John F. Kennedy, and Senator Robert F. Kennedy. Most visitors come to pay their respects at the graves of the Kennedy brothers and the Tomb of the Unknowns.

The grave of President Kennedy is marked by an eternal flame and quotations from his inaugural address. Near his tomb are the graves of his two infant children and that of Senator Robert Kennedy.

The Tomb of the Unknowns is guarded by elite sentinels from the "Old Guard" 3rd U.S. Infantry Regiment, whose precision—as they march exactly 21 steps, pause 21 seconds, and march back—is as measured as if they were automatons. The tomb is guarded 24 hours a day, with a change of the guard every half-hour in daytime from April 1–September 30 and every hour for the rest of the year, every two hours at night. The tomb originally was constructed for the body of an unknown World War I soldier returned from France. In 1958 the bodies of unknown American servicemen from World War II and the Korean War were interred there. And on Memorial Day 1984, an unidentified serviceman from the Vietnam War was finally laid to rest here.

A Memorial Amphitheater of white marble also honors the service dead and forms a background for the Tomb of the Unknowns. Memorial and Veterans Day ceremonies, Easter Sunrise Services, and other special ceremonies are held here. There is a display room of flags, medals and plaques inside the amphitheater.

A granite memorial marks the mass grave of over 2,000 unknown from Civil War battles. The mast of the battleship *Maine* marks the graves of 62 known and 167 unknown who lost their lives in the explosion that sank the ship in Havana in 1898.

The cemetery is open 8 A.M.–7 P.M. daily from April 1 to September 30, 8 A.M.–5 P.M. the rest of the year; Arlington House 9:30 A.M.–6 P.M. daily from April 1–September 30, 9:30 A.M.–4:30 P.M. the rest of the year. Arlington House is closed on Christmas and New Year's Day. No private autos are allowed within the grounds except those of relatives or friends who wish to visit gravesites. A narrated tour by Tourmobile is available at the visitor center. There is a Metrorail stop near the cemetery entrance.

Just outside the cemetery is the U.S. Marine Corps War Memorial, more familiarly known as the Iwo Jima Statue. This is a 78-foot-high, 100-ton bronze casting from a model by Felix de Weldon, recreating Joseph Rosenthal's Pulitzer Prize-winning World War II photo of Marines raising the flag on Iwo Jima's Mt. Suribachi. From early June to late August on Tuesday evenings at 7 P.M. visitors may watch a Marine Corps color ceremony and drill. There's free shuttle bus service from the Arlington Cemetery visitor's parking area to the Sunset Review and return.

Immediately south of the Iwo Jima Statue is the Netherlands Carillon Tower, a gift of the people of The Netherlands expressing their thanks for aid during and after World War II. Each of 49 chimes was a gift from a different segment of that country. On Saturdays, 2–4 P.M. during April, May, and September there is a live concert; 6:30–8:30 P.M. June, July, and August."

Not far from Arlington Cemetery is the world's largest office building surrounded by the world's largest parking lots and one of the world's biggest array of access roads. It's the Pentagon, headquarters of and symbol of the U.S. Department of Defense. The five-sided (hence the name) building covers 29 acres, has 17½ miles of corridors, and houses some 23,000 employees.

For years the Pentagon, like practically all other government buildings, was fairly wide open to visitors in peacetime. However, some bombing incidents brought about strict controls. To get into the building you must have business and be vouched for, or you can participate in a free 1¼-hour, 1½-mile-long tour. These begin every half hour from the Tour Office located near the Metro Entrance. The hours are 9:30 A.M.–3:30 P.M., Monday through Friday. You see a film, *History of the Pentagon,* and are taken down corridors of the Army, Navy, and Air Force branches lined with paintings of World War II and photos from the Korean and Vietnam conflicts. Highlight is a visit to the Hall of Heroes, dedicated to 3,400 Medal of Honor recipients. For more information call 703–695–1776.

Other Excursions in Virginia

Great Falls of the Potomac

The Great Falls of the Potomac have in recent years become a part of the National Park system. The 800-acre park on the Virginia side of the river is a favorite place for outings for local residents, and is easily accessible to tourists. The steep, jagged falls roars into a narrow gorge providing one of the most spectacular scenic attractions in the East. The park also includes the ruins of the Patowmack Canal, a business venture of George Washington's. There is a visitor's center with exhibits, a film, and on weekends a conducted walking tour. The park is open daily 8 A.M. to dark. Call (703) 285–2966.

Tysons Corner

Tysons Corner has grown into one of the largest shopping and office complexes in the Washington metropolitan area. And it is still growing with the recent addition of several luxury hotels. Only a few miles west of Tysons is the Colvin Run Mill Park operated by the Fairfax County Park Authority. The old mill grinds meal much as it has since 1811. On the grounds there is an exhibit in the miller's house, a general store, and a blacksmith shop. Open daily, except Tuesdays, 11 A.M.–5 P.M. mid-March through December, on weekends January–mid-March. Call (703) 759–2771.

Leesburg

Leesburg, whose name is more evidence of the influence of the Lee clan, was founded in 1758 and named for Francis Lightfoot Lee, one of the signers of the Declaration of Independence and a cousin of "Light Horse Harry," Robert E.'s father. President Madison and his cabinet fled to Leesburg after the British burned the White House in the War of 1812. There are many beautiful and historic homes here, but most are privately owned and are only open on special occasions such as Historic Garden Week in late April each year. Oatlands, a property of the National Trust for Historic Preservation, is a stately mansion of the Federal period. It is six miles south on U.S. 15. The house and formal gardens are attractive, but the estate is more renowned for its point-to-point races and other equestrian events. Open mid-March–mid-December, 10 A.M.–5 P.M. Monday–Saturday, 1–5 P.M. Sunday. From mid-February, by appointment for groups, (703) 777–3174. Morven Park, north of Leesburg off Va. 7, is the 1,200-acre estate of a former Virginia governor, Westmoreland Davis. The park includes an antique carriage collection and a museum about hounds and hunting. Open Memorial Day through Labor Day, Tuesday–Saturday 10 A.M.–5 P.M., Sunday 1–5 P.M. Open weekends May and September and first weekend of October. Call (703) 777–2414.

Quantico

Quantico is U.S. Marine Corps country, as you can plainly see by the replica of the Iwo Jima statue at the entrance to the huge Quantico Marine Reservation, some 30 miles south of Washington off I-95 and U.S. 1. Open to tourists is the Marine Corps Air and Ground Museum, which has interesting dioramas tracing the Marine Corp history, and includes a display of World War II aircraft. Open April 1–Nov. 27; Tuesday through Sunday 10 A.M.–5 P.M.; (703) 640–2606.

Fort Belvoir

Fort Belvoir, a bit south of Mount Vernon, on U.S. 1, is the home of the U.S. Army Engineers, and the location of the Engineer Museum, which has many military artifacts relating to the history of the Corps. Open 10 A.M.–4:30 P.M. Wednesday–Friday, noon–4:30 P.M. Saturday; (703) 664–6104.

Manassas National Battlefield Park

Manassas National Battlefield Park is 34 miles southwest of Washington via either I-66 or U.S. 29–211. Here two great battles of the Civil War, known as the Battles of Bull Run, were fought. The first in 1861, was when Gen. "Stonewall" Jackson got his nickname. The Confederate forces routed the Union armies then and in 1862. The grounds are open daily from 8:30 A.M. to dark. The interpretive Visitors Center on Va. 234 has a three dimensional map which graphically illustrates the course of both battles; open 8:30 A.M.–6 P.M. Memorial Day to Labor Day; 8:30 A.M.–5 P.M. remainder of year; (703) 591–3275. Also of interest is a Civil War Hospital in what was known as The Stone House. Open daily 10 A.M.–5 P.M. from June 15 to Labor Day.

Mountains and Shore

Virginia is a big state filled with diverse and far-ranging attractions. However, here is capsule information about the two areas which most appeal to Washington area weekenders: It's a classic mountains-or-shore selection—Virginia Beach or the combination of the Shenandoah National Park's Skyline Drive and Blue Ridge Parkway.

Virginia Beach, in the very southeast corner of the Old Dominion, claims to be the country's largest resort city in area and has a 29-mile coastline. Although farther away from Washington than the surfing resorts of Maryland and Delaware, it has a longer season and other attractions, including its proximity to the "historic triangle" of Jamestown, the first permanent colony in what was to become the U.S., Williamsburg, the beautifully reconstructed colonial capital, and Yorktown, where in 1781 Cornwallis surrendered to the upstart Yankee Doodle Dandies, ending the Revolutionary War. Still another attraction: the Lynnhaven oyster from nearby waters.

The Shenandoah Mountains are only about a two-hour drive west of Washington and are an oasis of respite from the miasma of heat and humidity which hangs over Washington for much of the summer. A miracle of engineering is Skyline Drive, which runs along the mountain crest for 105 miles from Front Royal to Rockfish Gap, where it then becomes the Blue Ridge Parkway for another 470 miles down to Great Smoky Mountains National Park in North Carolina and Tennessee. There are parking overlooks all along the way with great views across the Shenandoah Valley to the Massanutten Mountains and, still farther, the Alleghenies.

POINTS OF
This Week • INTEREST

IN MARYLAND

AUDUBON NATURALIST SOCIETY--
8940 Jones Mill Rd., Chevy Chase, Md.
(652-9188). Built in 1928 by John Russell
Pope, architect of the Jefferson Memorial,
this 40 acre estate, known a Woodend, is
now home to this conservation organization. Grounds are maintained as a wildlife sanctuary and include a 3/4 mile self-
guided nature trail. Gift shop carries
books, cards and items with a nature
theme. Grounds open every day dawn to
dusk. Building open Mon.-Fri., 9 am-5
pm. Bookshop open daily 9 am-5 pm, 12-
5 pm Sun., Thurs. until 7 pm.

GLEN ECHO PARK--MacArthur Blvd.
and Goldsboro Rd., Glen Echo, Md. (492-
6282). Once a Chautauqua meeting
ground, and later an amusement park,
this turn-of-the-century park is currently
undergoing restoration. Experience
music, dance, theater, arts, and crafts and
special events almost every weekend. Art
Gallery open Tues.-Sun., 12-5 pm,
grounds open to public daily.

GREAT FALLS TAVERN MUSEUM--
11710 MacArthur Blvd., Potomac, Md.
(229-3613). Built in 1830 to attract visitors
to Great Falls, a nearby scenic attraction.
The Crommelin House now houses a
museum devoted to the history of the
C&O Canal. Pinicking, hiking, guided
tours, and refreshments. Open daily 9
am-5 pm.

**NASA/GODDARD SPACE FLIGHT
CENTER--**Soil Conservation Road,
Greenbelt, Md. (286-8981). Rocket models, weather satellites, Delta Launch ve-
hicle and specimen of a moon rock are just
a few of the displays. Televised lectures,
films, and self-guided tours of Visitors
center Wed.-Sun. 10 am-4 pm. Computer
and Communications Center, which
tracks launch vehicles in flight, open for
public tours Thurs. 2 pm.

OXON HILL FARM--6411 Oxon Hill
Rd., Oxon Hill, Md. (839-1177). A working farm with animals, crops, and equipment typical of those used on farms at the
turn of the century. Seasonal activities
include cider pressing, corn harvesting,
gardening, spinning and sheep-shearing.
Self-guided nature walk explains how
farmers made use of the surrounding
area.

POINTS OF INTEREST

Adas Israel 3
Archives 41
Arlington Cemetery 70
B'nai B'rith 10
Botanic Garden 19
Bureau of Engraving 66
Cannon House Office Bldg 68
Capital Children's Museum 20
Capitol 49
Constitution Hall 33
Convention Center 16
Corcoran Gallery 27
DAR Headquarters 33
Dumbarton Oaks 4
Embassy Row 7
F.B.I. 37
Folger Library 63
Ford's Theatre 30
Franciscan Monastery 12
House Where Lincoln Died 29
Islamic Center Mosque 5
Iwo Jima Memorial 64
Jefferson Memorial 71
Justice Dept. 40
Kennedy Center 22
Kennedy Graves 40
Library of Congress 62
Lincoln Memorial 53
Longworth House Office Bldg 67
Martin Luther King Library 19
Nat'l Academy of Sciences 38
Nat'l Gallery of Art .... 47 & 48
Nat'l Geographic Society 11
National Theatre 35
Old Exec. Office Bldg 22
Old Post Office Pavilion 36
Org. of American States 39
Phillips Collection 8
Rayburn House Office Bldg 66
RFK Stadium 69
Seabee Memorial 69
Senate Office Bldgs .... 43 & 44
Shops at National Place 33
Shrine of Immaculate Conception 13
Smithsonian Institution
 Air & Space 40
 American Art 25
 American History 45
 Arts & Industry 38
 Castle Bldg 57
 Freer 38
 Hirshhorn 56
 Natural History 46
 Nat'l Portrait Gallery 25
 Renwick Gallery 18
St. Matthew's 9
Starplex Armory 69
State Dept. 31
Supreme Court 50
Sylvan Theatre 55
Treasury Dept. 24
Union Station 52
Vietnam Memorial 51
Wash. Dolls House & Toy Museum 2
Washington Cathedral 1
Washington Monument 54
White House 23
Zoological Park 3

PRACTICAL INFORMATION FOR
THE WASHINGTON AREA

HOTELS AND MOTELS. We have categorized our selection (and it is only a selection) of Washington area hotels mostly by price but also with due regard for the quality and type of service, style, location, and distinction of accommodations. Price ranges are based on the cost of a double-occupancy room at press time.

The hotels classified as *Super Deluxe* charge over $150 a night for their basic double room and the charge is often well over that.

The *Deluxe* hotels are only marginally less desirable. They often are larger, a bit less personal in their services. Rates for a double room range from $110 to $150, possibly a bit more. Some thrive on convention and/or tour business but all still offer fine service and comfort.

The hotels in our *First Class* range charge between $80–$110 for a double room. All hotels in this category offer a good range of services.

Hotels listed as *Moderate* in price today would have charged far less a few years ago, but all hotel prices reflect the economy of today's world. This category is in the $60 to $80 range. It includes many chain motels. Many offer such amenities as free parking and swimming pools.

Other establishments are listed as *Inexpensive.* All of these offer double rooms for under $60. These may include few frills and some are in less desirable neighborhoods, but in today's market all are good buys, and some are exceptional bargains.

In making your reservations, be sure to ask the exact price of the room you will occupy and also for taxes and any other applicable charges. Hotel room taxes in the area now range from 10 percent in the city of Washington and the Maryland suburbs to 9 percent in Virginia's Arlington County, and 8 percent in the city of Alexandria. Hotels and motels in the District are also required to levy a $1-a-night (per room) occupancy tax.

If you'd like some personalized local advice, call Washington DC Accommodations, (800) 554–2220. They'll describe hotels that fit your budget and make the reservations for you while you're still on the line. The service is free to the caller (they make their money from hotel commissions). If you're already in the D.C. area, call 289–2220, 9 A.M. to 5 P.M. Monday through Friday.

Remember that many of these hotels offer very substantial discounts on weekends, and that some of these special rates are available during the week in the summer. Advanced reservations are usually required to qualify for these rates. The Washington Hotel Association, 910 17th St., N.W., Washington DC 20005, will send you a pamphlet detailing many of these special rates.

Listings for city hotels are followed by listings for the Virginia and Maryland suburbs.

For information on bed and breakfast and hostels see *Facts at Your Fingertips.*

Washington, D.C.

Note: The area code for the District of Columbia is 202.

Super Deluxe

The Embassy Row Hotel. 2015 Massachusetts Ave., N.W.; 265–1600; (800) 424–2400. Off Dupont Circle and near an enclave of major embassies, this 196-unit hostelry recently underwent major refurbishing. Especially popular with foreign visitors. The *Ambassador Grill* restaurant is new.

Four Seasons Hotel. 2800 Pennsylvania Ave., N.W.; 342–0444; (800) 268–6282. At the edge of Georgetown, with the C&O Canal on one side and Rock Creek Park on the other, it has the city's most idyllic location. A beautiful hotel, skillfully operated, with a concierge and 24-hour room service. Only 197 rooms and each of them a gem. *Aux Beaux Champs Restaurant.* The *Garden Terrace Lounge,* off the lobby, is lovely. *Desirée,* a private club, extends temporary privileges to hotel guests.

Georgetown Inn. 1310 Wisconsin Ave., N.W.; 333–8900; (800) 424–2979. Right in the heart of Georgetown, this 95-unit hotel, now managed by the Potomac Hotel Group, is newly renovated. Valet parking available (a boon in Georgetown, where parking is impossible). *Georgetown Bar & Grill* is a tony restaurant with a pianist.

The Grand Hotel. 2350 M St., N.W.; 429–0100; (800) 848–0016. This beautiful 160-room deluxe hotel, a striking construction of pink marble and polished brass, is located in the West End, midway between Georgetown and the business district. It has two restaurants, a pool, and a lovely atrium.

Grand Hyatt. 1000 H St., N.W.; 582–1234; (800) 228–9000. The newest hotel in town has 907 units (including 60 suites) built around a 12-story atrium with a lagoon. It's across the street from the Convention Center and half a block from Metro Center. Three restaurants and two lounges. Special weekend rates can drop the price considerably for a double.

Hay Adams. 16th and H sts., N.W.; 638–6600; (800) 424–5054. Overlooking both Lafayette Park and the White House, on the site of the former Henry Adams and John Hay mansions, this famous hotel occupies some truly upper-crust real estate. The paneled lobby, Tudor dining rooms and grill room give it the look and feel of a fine old London hotel. A sunny third restaurant, overlooking the park, serves breakfast, lunch, and weekend brunch. Over 150 units.

Hyatt Regency. 400 New Jersey Ave., N.W.; 737–1234; (800) 228–9000. Closest major hotel to the Capitol and Union Station. 842 rooms grouped around a 5-story atrium. A great view of the Capitol from *Hugo's* top-floor restaurant. Seafood in *Jonah's Oyster Kitchen.*

Jefferson Hotel. 1200 16th St., N.W.; 347–2200; (800) 368–5966. This small, elegant, recently refurbished hotel, within walking distance of the White House, features *The Hunt Club* for haute cuisine, and tea service every afternoon. 24-hour butler service.

Madison Hotel. 15th and M Sts., N.W.; 862–1600; (800) 424–8577 or –8578. Owner Marshall Coyne keeps his eye on things from an office right across the street from the entrance and he keeps all of the help on their toes. Superb service and a truly elegant hotel. 374 rooms or suites, each with a refrigerator and stocked bar. *Montpelier Restaurant* for gourmet dining and afternoon tea in the lobby.

J.W. Marriott Hotel. 1331 Pennsylvania Ave., N.W.; 393–2000; (800) 228–9000. The showcase of the Marriott chain, this striking building next to the revitalized National Theater, five blocks from the Convention Center, combines offices and a retail mall with 774 hotel rooms (including 60 suites), restaurants, lounges, pool, and a health club and exercise room.

The Mayflower. 1127 Connecticut Ave., N.W.; 347–3000; (800) HO-TELS–1. A Washington landmark with a block-long lobby, this recently renovated Stouffer Hotel is close to Metro stops and shopping. Two restaurants (Nicholas and Cafe Promenade) and the Town and Country Lounge. Over 700 rooms.

The Park Hyatt. 24th & M Sts., N.W.; 789–1234; (800) 922–7275. Located opposite the Grand on what some are now calling "hotel corner" in the West End, this 225-room luxury hotel features American Gourmet food in its *Melrose* restaurant, and daily high teas (and nightly champagne and caviar) in its lounge.

The Phoenix Park. 520 N. Capitol St.; 638–6900; (800) 824–5419. Ten million dollars in renovation money produced this gracious, pastel-toned 87-room executive-oriented hotel near the Capitol and Union Station. Two restaurants: the fancy *Powerscourt* and the fun *Dubliner* pub.

Ritz Carlton Hotel. 2100 Massachusetts Ave., N.W.; 293–2100; (800) 424–8008. Refurbished and refurnished with Federal antiques, this elegant 230-room hotel, formerly the Fairfax, caters to chairmen-of-the-board types and their ladies. Home of the *Jockey Club* restaurant.

Sheraton-Carlton. 923 16th St., N.W.; 638–2626; (800) 562–5661. Located near the White House, this distinguished hotel was undergoing a major renovation at presstime, but was expected to reopen in the fall of 1988. Restaurants, piano bar in the lobby.

The Sheraton Grand. 525 New Jersey Ave., N.W.; 628–2100; (800) 325–3535. This new luxury Capitol Hill hotel lives up to its name, with pink marble in the lobby and 268 tastefully decorated guestrooms and 35 suites. Facilities include a comfortable lobby bar, which serves a lavish Sunday brunch, and the gardenlike Cafe at the Grand.

Vista International Hotel. 1400 M St., N.W.; 429–1700; (800) VISTA–DC. The second Hilton International to open in the United States, this 400-unit deluxe hotel aims for a European ambience, with full concierge amenities. Designed by Givenchy, the 6 suites in the eight-story Tower Suite are part of the atrium. *American Harvest Restaurant, Verandah Restaurant and Wine Bar, Federal Bar.* Afternoon tea is served in the Lobby Court. String quartet in the evenings, from the mezzanine.

Washington Marriott Hotel. 22nd and M Sts., N.W.; 872–1500; (800) 228–9290. Built in conjunction with *Blackie's House of Beef.* 350 units. Indoor pool and sauna.

Watergate Hotel. 2650 Virginia Ave., N.W.; 965–2300; (800) 424–2736. Suites overlooking the Potomac River are favored by entertainers playing at the nearby Kennedy Center. 238 units. Indoor pool and health spa. The Nixon bugging scandal involved a neighboring office building. *Jean-Louis* at the Watergate boasts the only 2-star Michelin chef working in the United States.

The Westin Hotel. 2401 M St., N.W.; 429–2400; (800) 228–3000. A new hotel with over 400 rooms built around a huge interior courtyard in the newly-fashionable West End. Noted for its 16,000-sq.-ft. health club, with two racquet courts and pool; 185-seat theater for teleconferences; the *Colonnade* restaurant and *Bistro Cafe.*

The Willard. 1401 Pennsylvania Ave., N.W.; 628–9100; (800) 327–0200. After a long and meticulous renovation/restoration, this downtown landmark reopened in late 1986 as an Inter-Continental luxury hotel with 395 rooms, a cafe, two lounges, and a formal restaurant, the *Willard Room,* that probably best displays—in its restored original chandeliers and oak paneling—the care with which restoration was done.

Deluxe

The Canterbury. 1733 N. St, N.W.; 393–3000; (800) 424–2950. With just 99 units, each of them a suite, this jewel of a hotel was built "with the senior corporate executive in mind." The building is new but the location on a quiet street off Connecticut Ave. was at various times home to Presidents Theodore and Franklin D. Roosevelt. Excellent *Chaucer Restaurant.*

Capital Hilton. 16th and K Sts., N.W.; 393–1000; (800) 445–8667. A bustling hotel right in the middle of things, two blocks from White House. Popular for conventions and tour groups. *Trader Vic's* and *Twigs* restaurants. 533 newly renovated rooms; new health club; lounge, special amenities on top four floors (Towers).

Dupont Plaza. 1500 New Hampshire Ave., N.W.; 483–6000; (800) 421–6662 312 renovated units near the Dupont Circle Metro stop. Restaurant and bar.

Guest Quarters. 123 units at 2500 Pennsylvania Ave., N.W.; 333–8060; and 101 units at 801 New Hampshire Ave., NW; 785–2000; (800) 424–2900 for both. An apartment hotel whose one-bedroom suites have fully equipped kitchens. The New Hamsphire Avenue building is especially popular with performers at the Kennedy Center. There are also branches in Alexandria and Bethesda.

Henley Park Hotel. 926 Massachusetts Ave., at 10th St., N.W.; 638–5200; (800) 222–8474. This small, elegant British-style hotel opened in March 1983. A former apartment building, it contains only 96 units, but the small rooms are handsomely appointed, and the hotel is walking distance from the new Convention Center.

Holiday Inn Capitol. 550 C St., S.W.; 479–4000; (800) HOLIDAY. 529 rooms near the Mall. Outdoor pool, restaurant.

Loew's L'Enfant Plaza. 480 L'Enfant Plaza, S.W.; 484–1000; (800) 223–0888. One of the city's most dramatic locations, overlooking a plaza, just off the Mall. Close to museums, the Metro, and shopping. 372 units, often used for corporate meetings. Rooftop swimming pool.

Morrison-Clark Inn Hotel. Massachusetts Ave. and 11th St., N.E.; 898–1200; (800) 332–7898. The newest hotel in Washington is in one of the oldest buildings, elegantly restored with a modern addition. The decor in the historic section is mid-Victorian and there are verandas and a garden courtyard. On the modern side, there are computer data ports, video movies. 54 units, including junior and one-bedroom suites. 120-seat restaurant.

The Omni Georgetown. 2121 P St., N.W.; 293–3100; (800) THE–OMNI. Actually closer to Dupont Circle than Georgetown, this hotel's 300 rooms were all recently redone, as was its chic *Beaux Arts Cafe* restaurant.

The Omni Shoreham. 2500 Calvert St., N.W.; 234–0700; (800) THE–OMNI. A sprawling 770-unit hotel on the edge of Rock Creek. Like the neighboring Sheraton Washington, a popular convention hotel with extensive public rooms and a renovated Art Deco elegance. Two restaurants, drinks served in *Garden Court,* Broadway-style entertainment in the *Marquee Lounge.* An Omni-Dunfey Hotel.

One Washington Circle. 1 Washington Circle, N.W.; 872–1680; (800) 424–9671. Near George Washington University and its hospital and a few blocks from the Kennedy Center. The 151 units all include kitchens. The highly rated West End Cafe and piano bar is downstairs.

Ramada Renaissance Hotel. 1143 New Hampshire Ave., N.W.; 775–0800; (800) 228–9898. This is the first example in the Washington area of this nationwide chain's top-line hostelries, and all who have sampled it have been impressed. 356 units. Near subway stops and Georgetown. Cocktail lounge and *Summerfield's* and *La Cloche* restaurants.

The River Inn. 924 25th St., N.W.; 337–7600; (800) 424–2741. Near the Watergate and Georgetown, this former apartment house has 128 suites, each with kitchen. *Foggy Bottom Café.* Potomac Hotel Group.

Sheraton Washington. 2660 Woodley Rd., N.W.; 328–2000; (800) 325–3535. Formerly Sheraton Park Hotel. Completely rebuilt, but still the city's biggest hotel (1,505 units) and convention center. Near Rock Creek Park and the National Zoo, off one of the most pleasant stretches of Connecticut Ave. A Metro stops right at the front door. Four restaurants, two outdoor swimming pools.

Washington Hilton and Towers. 1919 Connecticut Ave., N.W.; 483–3000; (800) HILTONS. Another popular convention hotel with 1,150 rooms, large outdoor swimming pool, tennis courts, and other recreational facilities. Extra amenities on the top two floors. *Gazebo* restaurant.

First Class

Hotel Anthony. 1823 L St., N.W.; 223–4320; (800) 424–2970. In the heart of Washington's new business district, just off Connecticut Ave. All 99 units with refrigerators, half with kitchens.

Bellevue Hotel. 15 E St., N.W.; 638–0900; (800) DC–ROOMS. 140 rooms near Union Station and the Capitol. *Tiber Creek Pub and Restaurant* is popular with the "Hill" crowd.

Best Western—Skyline Inn. 10 I St., S.W.; 488–7500; (800) 458–7500. One of the few in-city hostelries offering free parking. Near the Capitol and waterfront. 203 units with large outdoor pool, dining room, cocktail lounge, and entertainment.

The Capitol Hill. 200 C St., S.E.; 543–6000; (800) 424–9165. A 153-unit, each-room-is-a-suite hotel especially popular with G.O.P. politicos because of its location near the Capitol Hill (Republican) Club and the House of Representatives office buildings. Potomac Hotel Group.

Channel Inn. 650 Water St., S.W.; 554–2400; (800) 368–5668. Right on the waterfront, near Areana Theater and fine restaurants. 100 units, pool, *Pier 7* restaurant.

Georgetown Dutch Inn. 1075 Thomas Jefferson St., N.W.; 337–0900. An intimate inn whose 47 housekeeping units are located near the C&O Canal in Georgetown. *Leo and Linda's* Restaurant.

Georgetown Marbury Hotel. 3000 M St., N.W.; 726–5000; (800) 368–5922. 164 rooms in the heart of Georgetown. Two restaurants, tavern, and lounge. Free parking.

Governor's House Holiday Inn. 1615 Rhode Island Ave., N.W.; 296–2100; (800) 821–4367. More than 150 newly renovated rooms at Scott Circle. Pool, outdoor patio, *Herb's Restaurant.*

Hampshire Hotel. 1310 New Hampshire Ave., N.W.; 296–7600; (800) 368–5691. Three-fourths of the 82 units have kitchenettes. *Lafitte* restaurant.

Highland Hotel. 1914 Connecticut Ave., N.W.; 797–2000; (800) 424–2464. Near the Washington Hilton, a former apartment building that was converted to 140 suites, about 20 with kitchens.

Holiday Inn—Central. 15th & Rhode Island Ave., N.W.; 483–2000; (800) HOLIDAY. Just off Scott Circle in an area of many mid-city motels. 214 rooms. Outdoor pool.

Holiday Inn—Georgetown. 2101 Wisconsin Ave., N.W.; 338–4600; (800) HOLIDAY. At the edge of Georgetown. 300 units, outdoor pool, dining room.

Holiday Inn—Thomas Circle. Massachusetts Ave. at Thomas Circle, N.W.; 737–1200; (800) HOLIDAY. 208 units, rooftop pool.

Hotel Lombardy. 2019 I St., N.W.; 828–2600; (800) 424–5486. Near George Washington University and the Corcoran Gallery, this former apartment house has 125 units, most with kitchens and dining areas. The *Cafe Lombardy* overlooks Pennsylvania Ave.

Hotel Washington. 15th St. at Pennsylvania Ave., N.W.; 638–5900; (800) 424–9540. A fine older hotel with 350 renovated rooms. *Roof Terrace* lounge offers finest view in city of July 4th fireworks and Pennsylvania Ave. parades, or of just everyday low-rise Washington, D.C. *Two Continents Restaurant.*

Howard Johnson's Plaza Hotel. 2505 Wisconsin Ave., N.W.; 337–7400; (800) 654–2000. 150 units in a hotel only a few blocks from Georgetown, now under management of Howard Johnson. Outdoor pool. Restaurant lounge. Free parking.

Howard University Inn. 2225 Georgia Ave., N.W.; 462–5400; (800) 368–5729. Adjacent to and owned by Howard University. 140 units. Supper club, coffee shop, entertainment, health spa, pool.

Normandy Inn. 2118 Wyoming Ave., N.W.; 483–1350; (800) 424–3729. Formerly Barbizon Terrace. European-style hotel. Off Connecticut Ave., near several embassies. 74 units. Continental breakfast.

Quality Hotel Capitol Hill. Capitol Hill, 415 New Jersey Ave., N.W.; 638–1616; (800) 228–5151. Near Union Station and the Capitol. 341 units. Rooftop pool and sauna. *Coach and Parlor Restaurant, Whistlestop Lounge.* Across street from the Hyatt Regency. Free parking.

Quality Hotel Central. 1900 Connecticut Ave., N.W.; 332–9300; (800) 228–5151. Just across the street from the huge Washington Hilton, this inn has 149 units. Outdoor pool and nonsmoking rooms. Garage.

Radisson Park Terrace. 1515 Rhode Island Ave., N.W.; 232–7000; (800) 424–2461. 221 stylish units off Scott Circle in the heart of downtown. Home of the elegant nouvelle American restaurant *Chardonnay.*

Ramada Inn—Central. 1430 Rhode Island Ave., N.W.; 462–7777; (800) 368–5690. 186 units, 148 of them efficiencies. Rooftop pool; restaurant/lounge.

State Plaza. 2117 E St., N.W.; 861–8200 (800) 424–2859. In the Foggy Bottom area close to the State Department, and popular with State Department staffers. A converted apartment building, with 215 suites containing kitchens and dining rooms. *Garden Restaurant.*

Washington Plaza Hotel. Massachusetts and Vermont Aves., N.W.; 842–1300; (800) 654–9122. 340 rooms. Outdoor pool. *Mickey Cooper's* restaurant. Lounge. Free parking.

Moderate

Connecticut Avenue Days Inn. 4400 Connecticut Ave., N.W.; 244–5600; (800) 325–2525. 155 rooms located uptown and out of the bustle, but a block from the Van Ness Metro.

Days Inn Downtown/Convention Center. 1201 K St., N.W.; 842–1020; (800) 325–2525. About 220 rooms near the Convention Center and downtown business district.

General Scott Inn. 1464 Rhode Island Ave., N.W.; 333–6700; (800) 424–2496. Each of the 65 units here is a suite with equipped kitchen, and the location is a few blocks from the White House.

Hotel Farragut West. 1808 Eye St., N.W.; 393–2400. A homey, 75-unit European-style hotel for the budget-minded.

Howard Johnson's Motor Lodge. 2601 Virginia Ave., N.W.; 965–2700; (800) 654–2000. Right across the street from the Watergate Complex and near Kennedy Center. 194 units. *Big Boy* restaurant.

Quality Inn—Downtown. 1315 16th St., N.W. at Massachusetts; 232–8000; (800) 368–5689. Just north of Scott Circle. Former apartment house converted to 136 units, most with kitchens.

Walter Reed Hospitality House. 6711 Georgia Ave., N.W.; 722–1600; (800) 222–8388. Adjacent to Walter Reed Army Medical Center, this attractive, small (72-unit) hostelry offers free parking and free HBO. Swimming pool. *Mr. Chan* restaurant and lounge. Close to Metro.

Inexpensive

Allen Lee Hotel. 2224 F St., N.W.; 331–1224. A favorite of students, many from abroad. Of the 84 rooms, 23 have private baths.

Best Western—Envoy. 501 New York Ave., N.E.; 543–7400; (800) 528–1234. On heavily traveled U.S. 50 and U.S. 1 Alt. Pool and restaurant. 78 units. Takes pets.

Gralyn Hotel. 1745 N St., N.W.; 785–1515. About 35 units, roughly half of which have air conditioning and private baths, but it's a longtime favorite of those who like cozy, European-style inns. Breakfast served in garden or room facing it.

Harrington. 11th and E sts., N.W.; 628–8140; (800) 424–8532. With 310 rooms, the largest of the budget hotels. Downtown near major department stores, theaters, art galleries and Metro.

Rock Creek Hotel. 1925 Belmont Rd., N.W., a block off Connecticut Ave.; 462–6007. Near to shopping and embassy area. 54 units. Coffee shop.

Alexandria, Virginia

Note: The area code for the northern part of Virginia is 703.

Deluxe

Guest Quarters. 100 S. Reynolds St.; 370–9600; (800) 424–2900. Apartment hotel near Landmark Shopping Center. 225 units. Pool and restaurant.

The Morrison House. 116 S. Alfred St.; 838–8000; (800) 367–0800. A gem of a small hotel (47 rooms) in the heart of Old Town. Federal-style antique reproductions, four-poster beds, and flowers everywhere. Afternoon tea is served in the mahogany-paneled library and contemporary French cuisine is served in the lauded *Chardon d'Or* restaurant. Meeting rooms available. Everything's brand-new but looks as though it's been here for years.

Old Town Holiday Inn. 480 King St.; 549–6080; (800) HOLIDAY. Colonial-style luxury hotel in heart of restored area. 227 units. Indoor pool. Nightly entertainment in the 101 Royal restaurant.

Radisson Mark Plaza Hotel. Seminary Road at I-395; 845–1010; (800) 228–9822. 500 deluxe rooms and convention facilities on a manmade lake in Alexandria's sprawling southern end. Indoor pool, complete health club and racquet courts, two restaurants and lounge. Popular Sunday brunch with Big Band dancing.

First Class

Best Western Olde Colony Inn. 1st and N. Washington Sts.; 548–6300; (800) 528–1234. At the north end of Old Town, with indoor-outdoor pool, restaurant and piano bar.

Holiday Inn—Eisenhower Metro. 2460 Eisenhower Ave.; 960–3400; (800) HOLIDAY. 204 units, 2 miles from Old Town, near Hoffman Complex. Outdoor pool.

Ramada Hotel, Old Town. 901 N. Fairfax St.; 683–6000; (800) 272–6232. 259 units 9 blocks from Old Town. Outdoor pool and rooftop restaurant. Shuttle bus to National Airport.

Ramada Inn. I-95 & Seminary Rd.; 751–4510; (800) 228–2828. 193 units. Facilities for people in wheelchairs. Indoor pool, sauna, restaurant, bar.

Inexpensive

Imperial Motor Inn. 6461 Edsall Rd.; 354–4400; (800) 368–4400. 207 rooms. Full-service restaurant with cocktail lounge. Straight out I-395 at Edsall Rd. exit.

Towers Hotel. 420 N. Dorn St.; 370–1000; (800) 368–3339. 186 suites with kitchens, near Landmark Shopping Center, just off I–395 south of D.C.

Arlington, Virginia

Super Deluxe

Crystal City Marriott. 1999 Jefferson Davis Hwy. 1; 521–5500; (800) 228–9290. In a high-rise office area at Metro stop. 340 rooms, with indoor pool and sauna. Airport shuttle. Restaurant, lounge overlooking the city of Washington across the Potomac.

Key Bridge Marriott. 1401 Lee Hwy.; 524–6400; (800) 228–9290. Right at west end of bridge across the river from Georgetown. Great view from many of 560 rooms and *The View* rooftop restaurant.

Marriott Crystal Gateway Hotel. 1700 Jefferson Davis Hwy.; 920–3230; (800) 228–9290. Another posh new hotel, this one with concierge and 24-hour room service, three restaurants, a lounge, indoor-outdoor pool, exercise room, and sauna. 702 units with new addition.

Deluxe

Hyatt Arlington. 1325 Wilson Blvd.; 841–9595; (800) 228–9000. Three blocks from Key Bridge, across the street from Rosslyn Metro station. 303 rooms. *Hugo's Restaurant.* Airport transportation.

Hyatt Regency Crystal City. 2799 Jefferson Davis Hwy.; 486–1234; (800) 228–9000. This 685-unit luxury hotel near National Airport is priced to meet the stiff competition among fancy Crystal City establishments. Outdoor pool, two restaurants (one rooftop), two lounges, concierge.

Stouffer Concourse Hotel. 2399 Jefferson Davis Hwy.; 979–6800; (800) HOTELS–1. On U.S. 1, half-mile from National Airport. 388 units. Heated indoor pool with sauna and exercise room.

Twin Bridges Marriott. West end of 14th St. bridges on I–395 and U.S. 1. (Mail address: P.O. Box 24240, Washington, D.C. 20024); 628–4200; (800) 228–9290. Two pools, one heated, with sauna. 447 units. Free shuttle to airport and Pentagon.

First Class

Rosslyn Westpark. 1900 Ft. Myer Dr.; 527–4814; (800) 368–3408. Best Western near Key Bridge. 307 units with indoor pool, two dining rooms, cocktails, entertainment.

Holiday Inn—Key Bridge. 1850 No. Ft. Meyer Dr.; 522–0400; (800) HOLIDAY. In Rosslyn area, just across the Potomac from Georgetown, 177 units.

Holiday Inn—National Airport. 1489 Jefferson Davis Hwy.; 521–1600; (800) HOLIDAY. On U.S. 1, ¼ mile from airport. Free shuttle. Pool. 306 units.

Howard Johnson—National Airport. 2650 Jefferson Davis Hwy.; 684–7200; (800) 654–2000. A half-mile from the airport. Free shuttle. 276 units. Pool. Dining.

National Clarion. 300 Army-Navy Drive; 892–4100; (800) 848–7000. Near U.S. 1 and I–395. Formerly the Pentagon Quality Inn, enlarged to 635 units. Heated indoor pool and sauna. Airport shuttle. *Sky Dome* revolving lounge and two dining rooms. Entertainment.

Moderate

Best Western Executive Inn. 2480 S. Glebe Rd.; 979–4400; (800) 528–1234. On I–395 at Glebe Rd. exit. 325 units with pool, playground, restaurant, lounge.

Cherry Blossom Motor Inn. 3030 Columbia Pike.; 521–5570. Near junction of Columbia Pike and Glebe Rd. A TraveLodge with 76 units, 12 efficiencies. Restaurant and pool.

Comfort Inn. Glebe Road at I-66; 247–3399. 126 new units. Restaurant. Shuttle service to both airports.

Days Inn Crystal City Hotel. 2000 Jefferson Davis Hwy.; 920–8600; (800) 325–2525. Another largish (245 units) motel on U.S. 1, close to National Airport.

Econo-Lodge. 6800 Lee Hwy. (at I-66); 538–5300. 47 new units, about equally convenient to downtown and Dulles Airport.

Imperial Inn. 2485 S. Glebe Rd.; 979–4100; (800) 368–4400. At Va.120 exit off I–395. Pool, movies, restaurant. 163 units.

Quality Inn—Arlington Hotel. 1190 N. Court House Rd.; 524–4000; (800) 228–5151. On U.S. 50 near Courthouse Metro stop. 400 units including 70 efficiencies. Dining.

Quality Inn—Iwo Jima. 1501 Arlington Blvd.; 524–5000; (800) 228–5151. On U.S. 50 near the Marine Corps Memorial. 73 units. Pool. Restaurant.

Inexpensive

Motel 50. 1601 Arlington Blvd.; 524–3400. On U.S. 50. 38 units.

Tysons Corner, Virginia

Deluxe

Embassy Suites at Tysons Corner. 8517 Leesburg Pike; 883–0707. Hotel built around an 8-story atrium. Over 200 suites. Complimentary breakfast and manager's reception daily. *Carnegie Deli* restaurant.

McLean Hilton. 7920 Jones Branch Dr.; 847–5000; (800) HILTONS. Brand-new 456-room hotel with a 9-story atrium, two restaurants, two lounges, indoor pool, exercise facilities, sauna, and VIP concierge floor. Near the Beltway and Tysons Corner Shopping Center. Popular Sunday brunch.

Tysons Corner Marriott. 8028 Leesburg Pike; 734–3200; (800) 228–9290. A new hotel in the Washington area's most bustling shopping center area, near junction of I–495 and Va. Rts. 7 and 123. Atrium indoor pool with exercise room and sauna. *Rumford's Restaurant* and *Raffles Lounge* with cocktails, entertainment, dancing. 393 units.

Moderate

Ramada Inn—Tysons Corner. 7801 Leesburg Pike; 893–1340; (800) 228–2828. Junction of I–495 and Va. 7. 404 units. Heated indoor pool with sauna. Dining plus nightly live entertainment and dancing in Teddy's lounge.

Dulles International Airport

Deluxe

Dulles—Marriott Hotel. On service road near terminal. (Mail address: P.O. Box 17450, Washington, D.C. 20041); 471–9500; (800) 228–9290. 370 units. Two pools, tennis. Airport transport. Dining and cocktails.

First Class

Holiday Inn—Dulles Airport. 1000 Sully Rd., Sterling, Va.; 471–7411; (800) HOLIDAY. 297 units. New indoor pool, sauna, and exercise room. Airport transport. Dining and cocktails.

Ramada Renaissance Hotel. 13869 Park Center Rd., Herndon; 478–2900; (800) 228–2828. A new and striking addition to the booming Dulles corridor with 301 rooms, two restaurants and lounges, convention facilities, and a free half-hourly shuttle to the airport.

Bethesda, Maryland

Note: The area code for Maryland is 301.

Deluxe

Hyatt Regency Bethesda. Wisconsin Ave. at Old Georgetown Rd.; 657–1234; (800) 228–9000. Towering over the newly opened Metro stop and Red Line extension that spurred much of the recent new construction in venerable old Bethesda, the Hyatt has 380 deluxe rooms, two restaurants, two lounges, indoor pool and health club, plus convention facilities.

Bethesda Marriott Hotel. 5151 Pooks Hill Rd.; 897–9400; (800) 228–9290. Just off I–495 at Wisconsin Ave., near the National Institutes of Health and Bethesda Naval Hospital. 410 rooms. Indoor/outdoor pool with hydrotherapy and sauna. Tennis. Three restaurants and cocktail lounge, free parking.

First Class

American Inn. 8130 Wisconsin Ave.; 656–9300. 75 units. Pool. Courtesy transportation to National Institutes of Health weekdays. Restaurant.

Holiday Inn—Bethesda and Rockville. 8120 Wisconsin Ave.; 652–2000; (800) HOLIDAY. Roof-top pool. 270 units. Two dining rooms. Dancing and entertainment.

Holiday Inn—Chevy Chase. 5520 Wisconsin Ave.; 656–1500; (800) HOLIDAY. Near one of the metropolitan area's finest shopping areas. 230 units. Pool. Two dining rooms.

Ramada Inn—Bethesda. 8400 Wisconsin Ave.; 654–1000; (800) 228–2828. 163 units, immediately adajent to NIH. Recent renovation. Pool. Dining with cocktails and entertainment.

Inexpensive

Colonial Manor Motel. 11410 Rockville Pike, North Bethesda; 881–5200. 171 units, restaurant/nightclub on premises, hourly shuttle to NIH.

Silver Spring, Maryland

Moderate

Holiday Inn—Silver Spring Plaza. 8777 Georgia Ave.; 589–0800; (800) HOLIDAY. 229 units. Pool. One restaurant, one lounge.

Sheraton Inn Washington Northwest. 8727 Colesville Rd.; 589–5200; (800) 325–3535. On U.S. 29 in heart of business area. 293 units. Heated indoor pool and sauna. Two dining rooms, cocktails.

Inexpensive

Quality Inn—Silver Spring. 8040 13th St. off Georgia Ave.; near U.S. 29; 588–4400. Pool. 142 units. Dining and cocktails.

Silver Spring Motel. 7927 Georgia Ave.; 587–3200. Block from D.C.—Maryland line and 1 mile north of Walter Reed Army Hospital. 43 units.

DINING OUT. Dining out in the Washington area can be an adventure. New restaurants open and close with such alarming frequency that it's hard even for residents to keep up with the changing scene. So no listing of restaurants can be complete.

It's been said that almost any restaurant in the District can do a big luncheon business. As one reporter put it, "All you have to do is hang out your sign, stand back and avoid the rush." The average Washington commuter, however, either dines at home or stops at a restaurant on one of the "commuter corridors," which is one reason restaurants in Georgetown, Alexandria (Virginia), and Bethesda (Maryland) do such a major dinner business.

While the expense accounts of the nation's movers and shakers have sent prices skyrocketing in many restaurants near the White House and along the K Street corridor, the capital area is also rich in ethnic restaurants that offer interesting food at reasonable prices. The proliferation of Middle Eastern, Latin American, Afghan, Ethiopian, Thai, and Vietnamese restaurants immensely enriches the local culinary scene. You won't find much Southern food in local restaurants, deli food is virtually nonexistent, Italian food (except a delicious garlicky "white pizza") tends to be terribly overpriced, Chinese food is better in San Francisco and New York (though the capital now has its share of expensive restaurants specializing in the food of mainland China), and seafood is disappointing, considering the area's proximity to the Chesapeake Bay. But generalizations about food in the nation's capital are out of date almost as soon as they are written. Washington has changed from a sleepy town with Southern airs to a lively center of international activity. The Southern charm is still there, but there's a new note of urbanity and adventurousness.

Prices in Washington restaurants vary as much as hotel rates do. Restaurants frequented by the expense account crowd are usually much more expensive than those in which the clientele reach into their jeans and pay cash. Our categorization by price range is as follows, based on a complete dinner for one, including soup, entree, and dessert, but no alcoholic beverages: *Super Deluxe*, over $30; *Deluxe*, $20 to $30; *Expensive*, $15 to $20; *Moderate*, $10 to $15; *Inexpensive*, under $10. Washington has fewer of the Super Deluxe establishments than New York City, and almost none of the rock-bottom prices of rural areas. We suggest that you call about a restaurant's hours, reservations and credit card policy, and dress code. *Note:* Our listings give only the phone numbers of restaurants. Please remember to use the proper area code (District of Columbia 202, Virginia 703, Maryland 301) when dialing from one state to another. The following credit card abbreviations are used: AE, American Express; CB, Carte Blanche: DC, Diners Club; MC, MasterCard; V, Visa.

Afghan

Moderate

Bamiyan. Two locations, (operated by two different owners): 3320 M St., N.W., Georgetown; 338–1896; 300 King St., Alexandria, Va., 548–9006. The distinctive and delicious Afghan cuisine suggests the foods both of India and the Middle East, and Bamiyan is one of the best of several Afghan restaurants in the area. Among dishes to try at any of the Afghan restaurants: *aushak,* leek- or scallion-filled ravioli topped with meat sauce, mint and yogurt; sauteed pumpkin or eggplant; kebabs; rice pilav;

and, for dessrt, baklava and an incredibly sweet pastry called elephant ears. AE, MC, V.

Kabul Caravan. 1725 Wilson Blvd., Arlington, Va.; 522–8394. This airy, attractive restaurant (a short hop across the Key Bridge from Georgetown) serves a variety of good turnovers on the appetizer menu, good kebabs, homemade Afghan bread, and a fine version of *firnee,* an Afghan pudding. AE, MC, V.

Kabul West. 4871 Cordell Ave., Bethesda, Md.; 986–8566. Appetizers, kabobs, and vegetable dishes are especially good in this pleasant corner restaurant. MC, V.

Khyber Pass. 2309 Calvert St., N.W.; 234–4632. This reliable second-story restaurant near the Shoreham, the Sheraton Washington, and the Calvert Street Bridge was one of the first of the local Afghan eateries. AE, CB, DC, MC, V.

American International

Super Deluxe

Inn at Little Washington. Washington, Va.; (703) 675–3800. You'll need a car, time for a long pleasant drive to the country, and a reservation made two weeks in advance to visit this elegant country inn; but the food, from apple-smoked trout on, is well worth the trouble. Closed for lunch but early seating on weekends. Prix-fixe dinners are $54 per person, $68 per person on Saturdays. MC, V.

Windows. 1000 Wilson Blvd., in the *USA Today* Building, Rosslyn, Va.; 527–4430. Haute California cuisine featuring inventive combinations and exotic individual pizzas smothered in buffalo mozzarella or Louisiana *andouillette.* Ambitious desserts and a complimentary plate of petits fours and truffles with coffee. Near the Rosslyn Metro with a view of the river and monuments. Valet parking after 6. AE, DC, MC, V.

Deluxe

Chardonnay in the Park Terrace. 1515 Rhode Island Ave., N.W.; 232–7000. An elegant surprise hidden away behind the small bar of a midtown hotel, the Chardonnay makes dining a spectacle of smartness, from its glittering and colorfully complementary decor to the kitchen's imaginative, sure hand with New American cuisine. Standouts include poultry and game dishes, and desserts that are as memorable as the view through tall arched windows into the hotel courtyard. Dining and dancing on summer weekends in the courtyard. AE, CB, DC, MC, V.

Duke Zeibert's. 1050 Connecticut Ave., N.W.; 466–3730. Long an institution among Washington power brokers and sports figures, Duke's, which reopened in a fancy new 350-seat location after the owner's premature retirement, now competes for the sporting crowd with Mel Krupin's. Expect a wait, because Duke takes no reservations for lunch. House specialties include pickles, onion-poppy seed rolls, matzo balls, herring, crabcakes, beef stew, and roast beef hash. AE, CB, DC, MC, V.

Mel Krupin's. 1120 Connecticut Ave., N.W.; 331–7000. Popular lunching spot for the sporting crowd, run by the former maitre d' of Duke Zeibert's and serving the same type of fare, including fresh fish and cheesecake. No reservations for lunch. All major credit cards. (Insider's tip: Mr. M's, an inexpensive luncheonette at 1120 Connecticut Ave., N.W.;

331–7005, shares a kitchen with and serves the same soups, sandwiches, and daily specials as Mel Krupin's—in a more plebeian setting but at half the price.) AE, CB, DC, MC, V.

New Heights. 2317 Calvert St., N.W.; 234–4110. A trés chic new restaurant serving new American cuisine. Airy and bright upstairs dining room plus an elegant burled-wood bar downstairs and an outdoor cafe. Across the street from the Shoreham Hotel. AE, CB, DC, MC, V.

Nora. 2132 Florida Ave., N.W.; 462–5143. Fresh and seasonal ingredients, including herbs grown outside the restaurant, are used imaginatively in this popular little restaurant. Additive-free meats. Save room for the chocolate almond cake. No credit cards (personal checks accepted).

The Occidental. 1475 Pennsylvania Ave., N.W.; 783–1475. A reborn tradition on the Avenue. The downstairs Grill serves great soups, grilled meats, fish, and sausages, and is making a name for itself with a fabulous swordfish sandwich, all in a clubby brass and leather room with photos of presidents and politicos papering the walls. Upstairs is more formal and austerely elegant, with new American cuisine that's exciting, first class, and definitely Super Deluxe. AE, CB, DC, MC, V.

219. 219 King St., Alexandria, Va.; 549–1141. Creole and Cajun specialties include jambalaya, gumbo, barbecued shrimp, and shrimp Creole. Sunday brunch, 11 A.M. to 4 P.M. AE, MC, V.

Expensive

City Cafe. 2213 M St., N.W.; 797–4860. A trendy New York–style cafe with mirrors, marble, and faux granite, all pink and gray and very Deco. Serves au courant light cuisine—individual pizzas, grilled meats, and fish and salads. Great for beautiful people watching. No credit cards.

Portner's. 109 So. St. Asaph St., Alexandria, Va.; 683–1776. A beautifully appointed, noisy pub where your best value is probably drinks and appetizers, or entrees from the light fare menu. Sunday brunch. AE, DC, MC, V.

Moderate

American Cafe. Several locations: Georgetown, 1211 Wisconsin Ave., N.W., 944–9464; Capitol Hill, 227 Massachusetts Ave., N.E., 547–8500; Chevy Chase, 5252 Wisconsin Ave., N.W., 363–5400. National Place, 13th & F Sts. N.W., 737–5153; Fair Oaks Hall, Fairfax, 352–0201; Tysons Corner, 790–8858. Food, decor, and service are first-rate in every branch of this very American cafe. Good vegetable soups, imaginative salads and sandwiches (including rare roast beef on a superb croissant), smoked meats, yummy brownies, and carrot cake are some of the reasons this is one of our favorite lunch spots. Sunday brunch. AE, DC, MC, V.

Brickskeller. 1523 22nd St., N.W.; 293–1885. Reasonably priced pub food, lots of games, and an extraordinary list of domestic and imported beers. AE, CB, DC, MC, V.

Bullfeathers. 410 First St., S.E.; 543–5005. Beef and seafood in a popular hangout with a Teddy Roosevelt theme. The *New York Times* comes with the Sunday brunch. AE, CB, DC, MC, V.

Clyde's. 3236 M St., N.W.; 333–0294 (recorded message), 333–9180 (reservations). Omelets, cheeseburgers, chili, breakfast, and brunch are highlights at this popular Georgetown pub. Highlight at the newer Tysons Corner branch (8332 Leesburg Pike, Vienna, Va.; 734–1900) is a 22-foot high skylight and spectacularly extravagant decor; at the Columbia (Md.) Clyde's, it's the splendid lakeside view (596–4050). AE, CB, DC, MC, V.

Foggy Bottom Cafe. 924 25th St., N.W.; 338–8707. One of the few good cafes—albeit a small one—near the Kennedy Center. AE, CB, DC, MC, V.

Hamburger Hamlet. 3125 M St., N.W., in Georgetown, 965–6970; 5225 Wisconsin Ave., N.W., 244–2037; and 10400 Old Georgetown Road, Bethesda, Md., 897–5350. Readers of *Washingtonian* magazine voted this the best place for hamburgers. Sunday brunch. AE, CB, DC, MC, V.

Old Ebbitt Grill. 675 15th St., N.W.; 347–4800. An old D.C. tavern now in a stylish new location in Metropolitan Square. Sunday brunch. All major credit cards. AE, CB, DC, MC, V.

Suzanne's. 1735 Connecticut Ave., N.W.; 483–4633. Clever salads, tempting desserts, fine wine by the glass, fabulous homemade desserts, and bistro atmosphere are among the features that made Suzanne's second-story cafe (and first-floor carryout) an instant success. MC, V.

Timberlake's. 1726 Connecticut Ave., N.W., near Dupont Circle, 483–2266. A friendly, extremely popular neighborhood pub. Weekend brunch. AE, CB, DC, MC, V.

West End Cafe. 1 Washington Circle, N.W.; 293–5390. A pretty, light and airy place to enjoy a drink and light meal, a short taxi ride or healthy walk away from the Kennedy Center. Pleasant piano bar evenings. AE, DC, MC, V.

Inexpensive

Florida Avenue Grill. 1100 Florida Ave., N.W.; 265–1586. Ham hocks, fried chicken, cornbread, grits, and other downhome Southern dishes make this diner a favorite among taxi drivers, especially for breakfast. Hours: 6 A.M. to 8:55 P.M., Monday through Saturday. No credit cards.

Hard Times Cafe. 1404 King St., Alexandria, Va.; 683–5340. A variety of good chilis, including Texas and Cincinnati styles, and a lively crowd dancing to the jukebox's country & western music keep this small cafe jammed. Top price, $4.20. MC, V.

Kramerbooks and Afterwords Cafe. 1517 Connecticut Ave., N.W.; 387–1462. A friendly cafe-bookstore with a small but pleasant menu and an outdoor cafe. Open round the clock from Friday morning to Sunday night. Sunday brunch. AE, MC, V.

New Orleans Café. 1790 Columbia Rd., N.W.; 234–5111. Gumbo, crayfish, jambalaya, oyster loaf, and eggs Sardou are among the Creole offerings in this Adams-Morgan cafe, or you can start the day with chicory-flavored *café au lait* and *beignets.* Louisiana's answer to the doughnut. Sunday brunch. AE, MC, V.

O'Brien's Pit Barbecue. 1314 E. Gude Dr., Rockville, Md., 340–8596; 7305 Waverly St., Bethesda, 654–9004; and 6820 Commerce St., Springfield, Va., 569–7801. Formica tables, plastic beer mugs, good chili, and Texas barbecue local food critics rave about, especially the ribs. Cafeteria-style service; no reservations. AE, MC, V.

Reeves Bakery. 1209 F St., N.W.; 347–3781. This beloved bakery/restaurant—famous for such goodies as strawberry pie—has been a Washington landmark since 1886. Rebuilt completely since a fire destroyed it in 1983, and the only thing that's no longer as authentic and nostalgic is the decor. Convenient to Metro Center and downtown department stores. No credit cards.

Roof Terrace. Kennedy Center; 833–8870. You can catch a bite before the show at three different places in the Kennedy Center: the Encore Cafeteria, which serves soups, salads, hot entrees and desserts; and Curtain Call Cafe (often closed summers), which serves more formal meals; and the Hors D'Oeuvrerie, a pretty room that serves light snacks. Hours vary, depending upon theater schedules. AE, CB, DC, MC, V.

British

Expensive

Gadsby's Tavern. 138 N. Royal St., Alexandria, Va.; 548–1288. Welcome to colonial Virginia, with costumed waiters and serving wenches, game pyes, seafood and beef. In a 1791 hotel, this candlelit, authentic restaurant also features a Publick Table Sunday and Monday nights in which 30 or so people sit down at one big table for a colonial feast hosted by Kathleen Baker, who sings, gossips, and makes jokes, 18th-century style. It's fun, and it's $20 per person. AE, MC, V.

The Wayfarers. 110 S. Pitt St., Alexandria, Va.; 836–2749. Hurricane lamps light the attractive rooms of this British Colonial restaurant, an echo of Williamsburg. The menu leans toward British fare, from veal chops to kidney pie, and British beers to trifle. DC, MC, V.

Moderate

Scotland Yard. 728 King St., Alexandria, Va.; 683–1742. Scottish food, in a cozy setting, with plaid tablecloths, lace curtains, and imported Scottish ales. Dinner only. AE, MC, V.

Cafeterias

Most cafeterias take cash only, and those in Federal office buildings are often open only weekdays, for breakfast and lunch. Call ahead to check on hours.

Inexpensive

Chamberlin. 819 15th St., N.W.; 628–7680. Standard fare, lunch only, open from 10:30 A.M.

Connecticut Connection. Underground in the Farragut North Metro station, Connecticut at L St., N.W.; 783–1101. A collection of fast-food counters in the heart of the Connecticut Ave. shopping area.

Health's a-Poppin! 2020 K St., N.W.; 466–6616. Soups, salads and sandwiches *au naturel.*

Kitcheteria. Harrington Hotel, 11th and E Sts., N.W.; 628–8140. Standard fare; open all week, 7 A.M.–9 P.M.

Library of Congress. James Madison Memorial Building. 101 Independence Ave., S.E.; 287–8300. The cafeteria on the sixth floor of the new Madison annex (in the "red" section of the building) offers a great view of the city, and serves breakfast 8:30 A.M.–10:30 A.M., lunch 11:00 A.M.–2 P.M. Buffet served in the ground-floor coffee shop in "yellow" part of building for $6.95 plux tax (11:30 A.M.–2:30 P.M.).

Metro Market. Underground in the Farragut West Metro shop, or through International Square, between 18th and Eye Sts. and 19th and

K Sts., N.W. A subterranean potpourri of fast-food counters near Connecticut Ave. shops. Try the gyros at the Mykonos and the fruit bowl at Yummy Yogurt.

National Gallery of Art Cafeteria. On the concourse walkway between the East and West wings, near Constitution and 4th St., N.W.; 737–4215. Watch the concourse waterfall from the lower level, where you can buy inexpensive sandwiches, salad or hot entrees. Hours 11–6. Monday through Saturday; Sundays, noon to 6.

Organization of American States. 1889 F St., N.W. at 19th; 458–3829. Occasionally offers Latin American specialties. Open 7:30–10:30 A.M. 11:30 A.M.–2, and 3 P.M.–4 P.M.

Patent Pending. 9th and G Sts., N.W. This charming cafeteria in what was once the old patent office (in a building that now houses the National Collection of Fine Arts and National Portrait Gallery) serves soup, salads, sandwiches, pastries, wine, and imported beer. Dine among outdoor sculptures in good weather. Open weekdays 11 A.M.–3:30 P.M., weekends and holidays 11:30A.M.–4:00P.M..

Pavilion at the Old Post Office. 1100 Pennsylvania Ave., N.W.; 289–4224. Food stalls in the revitalized old Post Office building (worth strolling through) offer a better value than the restaurants, but close around 9 P.M., 6 on Sunday. If you can find a table in the open area, pick up a platter from the curry stand or whatever takes your fancy, listen to whoever is performing that day, look up at the play of light in the crystal-palace-like ceiling, and watch the passing parade. Some days it's lovely, some days a madhouse.

Senate Cafeteria. Dirksen Senate Office Building, Constitution Avenue and 1st St., N.E.; 224–2560. Open to the public for breakfast 10:30 A.M.–noon, and 1:30–3:30 P.M. for lunch (reserved for staff, noon to 1:30). Famous for bean soup (65 cents a bowl).

Sholl's. 1990 K St., N.W.; 296–3065. A Washington institution, welcomed by bargain-hungry visitors who often arrive by the busload. Homemade pies, fresh vegetables and frequent lines, so arrive early. Open for breakfast, lunch and dinner 7 A.M.–8 P.M.; closed Sundays. Also 1735 N. Lynn, Rosslyn, Va.; 528–8841. Virginia address closed Saturday and Sunday.

Le Souperb. 1221 Connecticut Ave., N.W.; 347–7600. Soups, sandwiches, stews, special stuffed baked potatoes, homemade bread and pastries, beer and wine. Scruffy but economical.

Supreme Court Building Cafeteria. East Capitol and 1st St., N.E.; 479–3246. Sandwiches, salads, and hot entrees. Hours, 7:30 A.M.–2 P.M. weekdays only.

Chinese

Super Deluxe

Mr. K's. 2121 K St., N.W.; 331–8868. Extravagantly priced dishes from the four main regions of mainland China: the northern Chinese food of Peking, the spicier Hunan and Szechuan (or Sichuan) food of central China, milder dishes from Shanghai, in eastern China, and the classic Cantonese dishes of the south. AE, CB, DC, MC, V.

Sichuan Garden. 1220 19th St., N.W.; 296–4550. Nearly 20 chefs were imported from the regional provinces of China to prepare the food served in this luxurious mainland-Chinese restaurant—the first of its kind in Washington and the best, according to the *Post's* food critic. AE, CB, DC, MC, V.

Sichuan Pavilion, 1820 K St., N.W.; 466–7790. Sister restaurant to the original Sichuan Pavilion in New York, the one that started the whole business of importing chefs from the regional provinces of mainland China. Dim sum served on weekends, noon to 4 P.M.. AE, CB, DC, MC, V.

Expensive

China Coral. 6900 Wisconsin Ave., Chevy Chase; 656–1203. Imaginative seafood dishes, Chinese style. AE, MC, V.

Moderate

China Garden. Upstairs at 1901 North Moore St., Rosslyn, Va. (across Key Bridge from Georgetown); 525–5317. First-rate Cantonese food, including dim sum Saturdays and Sundays (11:30 A.M.–3 P.M.), in a spacious dining room with a lovely view of Georgetown and the Potomac. Also in Bethesda, 657–4665. AE, DC, MC, V.

Szechuan. Upstairs at 615 I St., N.W.; 393–0130. Chinatown's best-known Szechuan restaurant has some nice dishes, but it was never known for its decor. It's not on the menu, but ask for the barbecued pork with bean curd—it's delicious, as is the Szechuan shredded beef. Weekend brunch (*tien hsin*) is a delicious northern Chinese variation on dim sum. Noodle dishes are good here, and such specialties as the cold marinated appetizers. AE, MC, V.

Yenching Palace. 3524 Connecticut Ave., N.W.; 362–8200. Well known as the scene of important East-West visits and negotiations and the source of Peking duck ($18.95) that does not require 24 hours advance notice. Sunday brunch. Family dinners, $9 per person. All major credit cards. AE, DC, MC, V.

Young Chow. 312 Pennsylvania Ave., S.E.; 544–3030. First-rate Szechuan and Hunan dishes in an attractive setting, just a block from the Library of Congress. Also in Crystal City, at 420 S. 23rd St., across from the Stouffer Hotel. AE, MC, V.

Inexpensive

Big Wong. 610 H St., N.W.; 638–0116. Noisy and crowded, and for a good reason: the prices, and the consistent quality of largely Cantonese fare of this basic basement eatery. MC, V.

China Inn. 631 H St., N.W.; 842–0909 or 842–0910. One of a group of traditional Cantonese restaurants clustered in the old and rapidly changing Chinatown area. Some Szechuan dishes. Open till 3:30 A.M. AE, MC, V.

Duck Chang's. 4427 John Marr Dr., Annandale, Va.; 941–9400. Regulars crowd this tiny suburban restaurant (a good schlepp from downtown Washington) for its tasty Peking duck, which requires no advance notice. One duck serves two. Sunday brunch. AE, MC, V.

Shanghai Garden. 4469 Connecticut Ave., N.W.; 362–3000. Szechuan cuisine is featured in this popular upper Northwest restaurant. Try the Peking duck and finish your meal with taffy apples or bananas. AE, MC, V.

Continental

Super Deluxe

Aux Beaux Champs. In the Four Seasons Hotel, 2800 Pennsylvania Ave., N.W.; 342–0810. Inventive Continental cuisine with a strong French accent in an elegant room lush with greenery and Chinoiserie. The dish of three mignons of veal, lamb, and beef, with three different sauces, is spectacular, as is the creamy Breton cake. They also serve a low-cholesterol, low-calorie, highly imaginative menu. Impeccable service. AE, CB, DC, MC, V.

Deluxe

Chaucer's. In the Canterbury Hotel, 1733 N St., N.W.; 393–3000. Charming English grill with excellent seafood and prime ribs served in an intimate setting. AE, CB, DC, MC, V.

The Jockey Club. 2100 Massachusetts Ave., N.W.; 659–8000. This attractive room in the Ritz Carlton Hotel attracts Reagan people, who can apparently afford $24.75 crab cakes. (Of course, they're "as good as crab cakes get," according to the *Washington Post's* food critic.) Also recommended on the classical French menu: rack of lamb, the veal dishes, and vegetables. AE, CB, DC, MC, V.

Expensive

Tivoli. In Rosslyn Center, 1700 N. Moore St., Rosslyn, Va.; 524–8900. A spacious, beautifully decorated third-floor dining room sitting atop the Rosslyn Metro station. Imaginative Continental cuisine mixed with northern Italian dishes. Worth the Metro ride. AE, DC, MC, V.

Inexpensive

Bread and Chocolate. 1120 20th St., N.W., 887–0570; 2301 M St., N.W., 833–8360; 5542 Connecticut Ave., N.W., 966–7413; 611 King St., Alexandria, Va., 548–0992; Skyline Mall, Falls Church, Va., 379–8005. Dash into this European tea room for coffee and croissants or pastries, or grab a soup and sandwich for lunch. Closes early in the evening. AE, MC, V.

Ethiopian

Washington boasts many Ethiopian restaurants, where meat and vegetable dishes are scooped up and eaten in pieces of *injera,* a spongy, crepe-like bread which serves all at once as tablecloth, eating utensil, and side dish. Typical dishes, in brief: *wat,* a spicy stew of chicken, beef or lamb; *alecha,* a mild stew; *kitfo,* a peppery version of steak tartare (a favorite); and *tibs,* or *zilzil tibs,* sauteed cubes of beef.

Inexpensive

Meskerem. 2434 18th St., N.W.; 462–4100. In multi-ethnic Adams Morgan, an attractive, atmospheric scene in which to sample Ethiopian cuisine prepared and served with finesse. AE, DC, MC, V.

Red Sea. 2463 18th St., N.W.; 483–5000. Noisy and popular with students; more likely than its competitors to spice dishes to Ethiopian tastes. AE, CB, DC, MC, V.

Filipino and Polynesian

Expensive

Trader Vic's. Capitol Hilton Hotel, 16th and K Sts., N.W.; 347–7100. Giant tiki gods mark the entrance to Washington's Trader Vic, a popular source of Chinese, Polynesian and Continental nibbles, traditionally washed down by mai-tais and other crazy drinks. AE, CB, DC, MC, V.

Moderate

Manila in Georgetown. 3280 M St., N.W.; 965–7877. Filipino food is not to everyone's taste, but explorers of the world's cuisines may welcome a chance to sample the exotic food of the Philipines. You will find echoes of Spanish, Malaysian, and Chinese cuisine in such dishes as empañaditas, fried squid, and stuffed shrimp. AE, CB, DC, MC, V.

French

Note: French restaurants are almost invariably closed on Sunday and often for Saturday lunch as well.

Super Deluxe

Fourways. 1701 20th St., N.W.; 483–3200. No expense was spared turning the lovely old Fraser mansion into one of the city's most beautiful restaurants, with food and service to match. French food with finesse. AE, CB, DC, MC, V.

Jean-Louis. In the Watergate, 2650 Virginia Ave., N.W.; 298–4488. A shrine of nouvelle cuisine supervised by a chef who earned two Michelin stars before he was 30 and still runs an adventurous and well-regarded kitchen. Pretheater dinners, 5:30–6:30 P.M., are $35; set-price dinners are $35, $70, and $85, depending on the number of courses. Some of the best desserts in the world included. AE, CB, DC, MC, V.

Jean-Pierre. 1835 K St., N.W.; 466–2022. A mixture of traditional and new French cuisine, in a distinguished downtown restaurant. AE, CB, DC, MC, V.

Le Lion d'Or. 1150 Connecticut Ave., N.W.; 296–7972. A longtime fine French restaurant. The dining room is large and elegant, the service attentive, but it's often noisy in the early evening when drink-guzzling lobbyists gather. The restaurant's strength is the creative culinary skill of chef-owner Jean-Pierre Goyenvalle. Try his lamb with thyme, and finish with an exquisite orange soufflé. AE, CB, DC, MC, V.

Le Pavillon. Washington Square, 1050 Connecticut Ave., N.W.; 833–3846. Chef Yannick Cam serves nouvelle cuisine legendary for its beauty, tastiness, high cost, and minuscule portions in a gorgeous location. Tasting dinners offer small portions of several courses at lunch and dinner. AE, CB, DC, MC, V.

Maison Blanche. 1725 F St., N.W.; 842–0070. Don't count on a good table at lunchtime: this elegant restaurant near the White House (hence the name) has replaced the late Sans Souci as the "in" place for lobbyists and television correspondents to see and be seen with White House staffers. Pre- and post-theatre dinners. AE, CB, DC, MC, V.

1789. 1226 36th St., N.W.; 965–1789. The three dining rooms of this clubby but dignified Georgetown restaurant are old Washington and old

money. Menu mostly traditional French, but now also American, thanks
to the new ownership (by the company that owns Clyde's). AE, CB, DC,
MC, V.

Expensive

L'Auberge Chez François. 332 Springvale Road, Great Falls, Va.;
759–3800. (Call for directions.) When François Haeringer left the city to
set up this country inn, the clientele from his old cafe followed him out
to the Virginia countryside. It's a long drive, and you must often book
two weeks ahead, but the ambience is charming, the food (including Alsa-
tian specialties) a real pleasure, especially if you like butter and garlic. Two
seatings each evening, three on Sunday. AE, MC, V.

La Bergerie. 220 N. Lee St., Old Town Alexandria, Va; 683–1007. Delicious Basque and French food (including such specialties from the Pyre-
nees as *garbure,* a sophisticated bean and cabbage soup) beautifully presented, in one of the prettiest restaurants in the area. AE, CB, DC, MC,
V.

La Chaumiere. 2813 M St., N.W.; 338–1784. A fireplace in the center
of this pleasant Georgetown restaurant adds to the ambience, which is
reminiscent of a French provincial inn. Daily specials include bouillabaisse
(Tuesday), couscous (Wednesday), and cassoulet (Thursday). AE, DC,
MC, V.

Dominique's. 1900 Pennsylvania Ave., N.W.; 452–1126. A bustling restaurant, famous for unusual game dishes (and infamous at one point for
serving rattlesnake) and super-rich chocolate truffles. Take advantage of
the fixed-price, pre- and post-theatre dinners, a bargain at $14.95. AE, CB,
DC, MC, V.

Le Gaulois. 2133 Pennsylvania Ave., N.W.; 466–3232. The food at this
tiny restaurant is so good, and its fans are so numerous, that you'll have
trouble getting in and will feel cramped for space when you do, but it's
worth it. A real gem. AE, MC, V.

Moderate

Bistro Francais. 3128 M St., N.W.; 338–3830. A popular Georgetown
bistro open till 3 A.M. weekdays, 4 A.M. Friday and Saturday nights. Famous for roast tarragon chicken. AE, DC, MC, V.

La Colline. 400 N. Capitol St., N.W.; 737–0400. The wine bar in this
pleasant Capitol Hill bistro offers daily specials of wine by the glass, and
an outdoor cafe facing the courtyard fountains in good weather. Set-price
dinner, $15.75. AE, CB, DC, MC, V.

La Fourchette. 2429 18th St., N.W.; 332–3077. An Adams–Morgan bistro offering good value for the money. Seafood specialties. AE, CB, DC,
MC, V.

Tout Va Bien. 1063 31st St., N.W.; 965–1212. The imaginative menu
in this small, sunny Georgetown cafe includes tender calf's liver topped
with avocado and herbs, a picture-pretty spinach pate, and delightful fruit
tarts. AE, CB, MC, V.

Inexpensive

Au Pied de Cochon. 1335 Wisconsin Ave., N.W.; 333–5440. Both the
food (fabulous real French fries and onion soup) and the hours (until 3
A.M. weekends) will remind many of this bistro's Paris namesake in Les Hal-
les. AE, CB, DC, MC, V.

Cafe La Ruche. 1039 31st St., N.W.; 965–2684. It's possible to dine nicely for under $10 in this charming Georgetown cafe, even if you finish the meal with one of their mouthwatering fruit tarts (try to go during raspberry season). There's a branch in White Flint Mall, Rockville. Md.; 468–1155. MC, V.

Vie de France. 1990 K St., N.W., 659–0055; 600 Maryland Ave., S.W., 554–7870; 4250 Connecticut Ave., N.W., 364–8888, and a spiffy new location at 1615 M St., N.W. (659–0992) across the street from the National Geographic building. Flaky croissants, good soups, a variety of quiches, and good hamburgers draw crowds for breakfast and lunch. Vie de France also runs *Monsieur Croissant,* a carry-out at 1725 K St., N.W.; 775–9193. AE, DC, MC, V.

German and Austrian

Expensive

Old Europe. 2434 Wisconsin Ave., N.W.; 333–7600 or 333–7601. Hearty German food (schnitzel, sauerbrauten, wursts, and dumplings), and excellent values in German wine and beer. Daily specials, from $11. AE, CB, DC, MC, V.

Moderate

Café Mozart. 1331 H St., N.W.; 347–5732. Viennese restaurant and carryout with typical Austrian dishes such as schnitzel, goulash, wursts, German salads, strudels, Viennese pastries, and great German sandwiches. Piano or Viennese chamber music most nights. AE, CB, DC, MC, V.

Inexpensive

Café Splendide. 1521 Connecticut Ave., N.W.; 328–1503. A friendly Austrian café where you can dine nicely for under $10. Known especially for its desserts. No credit cards.

Greek and Middle Eastern

Expensive

Dar es Salam. 3056 M St., N.W., in Georgetown; 342–1925. This lively Moroccan restaurant specializes in couscous in three-course, eight-course, and fixed-course dinners, complete with belly dancers. MC, V.

Kazan. 6813 Redmond Dr., McLean; 734–1960. You'll find wonderful Turkish food at Kazan. Our favorite dish is *yogurtlu kebab,* sliced beef in a yogurt, tomato, and dill sauce on diced pita, but regulars also flock for *doner kebab* (like a gyro, but better), which Kazan serves Friday and Saturday evenings. AE, CB, DC, MC, V.

Marrakesh. 617 New York Ave., N.W.; 393–9393. At this ornate Moroccan casbah dining becomes a show in itself. A delicious multicourse meal is served by kneeling waiters to diners ensconced on low cushions. Dinner takes hours and makes for lots of fun since there's no cutlery—strictly hands-on. Best to go with a crowd. Set price is $20 per person. No credit cards.

Moderate

Bacchus. 1827 Jefferson Pl., N.W.; 785–0734. First-rate Lebanese food guarantees that this two-room midtown restaurant is jammed at lunchtime; dinnertime may be more serene. Start with mezze (an array of good appetizers) and try the lamb or chicken served on a bed of rice, minced meat, almonds and pine nuts. AE, CB, DC, MC, V.

Caspian Tea Room. Inside the Spring Valley Center, 4801 Massachusetts Ave., N.W.; 244–6363. French pastries and Persian food dominate in this elegant tearoom. Rice dishes, kebabs and a chicken-pomegranate dish called *fessenjan* are especially good. AE, CB, DC, MC, V.

Iron Gate Inn. 1734 N. St., N.W.; 737–1370. Charming summers (in the garden) or winters (by the fire in what was once a stable). Middle Eastern specialties include hummus and baba ghanouj (dipped in pita bread) and baked eggplant. AE, CB, DC, MC, V.

Taverna Cretekou. 818 King St., Alexandria, Va.; 548–8688. Whitewashed walls, blue tablecloths, a lovely garden, bouzouki music, and thin black-clad waiters convey a romantically Mediterranean aura, especially pleasant at Sunday brunch. At other times, you might make a meal of the appetizer platter and honey-sweet desserts. AE, DC, MC, V.

Inexpensive

Astor. 1813 M St., N.W.; 331–7994. The long-standing champion for budget-priced meals midtown. Belly dancing (and higher prices) upstairs evenings. AE, DC, MC, V.

Taverna the Greek Islands. 307 Pennsylvania Ave., S.E.; 547–8360. Reliably good value in a romantic setting near Capitol Hill. Try the souvlaki sandwiches, marinated octopus, moussaka, and a moist lamb pie called *exochiko.* AE, MC, V.

Hungarian

Csikos. 3601 Connecticut Ave., N.W. (in the Broadmoor apartments); 362–5624. Traditional dishes (roast duck with red cabbage, goulash, stuffed cabbage, and paprika-seasoned stews). Dinner only. Moderate. AE, CB, DC, MC, V.

Indian-Pakistani-Nepalese

Expensive

Apana. 3066 M St., N.W.; 965–3040. A quiet, romantic Georgetown restaurant that serves excellent north Indian food. Curry-type dishes take a back seat to main courses featuring shrimp, Cornish hen, fish and cubed meat, delicately seasoned unless you request otherwise. Dinner only. AE, CB, DC, MC, V.

Bombay Palace. 1835 K St., N.W.; 331–0111. Sophisticated decor, elegant Indian dishes. The sizzling tandoori is spectacular. AE, DC, MC, V.

Shezan. 913 19th St., N.W.; 659–5555. Tandoori chicken and grilled kebabs are among mildly spiced but sophisticated dishes at this pretty Pakistani restaurant. Pre-theatre dinners. AE, DC, MC, V.

Moderate

Katmandu. 1800 Connecticut Ave., N.W., at Florida Ave.; 483–6470. This pretty little corner restaurant serves gently spiced dishes (you may request them hot) from Nepal and Kashmir: kebabs, a flavorful ground mutton sausage, charcoal-grilled meats recooked in yogurt sauce, excellent *biriani* (rice), and a surprisingly good turnip curry. AE, MC, V.

Tandoor. 3316 M St., N.W.; 333–3376. Beef, lamb and seafood are charcoal grilled inside a clay urn-shaped tandoor oven (you can watch the chef cook through a window) but we *invariably* order the succulent, flavorsome tandoori chicken and tandoor-cooked bread. Start with Pimm's cup, an aperitif you stir with a cucumber stick. AE, CB, DC, MC, V.

Paru's. See listing under Vegetarian restaurants.

Inexpensive

Madurai. 3318 M St., N.W.; 333–0997. Washingtonians have warmly welcomed this new vegetarian restaurant, managed by the owner of the neighboring Tandoor restaurant. The *masala dosai* (potato and onion filled crepes) are great, and you can sample a variety curries at the all-you-can-eat Sunday buffet ($6.95). AE, CB, DC, MC, V.

Siddartha. 908 Thayer Ave., Silver Spring, Md.; 585–0551, and a new downtown branch at 1379 K St., N.W.; 682–9090. Plastic containers, self-service, minimal if not tacky decor, and rock-bottom prices that encourage experimentation: these are the features of this Indian vegetarian restaurant. The food? Very satisfying. Recommended: eggplant curry and *massala dossa*, a crisp rice pancake filled with curried potatoes and onions. No credit cards.

Italian

See also "Pizza."

Super Deluxe

Cantina d'Italia. 1214–A 18th St., N.W.; 659–1830. The northern Italian cuisine served in the small rooms of this comfortable restaurant is considered among the finest in the country. Delicate pasta (prepared fresh daily and cooked to order), antipasta and main dishes are prepared with imagination and care, from fresh ingredients of the season. Closed Saturday and Sunday. AE, CB, DC, MC, V.

Tiberio. 1915 K St., N.W.; 452–1915. Lobster and linguine with lobster. Fine food, but overpriced. You can get the same food at much lower prices at the just as elegant **Terrazza** in Alexandria, Va. (710 King St.; 683–6900), run by the same owners. AE, CB, DC, MC, V.

Deluxe

Il Giardino. 1110 21st St., N.W.; 223–4555. Pastas in this north Italian restaurant are worth writing home about, particularly *linguini alla puttanesca* (racy Italian for a sauce of capers and black olives), gnocchi, and spinach-stuffed agnolotti. AE, CB, DC, MC, V.

Vincenzo. 1606 20th St., N.W.; 667–0047. Simplicity and authenticity are the keywords at this Italian seafood restaurant, so much so that when Vincenzo first opened, talk was evenly divided between how good the fish was and why he refused to serve butter with the bread. AE, DC, MC, V.

Expensive

Trattoria da Franco. 305 S. Washington St., Alexandria, Va.; 548–9338. Large portions and high quality are the trademarks of this friendly family-run restaurant. Try the creamy rich *tortellini alla panna.* AE, MC, V.

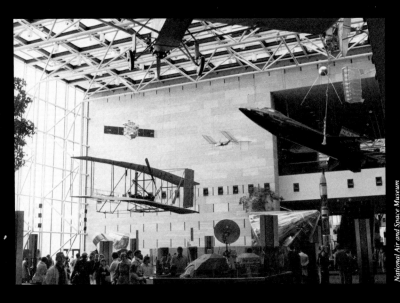

The bronze figure of Mercury stands in the center of the Rotunda at the National Gallery of Art (top). The National Air and Space Museum contains a spectacular array of air and space craft, including the Wright brothers' 1903 Flyer (bottom, at left).

The National Gallery of Art's domed West Building was designed by John Russell Pope and opened in 1941 (top). The East Building, which opened in 1978, was designed by I. M. Pei. Washington's ultramodern Metro subway system began operating in 1976 (bottom).

U.S. Department of the Interior

John F. Kennedy Center for the Performing Arts

Mule-drawn barges carry tourists down the scenic C&O Canal during summer months (top). The elegant John F. Kennedy Center for the Performing Arts features top entertainment in its four theaters (bottom).

he U.S. Capitol is perhaps the most famous structure in the United States.

Moderate

Cafe Capri. 301 Massachusetts Ave., N.E.; 546–5900. Good Italian food. This is one of a cluster of Capitol Hill pubs with outdoor cafes. Sunday brunch. AE, MC, V.

Candelas Ristorante. 3284 M St., N.W.; 338–0900. Nice veal, good Matriciana sauce, pleasant service. In Georgetown. AE, DC, MC, V.

Ecco. 220 N. Lee St., Alexandria, Va.; 684–0321; and Ballston Common (on the Orange Metro line), Arlington, Va.; 525–3226. Trendy, upscale; Italian soups, salads, pastas, individual pizzas, and crusty herbed breads. AE, MC, V.

Morrocco's. 1120 20th St. N.W.; 331–9664. This veteran family-style Italian restaurant has made a successful move to newer and much prettier quarters. Veal dishes are particularly good here, as are the squid, mussels and *spaghetti bolognese.* AE, DC, MC, V.

Inexpensive

Adams-Morgan Spaghetti Garden. 2317 18th St., N.W.; 265–6665 and 232–2929. A friendly neighborhood restaurant, jammed on weekend evenings, where pasta is served *al dente* and veal dishes are cheaper than you can make them at home. AE, MC, V.

Fio's. 3636 16th St., N.W. (in the Woodner Apartments, down the main hall to the left); 667–3040. One doesn't mind dining on these oilcloth-covered tables because Fio's affordable food ranges from fair to very good—especially the white pizza (like a divinely garlicky fried dough), a dish beloved of regulars at **A.V. Ristorante** on New York Ave. (owned by members of the same family). AE, DC, MC, V.

Japanese

Expensive

Ginza Restaurant. 1009 21st St., between K and L Sts., N.W.; 833–1244. Sushi, tempura and the like, midtown. AE, DC, MC, V.

Japan Inn. 1715 Wisconsin Ave., N.W.; 337–3400. In the Japanese Room you eat sukiyaki or shabu seated on the floor; in the Teppan-Yaki Room you eat grilled steak, shrimp and chicken Benihana style; or you may opt for sushi at the new sushi bar. AE, CB, DC, MC, V.

Takesushi. 1010 20th St., N.W.; 466–3798. Washington's branch of the well-known New York and Tokyo sushi bar turns out beautiful sushi at sometimes dollars-per-bite prices. Order carefully and you can get a nice lunch for under $10. AE, DC, MC, V.

Moderate

Matuba. 2915 Columbia Pike, Arlington, Va.; 521–2811; also at 4918 Cordell Ave. in Bethesda, Md.; 652–7449. Locals go for sushi and sashimi but you can also order hot dishes. AE, DC, MC, V.

Mikado. 4707 Wisconsin Ave., N.W.; 244–1740. A serene and gracious source of good Japanese food at reasonable prices. The special sukiyaki or shabu-shabu dinners for two give you soup, sashimi or tempura, salad or Japanese pickles, rice or noodles, the entree, and ice cream. New sushi bar. Closed Mondays. AE, CB, DC, MC, V.

Sushi-Ko. 2309 Wisconsin Ave., N.W.; 333–4187. A small sushi and sashimi restaurant above Georgetown, with a loyal clientele. AE, MC, V.

Yosaku. 4712 Wisconsin Ave., N.W.; 363–4453. Sushi, sashimi, traditional cooked entrees, and delicious appetizers in a small restaurant that offers very good value. AE, MC, V.

Latin American

Expensive

Las Pampas. 3291 M St., N.W.; 333–5151. Grilled chicken and empanadas are highlights at Georgetown's Argentinian grill, but beef is the real star. For steak, order a *churrasco;* for a wider sampling, try the *parrillada,* a mixed grill of short ribs, sausages, kidneys and sweetbreads. AE, CB, DC, MC, V.

Moderate

Dona Flor. 4615 41st St., N.W.; 537–0404. This attractive little restaurant just off Wisconsin Ave. serves interesting Brazilian dishes, including feijoada, Brazil's national dish of spicy meat, sausage, black beans, and rice; seafood in coconut milk and palm oil sauces, and grilled meat on skewers. AE, CB, DC, MC, V.

El Caribe. Three locations: in Georgetown, at 3288 M St., N.W., 338–3121; and in the Latino section of Adams Morgan, at 1828 Columbia Rd., N.W., 234–6969; and in Bethesda, at 8130 Wisconsin Ave., 656–0888. Huge portions of black beans and rice come with the well-prepared specialties of Spain, Argentina, Bolivia and Peru: fried squid, shrimp in garlic sauce, ceviche, and paella, among them. Strolling guitarists add to the festivities. The Adams-Morgan branch is smaller, more crowded, and somewhat less expensive. AE, CB, DC, MC, V.

Inexpensive

Il Migueleño. 2411 18th St., N.W.; 328–6532. Best bet, if you are new to the food of El Salvador, is the platter of Salvadorean specialties, which includes fried *yuca, pupusa* (corn meal pancakes stuffed with pork or cheese or both), and fried bananas. AE, MC, V.

Omega. 1858 Columbia Rd., N.W.; 462–1732. Large portions and low prices guarantee you a wait in line at this ever-popular old Cuban restaurant in the heart of the District's Latino section. Paella, rabbit, pork, and other dishes are served with black beans and rice. AE, DC, MC, V.

Mexican

Expensive

Enriqueta's. 2811 M St., N.W.; 338–7772. A cheerful, always-crowded Georgetown restaurant, where aficionados of authentic Mexico-Mexican food can find something more sophisticated than standard border fare (though tacos are available). Try chicken mole, or mussels with *ranchero* sauce. And now there's a new, roomier branch at 1832 Columbia Rd., N.W. in Adams Morgan; 328–0937. AE, DC, MC, V.

Moderate

La Fonda. 1639 R St., N.W.; 232–6965. In good weather, enjoy your *carne asada* outside, in this old restaurant's sidewalk café. Sunday brunch. AE, CB, DC, MC, V.

La Plaza. 1847 Columbia Rd., N.W.; 667–1900. Here's a restaurant in Adams-Morgan whose sophisticated menu proves there is more to Mexican food than tacos and enchiladas. The *pollo assado* is smothered in sweet browned onions, and the flan is the best in town. AE, MC, V.

Tía Queta. 8009 Norfolk Ave., Bethesda, Md.; 654–4443. Pleasant dining in two spacious rooms and a sidewalk café. Not quite as good as Enriqueta's (the owners are brothers), but cheerful and much less crowded. AE, MC, V.

Inexpensive

Casa María. 700 Water St., S.W.; 554–5302. This popular riverfront restaurant near Arena Stage serves giant margaritas and better food (California-Mexican) than the adjacent cluster of tourist-oriented seafood cafés. Other branches in Landmark, Va.; 370–9681; Tysons Corner, Va., 893–2443; and Rockville, Md., 984–5880. Sunday brunch. AE, CB, DC, MC, V.

La Casita of Capitol Hill. 723 8th St., S.E.; 544–0233. *Chiles rellenos* are delicious at this pretty and popular Tex-Mex restaurant, but above all order the brisket, barbecued Texas style. No credit cards at lunch; AE, MC, V, at dinner.

Pizza

The following is a list of the city's best and most popular pizzerias.

Armand's Chicago Pizzeria. 4231 Wisconsin Ave., N.W.; 686–9450; 111 King St., Alexandria, Va.; 683–0313; 226 Massachusetts Ave., N.E.; 547–6600. Deep-dish pizza draws crowds to these popular neighborhood restaurants. All-you-can-eat pizza and salad at lunch is a great bargain. AE, CB, DC, MC, V.

Geppetto. 2917 M St., N.W.; 333–2602 (333–4315 for carryout). AE, MC, V.

Ikaros Airborne Pizza. 3130 M St., N.W.; 333–5551. No credit cards.

Jerry's Subs. 1140 19th St., N.W.; 296–7390. No credit cards.

Luigi's. 1132 19th St., N.W., 331–7574. AE, DC, MC, V.

Maggie's. 4237 Wisconsin Ave., N.W.; 363–1447. (Half price Monday and Wednesday evenings.) AE, DC, MC, V.

Pizzeria Uno. 3211 M St., N.W.; 965–6333. AE, MC, V.

Vesuvios Pizza. 1601 Connecticut Ave., N.W.; 667–1500. No credit cards.

Volare. 2011 S St. N.W.; 234–9150. No credit cards.

Seafood

Maryland crabs are the most famous local seafood specialty. Try them in crabcakes, crab imperial, or softshell crab sandwiches, or put on something casual and order them steamed, flavored with a spice that will make your mouth tingle. Steamed crabs are traditionally served whole on a table covered with newspapers; you crack them open with a wooden mallet. Rockfish (a local bass) and Chincoteague oysters are other delicacies from local waters. Note that most seafood restaurants are closed on Sunday.

Deluxe

Harvey's. 1001 18th St., N.W.; 833–1858. Open since 1858, this large, dimly lit restaurant may be one of Washington's oldest. The rule here, as at most of the city's fish emporia, is to stay away from fancy sauces and stick to simple dishes. Harvey's stuffed, broiled fish dishes are excellent and Crab Imperial, which is said to have originated here, is still a favorite, as is the musty ale. AE, CB, DC, MC, V.

Vincenzo's. See listing under Italian restaurants.

Expensive

Charley's Crab. 1101 Connecticut Ave., N.W.; 785–4505. A bustling Raw Bar, a lovely dining room, pleasant service and good food make this a popular restaurant with seafood fans. Order the fresh catch of the day, poached or charcoal-broiled, and take advantage of sharply reduced prices for lunchers who arrive at 1:30 or after. AE, CB, DC, MC, V.

China Coral. See listing under Chinese restaurants.

Crisfield. 8012 Georgia Ave., Silver Spring, Md.; 589–1306. With its formica tables and tiled floors and walls, Crisfield is no garden spot, but Washingtonians consistently vote it their favorite fishhouse and wait in first-come, first-served lines to order good seafood, great French fries, and fresh cole slaw. No credit cards.

The Fishery, 5511 Connecticut Ave., N.W.; 363–2144. You can be sure the somewhat pricey fish at this Chevy Chase restaurant is fresh; it comes from the fish store next door. AE, CB, DC, MC, V.

Moderate

Aux Fruits de Mer. 1329 Wisconsin Ave., N.W.; 965–2377. A Georgetown fish restaurant in which dinner for two can be kept under $25 has got to be one of the best buys in town. Popular, pleasant, and open late (till 2 A.M. weekdays, 3 A.M. weekends). Sunday brunch. AE, CB, DC, MC, V.

Devon Bar & Grill. 2000 Pennsylvania Ave., N.W.; 833–5660. A wide choice of guaranteed-fresh seafood in an upscale Tiffany-skylit, brass-and-wood setting. Hot homemade biscuits are mouth-watering, and the portions are humongous. All-you-can-eat dinners go for as low as $11.95. Great quality and value. There's also a branch at Tysons Corner (442–0401). AE, CB, DC, MC, V.

Ernie's Original Crab House. 1623 Fern St., Alexandria, Va; 836–1623. You'll generally find the best steamed crabs (newspaper and mallet style) in the suburbs. Ernie's offers a $13.95 all-you-can-eat special. MC, V. Other basic crabberies include the **Bethesda Crab House** (4958 Bethesda Ave., Bethesda, Md.; 652–9754; $14.95 all-you-can-eat special, reservation required; cash only); **Chesapeake Crab House** (8214 Piney Branch Rd., Silver Spring, Md.; 589–9868; $14.95 to $19.95 all-you-can-eat specials. MC, V.); and **Capt. Pell's** (8815 Lee Hwy., Fairfax, Va.; 560–0060; $14 all-you-can-eat special). No credit cards.

Market Inn. 200 E. St., S.W.; 554–2100. Hefty drinks, a choice between three dining rooms, and a wide selection of fish dishes make this vestige of the old market area a favorite of many who work near the Capitol. AE, DC, MC, V.

O'Donnell's. 8301 Wisconsin Ave., Bethesda, Md.; 656–6200. A crowded local family restaurant with good crab dishes and many Norfolk specialties. AE, MC, V.

Potowmack Landing. Washington Sailing Marina (1½ miles south of National Airport on the George Washington Pky.); 548–0001. Mesquite-grilled seafood in an airy riverside restaurant with a panoramic view of the D.C. skyline, planes lifting off at National Airport and boardsailers skimming across the Potomac. (All facilities handicapped accessible.) AE, MC, V.

Inexpensive

Market Lunch. In the Eastern Market, 225 7th St. at C St., S.E.; 547–8444. The rule here: Arrive early and hungry. The breakfast line on a nice weekend stretches out onto the sidewalk after about 10 A.M., as locals carry their blueberry pancakes and crab omelettes to tables inside and outside the colorful Eastern Market. The crabcakes are first rate and great value. No credit cards, and the grills close for the day at 2:30 P.M.

Spanish

Deluxe

El Bodegon. 1637 R St., N.W.; 667–1710. Flamenco dancers, guitar music, and an owner-host who squirts wine down your throat from a *porron* contribute to a festive air. Specialties include paella, stuffed squid, and pork loin. AE, MC, V.

Inexpensive

Churreria Madrid. 2505 Champlain St., N.W.; 483–4441. Spanish food for the budget-minded, with churros (Spanish doughnuts) for dessert. AE, CB, DC, MC, V.

Steak Houses

Deluxe

Gary's. 1800 M St., N.W. (in the courtyard); 463–6470. Though more elegant than the Palm, where the owner was once chef, Gary's caters to the same high-wallet meat-and-potatoes crowd. AE, CB, DC, MC, V.

Joe and Mo's. 1211 Connecticut Ave., N.W.; 659–1211. Class A roast beef, good steaks and lobster, scads of political bigwigs. And a new branch in Bethesda, Md. at 7345 Wisconsin Ave.; 656–8501. AE, DC, MC, V.

Las Pampas. See listing under Latin American restaurants.

Morton's of Chicago. 3251 Prospect St., N.W.; 342–6258. *Washingtonian* magazine's food critic voted Gary's and Morton's the restaurants that serve the best steaks in towns, adding that Morton's has the best steakhouse salads, including a good Caesar salad. Despite stiff beef prices, Morton's is packing 'em in. Dinner only. AE, DC, MC, V.

Prime Rib. 2020 K St., N.W.; 466–8811. Good beef, legendary potato skins, good cheesecake, and elegant surroundings, popular with the expense account crowd. Readers of *Washingtonian* magazine voted it best place for "steaks." AE, CB, DC, MC, V.

Ruth's Chris Steak House. 1801 Connecticut Ave., N.W.; 797–0033. Located near the Washington Hilton, this new outpost of New Orleans' steakhouse chain serves a fine porterhouse on a platter, peppered and swimming in butter (which you can ask them to withhold). AE, DC, MC, V.

Washington Palm. 1225 19th St., N.W.; 293–9091. Washington's counterpart to the New York Palm, with large portions of beef and lobster, and prices to match. AE, CB, DC, MC, V.

Moderate

Blackie's House of Beef. 22nd and M Sts., N.W.; 333–1100. Red meat in a rambling restaurant with a New Orleans flavor. AE, CB, DC, MC, V.

Le Steak. 3060 M St., N.W.; 965–1627. Steak in the French manner is one of only two entrees (the other is swordfish) in this popular Georgetown bistro—$16.95 for a complete dinner. World-class French fries. AE, MC, V.

Paramount Steak House. Two locations: 1609 17th St., N.W., near Dupont Circle, 232–0395; and 1227 Wisconsin Ave., N.W., 333–0393. Proof that a smart man can produce a tasty steak for $7. AE, CB, DC, MC, V.

Swiss

Deluxe

The Broker. 713 Eighth St., S.E.; 546–8300. Classically simple decor shares star billing with elaborate pastries in this skylit restaurant, which serves moderately priced Swiss specialties such as *raclette* and fondue and artistic fish and veal dishes. The chocolate Diplomat cake is a winner too. AE, MC, V.

Thai

Inexpensive

Bangkok Gourmet. 523 So. 23rd St., Arlington, Va.; 521–1305. Coriander, lemon grass, and other unfamiliar seasonings contribute to the unique taste of Thai food, which may be too spicy for some palates but is ideal for people who like food "al diablo." Start with the unusually flavored Thai soups, by all means order sate (or satay) and a cold salad of spicy beef (sliced or ground), sample a soupy red Thai-style curry, and order plenty of rice and Thai beer to cool your mouth. DC, MC, V.

Thai Room. 5037 Connecticut Ave., N.W., 244–5933. Most local Thai food requires a trip to the suburbs; fortunately, D.C.'s Thai Room still serves good Thai food, from mild-flavored stuffed chicken thighs and a good satay, to a peppery squid appetizer that proves pain can be beautiful. AE, CB, DC, MC, V.

Thai Place. 4828 Cordell Ave., Bethesda, Md.; 951–0535. Delicious, imaginative, low-priced Thai food in a lovely, spacious dining room a block from Wisconsin Ave. Among dishes we've never tasted the likes of, the peppery tuna salad is a standout. AE, MC, V.

Thai Taste. 2606 Connecticut Ave., N.W.; 387–8876. One of the newer Thai restaurants and already a favorite with aficionados of spicy Thai food.

Daily seafood specialties. Within walking distance of the Shoreham and Sheraton Washington hotels. AE, CB, DC, MC, V.

Vietnamese-Asian

Deluxe

Germaine's. 2400 Wisconsin Ave., N.W.; 965–1185. The flair and good taste Germaine Swanson brings to her pan-Asian culinary experiments have helped this chic and airy restaurant maintain its popularity with Washington's upper crust. Daily specials such as pine cone fish are generally excellent, and on the regular menu you'll want to try the house spring rolls, sate, and lemongrass BBQ spareribs. Vietnamese, Thai, Indonesian, Korean, and Chinese dishes, with Germaine's unique accent. AE, CB, DC, MC, V.

Expensive

East Wind. 809 King St., Alexandria, Va.; 836–1515. Among specialties on East Wind's interesting menu are two grilled items that should provoke more imaginative home barbecuing: garlicky shrimp wrapped around sugarcane, and marinated beef wrapped around onions. AE, CB, DC, MC, V.

Moderate

Vietnam-Georgetown. 2934 M St., N.W.; 337–4536. Soups (especially a slightly sweet seafood concoction) and spring rolls are tasty in this economical Georgetown restaurant, and noodle dishes and lemongrass chicken are popular among regulars. No credit cards. **Viet Huong,** next door (2928 M St., N.W.; 337–5588), is a pleasant alternative, if there's a crowd. AE, MC, V.

Vegetarian

Many vegetarian dishes will be found on the menus of Afghan and Indian-Pakistani restaurants.

Moderate

Madurai. See listing under Indian-Pakistani restaurants.

Inexpensive

Food for Thought. 1738 Connecticut Ave., N.W.; 797–1095. Plain old vegetarian fare in a plain old dining room. No credit cards.

Kalorama Cafe. 2228 18th St., N.W.; 667–1022. A tiny neighborhood cafe with fish and vegetable dishes, and folk music in the evening. No credit cards.

Paru's Indian Vegetarian Restaurant. 2010 S St., N.W.; 483–5133. Indian pancakes and vegetable curries, rice and lentil dishes, are the specialties at this friendly Dupont Circle café, a formica-tabled hole in the wall in which you serve yourself good food at bargain-basement prices. No credit cards.

Siddartha. See listing under Indian-Pakistani restaurants.

Mostly for the View

Deluxe

The Dandy. Moors at foot of Prince St., Alexandria, Va.; 683–6076. Three-hour dinner cruises with dancing nightly and two-hour luncheon cruises several times a week aboard a glassed-in boat. AE, DC, MC, V.

Old Angler's Inn. 10801 MacArthur Blvd., Potomac, Md.; 365–2425. A dimly lit old country inn long favored for romantic tête-à-têtes near the fireplace, generally over drinks. So-so food, but the owners have recently upgraded the cuisine. Outdoor dining in the summer. AE, DC, MC, V.

The View. Atop the Key Bridge Marriott Hotel, 1401 Lee Hwy., Arlington, Va.; 524–6400. The nouvelle cuisine served in this luxurious dining room is overpriced, but the view of Washington's monuments and the Kennedy Center is spectacular. Best value: drinks at twilight, or Sunday brunch. AE, CB, DC, MC, V.

Expensive.

The Top O' the Town. Prospect House, 14th and North Oak Sts., Arlington, Va.; 525–9200. Ride the glass-enclosed elevator to a spectacular view of the nation's capital. Tuesday evenings in the summer you can hear the Marine Band playing at the Iwo Jima Memorial, from the terrace. Dinner dancing evenings. AE, MC, V.

Watergate Terrace. Watergate Hotel, 2650 Virginia Ave., N.W.; 298–4455. Enjoy drinks and a glimpse of the Potomac from an enclosed terrace near the Kennedy Center. Sunday brunch. AE, DC, MC, V.

Moderate

Hotel Washington Sky Terrace. 15th St. and Pennsylvania Ave., N.W.; 347–4499. Dinner in the glass-enclosed rooftop restaurant, Two Continents in the Sky, falls into the "deluxe" category, but most Washingtonians meet outside on the Sky Terrace for drinks, sandwiches and appetizers ($3 and up for both). The terrace affords a lovely view of the mall, the monuments, the White House, the city skyline, and the sunset. In hot weather (and sometimes just for fun) the management provides "artificial rain" to cool off the terrace awning. AE, DC, MC, V.

Pier 7. 650 Water St., S.W.; 554–2500. One of four neighboring seafood houses noted for their view of the riverfront, and regarded by locals (who go elsewhere for seafood) as having the best food value of the four. Pier 7 offers dancing nightly except Sunday and Monday. All these restaurants take AE, CB, DC, MC, V. Hogate's (Ninth and Maine St., S.W.; 484–6300) packs in tourists but serves average to mediocre seafood, as does Phillips' Flagship (900 Water St., S.W.; 488–8515), and the 700 Water Street Grill (554–7320). Choices at The Gangplank (600 Water St., S.W.; 554–5000) are more limited, and prices higher. Alternatives for the same view—and proximity to the Arena Stage—include Casa Maria (see Mexican).

HOW TO GET AROUND. Bear in mind that the city is laid out in four quadrants, with the Capitol as the center point. Every address in the District of Columbia is followed by N.W., S.W., S.E., or N.E. Remember the following: numbered streets run from north to south; lettered streets run from east to west; avenues named after the states run out from the Capitol at angles, like the spokes of a wheel. The Potomac River divides the District from Virginia; Maryland lies to the north, east, and south.

By car: Be forewarned. Never set forth without a map of the city and don't hesitate to ask for detailed directions.Try to avoid driving between 7 and 9 A.M., and 4 and 6:30 P.M., as commuters burden the main arteries and bridges during these hours. Also, some streets run one way during rush hours and even reverse their directions, inward in the morning and the other direction in the evening. Be prepared for many NO LEFT TURN signs in the downtown area and a state of confusion in the traffic circles. Read with care the parking signs before leaving your car. Some meters are for 20-minute parking only, most are for an hour, and occasionally you will find one for two hours. Carry a supply of quarters with you. Most meters accept only quarters. Should you commit a violation, such as unwittingly leaving your car parked along a main street after 3 P.M., the police may tow it away. Release of your car will cost you $50 (cash, money order, credit card, or personal check). For help call 727–5000. Some parking on the Mall is allowed, but finding your niche will be time-consuming. Try to arrive on the Mall just before 10 A.M., the earliest time cars are allowed to park there. On Saturday and Sunday in the city you will find relatively traffic-free avenues and easier parking.

By Tourmobile: We highly recommend sightseeing the Tourmobile way. (Leave your car at hotel or nearby parking lot and hop aboard at one of 18 stops at major attractions between the Capitol, Lincoln Memorial, and Arlington Cemetery. Locations with all-day parking are the Arlington Cemetery, West Potomac Park, and Ohio Drive, south of the Lincoln Memorial, all stops on the tour route.) You will enjoy a narrated tour of all the principal monuments and points of historical interest along the way, dispense with driving and parking worries, and go at your own pace, getting on and off as often as you like at no extra charge. The Washington-Arlington Cemetery tour costs $7 for adults and $3.50 for children (ages 3–11). A separate tour of Arlington Cemetery is $2.25 for adults and $1.00 for children. A combination tour of Washington, D.C., Arlington Cemetery, and Mount Vernon operates daily, between June and Labor Day. For $21 ($10 for children) you may have two consecutive days of touring, and a trip to Mount Vernon with admission to the estate included. Call (202) 554–7950 for detailed information.

By taxi: Taxis are relatively plentiful (except when it rains), and charge according to a potentially confusing zone plan displayed in each cab. There are no metered cabs. Note that taxis in Maryland and Virginia are metered.

By boat: *Spirit of Washington,* Pier #4, 6th and Water sts., S.W., offers cruises up and down the Potomac River. Summer disco cruises, with dancing, cocktails, snacks, and refreshments are also offered. The daily (twice a day on weekends) trip to Mount Vernon and back takes about 4 hours and costs $15.75 for adults, $8.50 for children ages 6–11; ages 2 to 5, $6.50. On Sundays and holidays a 3-hour brunch cruise is offered. Reservations for disco and brunch cruises are necessary. For information, call 554–8000.

By bus: Metrobus provides bus service for Washington, Maryland, and northern Virginia areas. Non-rush fares are 75 cents within the District (exact change or tokens required). Call 637–7000 for bus route informa-

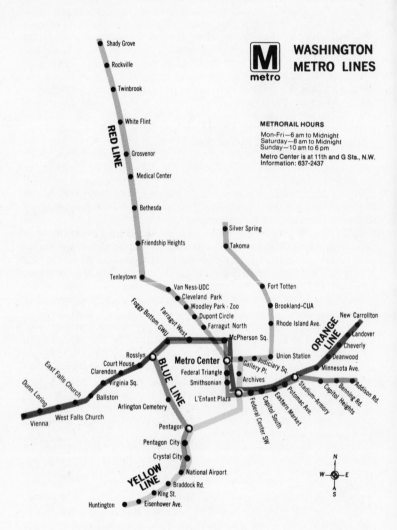

tion. As new legs of the subway are opened, riders may find it necessary to use a combination of bus and subway to reach their destinations.

By subway: Look for a capital "M" on a black pylon, a landmark showing an entrance to Washington's subway, the Metrorail. Base fare is 80 cents during nonrush hours, and varies according to destination. Trains operate from 6 A.M. to midnight Monday through Friday; 8 A.M. to midnight Saturday; and 10 A.M. to midnight Sunday. With its long escalators, vaulted ceilings, quiet, carpeted subway cars, and subdued lighting, the Metro will link outlying areas of Maryland and Virginia in its 100-mile system. Payment is by a computerized Farecard; the system is not as difficult to use as it first might seem. Any "native" will show you how, except maybe during rush hour. Metro Center, the central link for all subway lines, is located at 11th and G Sts., N.W.

GETTING TO ARLINGTON AND ALEXANDRIA. By car: To Alexandria, the Crystal City section of Arlington, and National Airport, over the 14th Street Bridge complex. To Arlington Cemetery and Arlington House, over Arlington Memorial Bridge. To the Rosslyn section of Arlington, over the Theodore Roosevelt Bridge or Key Bridge.

By bus: Sightseeing tours to Arlington, Alexandria, and Mt. Vernon operate all year from Washington. Local transit buses run frequently to Arlington and Alexandria and provide service to most suburban Virginia communities. Arlington and Alexandria are both also served by the local subway system (Metrorail), which also runs to National Airport. For local transit information call 202–637–7000.

Alexandria has its own intracity bus system. One of the routes goes directly from Metrorail's King Street station (adjacent to the Washington Masonic Memorial and the Amtrak Station) to Old Town.

TOURIST INFORMATION SERVICES. Contact the *Washington Convention and Visitors Association,* 1575 I (Eye) St., N.W., Washington, D.C. 20005, (202) 789–7000, for pamphlets and brochures on hotels, motels, and sightseeing here and in the environs. Open Mon.–Fri., 9 A.M.–5 P.M.. For daily recorded event information call 737–8866.

The Washington Visitor Information Center in the Willard Hotel complex at 1455 Pennsylvania Ave., N.W., provides sightseeing information. It's open 9 A.M.–5 P.M. daily, July 1–Labor Day.

During the summer the *National Park Service* maintains kiosks at several downtown locations such as the Lincoln Memorial, Lafayette Park, and the Washington Monument. At the *Smithsonian* museums free pamphlets are distributed. The *National Gallery of Art* offers excellent free guides to the East and West Buildings.

IVIS, the International Visitors Information Service, 733 15th St., N.W., Suite 300, Washington, D.C. 20005; (202) 783–6540, stands ready to help foreign visitors with free maps in foreign languages and some multilingual pamphlets. The IVIS Language Bank helps visitors with a language problem.

The *Washington Post* carries information on movies, theater, sports, and cultural events in the Friday supplement, *Weekend* and in its Sunday *Show* section. The new *Washington Times* is also a good source.

Especially helpful to the tourist is the top-flight monthly *Washingtonian* magazine ($1.95) which details current happenings in its "Where and When" section.

The *Theatre Guide,* published semi-annually, provides theater schedules, seating plans, curtain times, and box office hours. On sale at news stands for $2.50.

SEASONAL EVENTS. If you are free to plan your trip at any time of year, consider the advantages of visiting Washington in fall or winter. With the first crocus, buses from Keokuk to Kalamazoo disgorge their loads of eager high school students, and this state of affairs continues until early June. Summer brings family groups, long lines, hot weather, and a wealth of things to do. Some city hotels offer lower rates in July and August, however, because business travel is slow then. They also offer attractive weekend and holiday rates year-round for the same reason. With Labor Day, the residents return and the city gets back to normal. Washington's fall is justifiably famous, with day after day of mild, sunny weather often lasting well into November. Winters are passable, with few snowy or bitterly cold days.

The *Washington Convention and Visitors Association* (address above) publishes a quarterly calendar of events called "Sights and Sounds." Detailed schedules of museum exhibits, sporting events, musical and theatrical presentations, with helpful ticket information are yours for the asking.

The following calendar of events will help to acquaint you with "what goes on where."

January (first week). Congress opens. January 18, Martin Luther King, Jr. Day. Every fourth year on January 20th a President is inaugurated on the steps of the Capitol. An inaugural parade follows.

February. February 12, Abraham Lincoln's birthday, special services are held at the Lincoln Memorial. February 22, George Washington's birthday, special services are held at Mount Vernon and at the Washington Monument. There are also traditional George Washington's Birthday sales with almost ridiculously low prices on some special items.

March (late, or early April). The famous cherry blossoms begin to bloom around the Tidal Basin (and in Kenwood, Maryland, where they can be enjoyed under less crowded conditions). The white single blossoms at the Tidal Basin appear first. The pink double blossoms, mostly around Hains Point, bloom about two weeks later.

Cherry Blossom Festival, including a pageant, parade, and the crowning of a Cherry Blossom Queen from among the princesses representing the 50 states, is held.

Flower Show takes place early each year at the D.C. National Guard Armory. Forsythia in Dumbarton Oaks Garden, Georgetown, present a glorious sight. Botanic Gardens feature stunning displays of azaleas and lilies.

April (or late March). Easter sunrise services are held outdoors at Arlington National Cemetery, on the grounds of Walter Reed Army Hospital and at the Carter Barron Amphitheater. Easter Monday egg rolling is held on the White House lawn, with adults admitted only when accompanied by a child.

National Arboretum displays thousands of azaleas in a natural, 415-acre parklike setting.

House, Garden, and Embassy Tours offer a rare opportunity to see the interiors of some of Washington's most elegant embassies and private residences. Proceeds go to charity; tickets cost about $12 and may be bought at the first house or embassy visited. See local papers for details.

May (first Friday). An outdoor fair is held on the grounds of the Washington Cathedral, with proceeds going to the upkeep of the Cathedral Close. This colorful event features international booths, herbs and perennials, antiques, and rides for the children. (Third week) Armed Forces Day allows the public to visit military installations in the area. Of particular interest are the events at Andrews Air Force Field and the David Taylor Model Basin (Navy).

Memorial Day at Arlington National Cemetery is marked by special services at the Amphitheater. The President (or his representative) lays a wreath at the Tomb of the Unknowns, and each grave in the cemetery is decorated by a flag placed there by volunteer groups.

President's Cup Regatta, with world-famous unlimited hydroplane powerboats competing for presidential awards, are usually held over Memorial Day weekend.

July 4. Spectacular display of fireworks erupts on the grounds of the Washington Monument and an all-day program at Wolf Trap Farm Park. For several days preceding the Fourth, a Festival of American Folklife is staged on the Mall.

June–August. An outstanding program of musical events (including ballet, opera, symphony, and other performing arts) is presented throughout the summer at the following places: The Kennedy Center for the Performing Arts, Wolf Trap Farm Park, Merriweather Post Pavilion, and Carter Barron Amphitheater. A detailed program of each week's activities is published in the *Washington Post* "Weekend" section on Friday.

The Smithsonian Institution offers a wide variety of special summer programs for children and adults. Call 357–2020 for detailed information.

Branches of the Armed Forces offer varied programs as follows:

Marine Corps Barracks Dress Parades, with the Marine Corps Drum and Bugle Corps, Marine Band, and the Silent Drill Team at the barracks, 8th and I Sts., S.E.; free; Friday. This is a not-to-be forgotten ceremony, but must be planned well in advance. Advance reservations are necessary. Call 433–6060. Begins promptly at 8:20 P.M.

Sunset ceremonies at the Iwo Jima Statue, Tuesday at 7 P.M.; free.

The Netherlands Carillon, located near the Iwo Jima War Memorial in Arlington, Virginia, is a landmark 127 feet high; its 49 bells are played manually. Concerts are given during the summer months each Saturday from 6:30 to 8:30 P.M. Free; no tickets required. (202) 285–2601.

U.S. Military Bands give outdoor concerts on the plaza in front of the West Front of the Capitol, on the West Terrace of the Air and Space Museum, at the Sylvan Theater, at the Washington Navy Yard, and at the Jefferson Memorial. Dates and times listed in Washington's summer edition of "Sights and Sounds." pamphlet, available from the Washington Convention and Visitors Association.

September. The Washington Redskins professional football team opens its season at R.F.K. Stadium.

October. Supreme Court reconvenes on the first Monday. This date traditionally marks the beginning of Washington's social season.

Library of Congress concerts begin (see *Music*).

November. International horse race at Laurel Racetrack, Laurel, Maryland.

Veterans' Day services are held at Arlington National Cemetery.

December. Christmas Pageant of Peace starts around December 15 with the President lighting the National Christmas Tree at the Ellipse near the White House. Carols and musical programs continue until New Year's Day.

Special Christmas-week programs take place at the Washington Cathedral, the Kennedy Center, L'Enfant Plaza, and at churches throughout the area. The National Geographic Society always has a special exhibit in its Explorers Hall.

If it's cold enough, ice-skating is offered at the Sculpture Garden Rink on the Mall and at other outdoor rinks downtown.

Note: With federal budget cuts now in effect, it is important to check above attractions in the newspaper.

Alexandria: In **February** there are parades, balls, and other *Washington Birthday events* to celebrate the city's most famous citizen.

In **June** is the *Alexandria Red Cross Waterfront Festival* drawing 100,000 persons.

In **July** the Scottish heritage is revived with Scottish athletic games, Scottish foods, highland dances, and bagpipers.

The **Christmas season** is ushered in with the popular Scottish Christmas Walk led by bagpipe bands.

Arlington: First weekend in **November** is the *Marine Corps Marathon* with more than 12,000 runners from around the world.

In **December,** Arlington House is decorated in 1860s Christmas regalia as the Lees would have done. Candlelight tours of the home are also sometimes presented.

Note: For special free events we suggest you read the "Weekend" section of the *Washington Post.*

TOURS. The tour's the thing for the more than 50 sightseeing companies whose concern is the patronage of Washington's 18 million annual visitors. The larger companies (see Yellow Pages for complete list) will pick you up at your hotel or motel 30 minutes before the scheduled time of your tour's departure, and return you without extra charge. The *Washington Convention and Visitors Association* also will provide a list of sightseeing and guide services.

Half-day tours include a drive around downtown Washington, and viewing from the outside the principal monuments and government buildings. An all-day tour might include Alexandria, Mount Vernon, and Arlington Cemetery.

The **National Fine Arts Associates** (NFAA) will arrange custom-made tours for individuals, small or large groups. Museum-trained guides conduct general sightseeing tours and/or special tours highlighting museums, historic houses, gardens, and walking tours. Write in advance for detailed information to NFAA Inc., 4801 Massachusetts Ave., N.W., Suite 400, Washington, D.C. 20016, (202) 966–3800.

Tailored Tours Ltd., 6211 Crathie Lane, Bethesda, Md. 20816, (301) 229–6221, will design short or long tours for small or large groups.

Washington à la Carte calls itself "the premier custom tour service organization in the nation's capital." Write to them at 1706 Surrey Lane, N.W., Washington, D.C. 20007, or call (202) 337–7300.

Information on the highly recommended **Landmark Service Tourmobiles** is presented under *How to Get Around.*

SPECIAL-INTEREST TOURS. Few sightseers know of the **Voice of America** tour at the Health, Education and Welfare building, 4th St. and Independence Ave., S.W., second floor. The tour views the V.O.A.'s use of short-wave radio, magazines, books, and television to gain support abroad for U.S. policies. Free guided tours; open 8:40 A.M.–2:40 P.M. weekdays. For tour hours, call 485–6231.

A very special (and highly recommended) tour of the eighth-floor **Diplomatic Reception Rooms** of the State Department, 23rd and C Sts., N.W., can be arranged by writing at least 6 weeks in advance for reservations. Tours are given Monday–Friday, take about 40 minutes, and are free. Numbers are limited. On view are the exquisitely decorated rooms where the Secretary of State entertains important foreign dignitaries. The 18th-century antique furniture and paintings are all of museum quality. For tour information call 647–3241.

The **FBI tour** is described under *Historic Sites.*

The **National Building Museum,** 440 G St., N.W., recently opened, displays its exhibits in a truly historic and fascinating Victorian brick building dating back to 1882. Known as the Pension Building, this huge edifice originally housed 1,500 clerks who administered pensions to Civil War veterans. Open weekdays 10 A.M.–4 P.M.; tel. 272–2448.

The **National Housing Center,** 15th and M Sts., N.W., is the showcase headquarters of the National Association of Home Builders. The first floor public rooms always have an interesting exhibit about housing developments in the U.S. and sometimes elsewhere. Open 8:30 A.M.–5 P.M.; tel. 822–0200.

The **National Rifle Association,** 1600 Rhode Island Ave., N.W., maintains a museum of antique and modern weapons. Open 10–4 daily; tel. 828–6194.

The **Bureau of Engraving and Printing,** 14th and C Sts., S.W.; (tel. 447–1391), offers self-guided tours to observe how our money is printed. Open weekdays 9 A.M.–2 P.M. Come early; tickets issued on a first-come basis, and during the summer there is often a long wait. This is a popular tour.

The **Navy Memorial Museum** is on the grounds of the Navy Yard and is reached via the Ninth and M Sts., S.E., sentry station. They don't make ships in the Navy Yard anymore, so there's generally plenty of free parking. The 5,000 or so artifacts include ship models, a submarine conning tower and periscope, and biscuits reputedly baked in 1854 on "Old Ironsides." 433–4882. Open weekdays, 9 A.M.–4 P.M., to 5 P.M. during summer; weekends, 10 A.M.–5 P.M.

The **Naval Observatory,** Massachusetts Ave. at 34th St., N.W., offers one-hour tours of the Observatory, Monday–Friday. Reservations are not required for this tour unless a group of 10 or more is involved. Evening tours are given every Monday night; tickets are handed out at 8:30 P.M. to the first 100 arrivals. Daytime tours last about 1 hour; evening tours last 2 hours. Children under 14 are discouraged; reservations for evening

tour *must* be made in advance by calling (202) 653–1543, or writing well
in advance to Superintendent, U.S. Naval Observatory, Washington, D.C.
20390. (Your congressman can also make reservations for you.) Call for
current schedule of tours.

The Organization of American States *(The Pan American Union),* 17th
St. and Constitution Ave., N.W., 458–3000. Take a conducted tour of this
beautiful building representing *The House of the Americas.* Open 9:30
A.M.–5 P.M., Monday–Friday. Visit the new art gallery, the only museum in
the world dedicated solely to Latin-American art. Open Tuesday through
Saturday, 10 A.M.–5 P.M.

B'nai B'rith Museum, 1640 Rhode Island Ave., N.W. Judaica. Open
Sunday–Friday, 10 A.M.,–5 P.M. See *Museums and Galleries* section for details.

GARDENS. Visitors to Capitol Hill will enjoy a change of pace by
spending some time at the **Botanic Gardens,** Maryland Ave. between 1st
and 2nd Sts., S.W., 225–8333. If you are here during March and April,
you will see one of the most colorful azalea displays imaginable. Other
seasonal flower extravaganzas include Easter lilies, tulips, poinsettias, and
chrysanthemums. Open daily during summer (June through August), 9
A.M.–9 P.M.; winter (September through May), 9 A.M.–5 P.M.

A trip to Georgetown should include a visit to **Dumbarton Oaks Gardens** at the corner of 32nd and R Sts., N.W., adjacent to the Dumbarton
Oaks Museum, 342–3200. These beautiful formal gardens are open to the
public daily, weather conditions permitting. Considered to be one of the
loveliest spots in all of Washington, the gardens cover 16 acres and are
particularly colorful in early spring when narcissus, tulips, and forsythia
are in bloom. Entrance to the gardens is at 31st and R St. Open daily,
2–6 P.M. Museum is open 2–5 P.M., closed Monday. Admission $1 for gar-
dens, April 7–November 1.

If your schedule permits (several hours are necessary) plan to see the
Kenilworth Aquatic Gardens at Kenilworth Ave. and Douglas St., N.E.,
near Eastern Ave., 426–6905. Guided tours are offered weekends and holidays. Water lilies, lotuses, hyacinths, and some 40 species of pond and
marginal plants may be seen in the 14 acres of quiet pools and marshy
fringe. Wild irises in May, hardy water lilies in June, and lotuses by mid-
July are best seen in the morning. Open daily, 7 A.M.–sundown.

The **National Arboretum,** 3501 New York Ave., N.E., 475–4815, is a
must to visit in the azalea season. Located near the Kenilworth Aquatic
Gardens, it is open year-round. During the summer the rhododendrons,
clematis, ferns, and roses bloom in profusion. Many varieties of trees and
shrubs covering 444 acres make this a relaxing place for a stroll. The *Bonsai Collection* of dwarf trees was a Bicentennial gift of the Japanese people
to the people of the United States. A most popular new attraction is the
National Herb Collection, with "zillions" of varieties in five plantings.
Open weekdays, 8 A.M.–5 P.M.; weekends and holidays, 10 A.M.–5 P.M. Bonsai
collection daily, 10–2:30 P.M.

Note: If you are in Washington in April or May you will have an unusual
opportunity to see some of the finest houses and gardens in Georgetown,
Cleveland Park, Chevy Chase, and Alexandria, and support a worthy
charity at the same time. See daily newspapers for details. Admission
about $12.

The newest garden open to the public is that of **Hillwood,** 4155 Linnean Ave., N.W., 686–5807, the former estate of Marjorie Merriweather Post. Open year-round, (except February) it contains a *Japanese Garden, Rhododendron Walk,* a formal *French Garden,* the *Friendship Walk* (a gift of 150 of her friends), a *Rose Garden,* and greenhouses in which 5,000 orchids grow. Tours of the museum and grounds are conducted daily (except Tuesday and Sunday). $7 per person; children under 12 not admitted. Reservations are a must, and make them far in advance. There's also a tour of the gardens for $2, between 11 A.M. and 4 P.M.; no reservations required. Newly opened is a large room similar to one in Mrs. Post's Adirondack lodge, housing an outstanding collection of American Indian artifacts. There's a pleasant cafe for lunches and afternoon teas.

Springtime visitors to the capital will marvel at the dramatic displays of daffodils, tulips, and azaleas in flower beds, mini-parks, and unlikely places throughout the downtown area. Many of these treats for the eye are thanks to Lady Bird Johnson, who, during her years as First Lady, carried out the mandate to "Keep America Beautiful."

CHILDREN'S ACTIVITIES. It seems that a favorite outdoor sport among children visiting Washington is pigeon-chasing. And the Mall between the Smithsonian Museums abounds in pigeons. A carousel ride (75 cents) located on the Mall in front of the Arts and Industries Building any summer day 10 A.M.–4:30 P.M. (5:30 on weekends) except Monday is a must for youngsters of all ages.

Running a close second in popularity with youngsters is feeding peanuts to the squirrels on the Capitol grounds. The rolling lawns on the west side (toward Pennsylvania Avenue) harbor hundreds of polite but hungry squirrels that will come to within three or four feet of you at the drop of a peanut. Their performance is a delight, especially if the peanuts are still in the shell, which they daintily remove. The trick is to find a foraging squirrel or two, then stand still and make clicking noises, ignoring stares of passersby. As soon as other squirrels gather, turn the feeding over to the child and enjoy the show.

Beyond the pigeons and squirrels, there is a world of wonder for children throughout the Washington area. Much of it is free and fun.

We will suggest things to see and do for children up to about age 12. For those past 12, we recommend dropping them off at the National Air and Space Museum and forgetting them. Lost in outer space, they will happily forget you.

Note: *Access Washington* lists what is accessible to handicapped people. Available from Information, Protection & Advocacy Center for Handicapped Individuals, Inc., 360 I St., N.E., Suite 202, Washington DC 20002; 547–8081. It costs $3.75, or $4.20 if mailed.

Major Monuments That Attract Children

For detailed information, see the *Historic Sites* section.

Washington Monument. Draws kids like a magnet. Go early on a clear morning, if possible, or late at night.

Bureau of Engraving and Printing. Money has a special allure for youngsters and here they can see millions of dollars being printed and counted.

Capitol. After the tour, take a ride on the subway cars that shuttle from the Capitol's basement level to the Rayburn House Office Building. Romp on the lawn (don't forget the peanuts) and explore the little sunken grotto on the right side of the lawn facing Constitution Avenue, halfway up Capitol Hill. Hidden among trees and bushes, it has benches and water fountains and a mossy cave with water spraying over the rocks in mild weather. Many pass without seeing it, and miss its secret magic.

The White House. Try and arrange a VIP tour with your congressman at least a month in advance. The tour gets you in early in the morning, and avoids the usual wait. The White House is at its loveliest at Christmas time (closed Christmas Day).

Lincoln and Jefferson Memorials. To make the most lasting impression, take the child at night, as a special, stay-up-late treat. These hallowed shrines are luminous and unforgettable after dark.

Favorite Museums

For detailed information, see the *Museums and Galleries* section.

The Smithsonian Museums along the Mall are incomparable for education made enjoyable. Before going through "The Nation's Attic," Dial-A-Museum, 357–2020, for announcements of special events.

We have focused on exhibits that especially capture children's interest, but have not included all of the Smithsonian Museums. (Locations given are oriented to the Mall, though there are also street entrances.)

Outside the *Museum of Natural History,* on the Mall side, there is a dinosaur (Uncle Beasley) to climb and, in summer, a carousel to ride near the Castle.

The *Air and Space Museum* is the most exciting and most popular spot in town for children. The planes in mid-air, the Apollo moon-landing module, the walk-through Skylab, the rockets and moon rock are all real—that's the best part. The action exhibits are riveting, and the alternating IMAX films, including "To Fly," "The Living Planet," "Flyers," and "Hail Columbia," are the biggest thrill of all. Films are $2 for adults, $1 for senior citizens, and $1 for children. There is often a wait. Take in the show at the Planetarium, too. "Stars" is a marvelous new exhibit on astronomy which includes a holographic "journey" through deep space. South side of the Mall, far east end.

The *National Gallery of Art* offers a priceless opportunity to introduce a child to some of the greatest masterpieces of the world. Limit the visit to a few paintings and pieces of sculpture, and let the child visually explore the selection while you both discuss what you see. For example: Desiderio's *Head of a Little Boy,* the dazzling colors and details of a Renaissance Nativity Scene, Sansovina's sculpture of *Bacchus and a Young Fawn,* the Impressionists' seashores, the *Mercury* of the central fountain, with wings on his running shoes.

The Gallery's *East Building* features the city's biggest toy: the Calder mobile. The clownish figures in the glassed court are whimsical. But often children find the enclosed waterfall and the people-mover ramp in the passage connecting the buildings the most fun of all. The Galleries are on the north side of the Mall, far east end.

The *Museum of Natural History* bowls them over from the start with the gigantic African bush elephant at the Mall entrance. Take your choice of fossils, sea life, birds, mammals, meteorites, minerals and gems (see them under black light), or American Indian life—a favorite. The Dinosaur Hall is another delight. Two exhibits are especially designed for children: The Insect Zoo and Discovery Room. To the sound of chirping crickets as background, children at the Insect Zoo can watch live bees swarming in the hive, ants gnawing leaves, and maybe see a staff member handle a live tarantula while explaining its habits. The Discovery Room is a great hands-on children's laboratory for exploring the world of animals, vegetables, and minerals, with necessary equipment provided. Limited hours, free tickets required at the Discovery Room door. North side, opposite the Castle. Call 357–2700.

The Museum of American History has a mind-boggling variety of attractions, highlighted by the turn-of-the-century ice-cream parlor (with real ice cream to buy), and the tremendous "A Nation of Nations" exhibit, which brings America's past into the present via films, multimedia shows, period rooms, stage coaches, the voice of George M. Cohan, and Archie Bunker's chair. Fabulous old-favorite exhibits for children are still the huge railroad displays with sound effects, and the Foucault Pendulum, that hypnotic wonder that swings from a three-story height, demonstrating the rotation of the earth and knocking down little red pegs. The fascination is in waiting for the next peg to drop. North side of Mall, far west end. Call 357–2700.

National Museum of African Art reopened in September 1987 in a new building that's mostly underground behind the Smithsonian Castle. Dazzling displays of African art and culture and lots of scary masks. Next door, also underground, is the new Arthur M. Sackler Gallery of Asian and Near-Eastern Art, which has special tours and a gallery guide just for children. Both open 10 A.M.–5:30 P.M. daily. Call 357–2700.

Smithsonian Discovery Theater in *Arts and Industries,* next to the Castle, presents a variety of programs for children—music, drama, puppets, many with an international flavor. There is a central theme each season, which runs from early October–May, with a different program each month. Wednesday–Friday, 10 and 11:30 A.M.; Saturday, Sunday, 1 and 3 P.M. Adults $3, children under 12, $2.50. Call (202) 357–1500.

Capital Children's Museum promises little from the outside; inside it is a child's fantasy turned into reality—ladders to climb, bells to ring, cars to drive, mock sewers to crawl through, uniforms to try on, telephones and computers to use, a food store where the goods can be handled, weighed, and priced. All the untouchables become touchable here as children are invited to take part in the exhibits. And all the while children are learning the metric system, how levers work, what gears do, how to build a machine, and what fun learning can be. A gem of a museum. 800 3rd St., N.E. (near H St.). Parking across the street. Open daily 10 A.M.–5 P.M. Call 543–8600. Admission $4, age 2 and up.

National Aquarium shows fish in their natural environment, relatively speaking. Shark feeding, Monday, Wednesday, Saturday, 2 P.M. Dept. of Commerce Building, 14th Street, between Constitution Ave. and E St., N.W. Open daily, 9 A.M.–5 P.M. Closed Christmas. Admission $1 for adults; 50¢ for children. Call (202) 377–2826. Cafeteria open 8 A.M.–2:30 P.M. weekdays.

Naval Yard and Navy Memorial Museum provide a great refuge after the hassle of downtown crowds and parking. Turn the youngsters loose to climb old tanks and cannons in the outdoor playground, on the Anacostia River. Then go into the adjoining museum to see the model ships and Naval history exhibits, and best of all, to man the working periscopes and to operate the—unloaded—anti-aircraft guns. The Visitors Center has a slide show and a map of the Yard's Historic Precincts. Free. Abundant parking. *Washington Navy Yard,* 9th and M Sts., S.E. (202–433–2651). Open Monday–Friday, 9 A.M.–4 P.M., to 5 in summer; weekends, 10 A.M.–5 P.M. (See *Special Interest Tours.*) Also at the Navy Yard, kids can board the destroyer *Barry,* a retired Navy ship, and explore it from top to bottom, including the combat center, torpedo deck, galley, and mess. It's open 10 A.M.–5 P.M. daily, and it's free. Call (202) 433–3371.

National Geographic Explorers Hall is like walking into the pages of the *National Geographic* for children raised on the magazine. Small but select. 17th and M sts., N.W. Open 9 A.M. to 5 P.M. Monday–Saturday and on holidays. Sunday 10 A.M.–5 P.M. Closed Christmas. Free. Parking difficult. Commercial garages nearby. Call (202) 857–7588.

Dolls' House and Toy Museum of Washington is a charmer. From an ornate Mexican mansion to an austere, antique German kitchen, all the exhibits are in miniature and displayed in subdued-lighting intimacy that allows imagination a free rein. Dolls, doll houses, and furniture tastefully fill two floors. Dolls and furniture on sale in the lobby, and a unique toyshop on the second floor, plus an "ice cream parlor" for birthday parties (arrange well in advance). 5236 44th St., N.W. (next to Lord & Taylor's parking garage). Open Tuesday–Saturday 10 A.M.–5 P.M., Sunday, noon–5 P.M. Admission $2 for adults, $1 for children under 14. Street parking and in nearby garages. Call (202) 244–0024.

Daughters of the American Revolution Children's Attic is full of toys from Revolutionary times, especially dolls. There is also a children's tour of the rest of the extensive museum that allows them to touch and examine everyday things of the Colonial era. 1776 D St., N.W. Open Monday–Friday, 10 A.M.–3 P.M., Sundays, 1–5 P.M., closed holidays. Free. Call (202) 628–1776. Closed two weeks in April.

The London Brass Rubbing Center near the Gift Shop in the crypt beneath the National Cathedral, provides children and their parents an opportunity to create a handsome rubbing suitable for framing. Fee. Wisconsin and Massachusetts Aves., N.W. Open daily 9:30 A.M.–7:30 P.M. weekdays, till 5, weekends. Call (202) 364–0030.

Things That Move

Metrorail, Washington's horizontal elevator, can be fun to ride. Much of the system is above ground, but underground is fun, too. You can ride all day—provided you don't go through the exit gates—for 80 cents, from 9:30 A.M.–3 P.M. Fares are more expensive at other times and the amount depends on distance traveled. Each person six and over must have an individual fare card. Call (202) 637–7000 for bus and rail route information.

Washington National Airport has planes taking off or landing just about every minute. Watch them from the observation deck for a minimal fee—a small price for so much action. Metrorail goes direct to the airport. A bit farther afield, but worth the trip, is *Dulles Airport,* 25 miles west of Washington. Designed by the famous Finnish architect Eero Saarinen, this terminal may well be the most distinguished in the world.

Paddle boats are a special attraction at the Tidal Basin. They are great fun for the children, and adults, too, if your leg muscles are up to the "paddling." Rentals are available at the Tidal Basin Boat House, 15th St. and Maine Ave., S.W., during the summer, daily starting at 10 A.M. Fee: $5.50 an hour. At *Thompson's Boat Center,* Rock Creek Parkway and Virginia Ave., N.W. (333–4861), canoes and rowboats are for rent by the hour or day. Open daily, dawn to dusk. Or hire a boat at *Fletcher's Boat House,* 4940 Canal Rd., N.W. Call 244–0461. Open late April to mid-October, depending on weather.

Riding the **Canal Clipper** down the C&O Canal is like living on a barge with a family of the 1890s, hearing them talk about their life, listening to the music of the period. It's all live, including the two mules that pull the barge for the 1½-hour trip. And it is a lifetime memory for any child lucky enough to be a part of this living history experience. It generally runs from April to October, from Great Falls, Md., at the western end of MacArthur Blvd. Tickets must be purchased two hours before the barge leaves. Ticket office is in the historic Great Falls Tavern. For current schedule and prices, call (202) 299–2026. A newly constructed barge, the *Georgetown,* leaves from the Foundry at 30th and Thomas Jefferson Sts., N.W. The barges run only Wednesday–Sunday; fares are $4 for adults, $2 for children. Call 472–4376 for information.

Spirit of Washington runs two boat trips on the Potomac, both beautiful and thrilling for children. In the summer there is a cruise down the Potomac to Mount Vernon at 9 A.M. and 2 P.M. daily (except when chartered), for a four-hour trip including a sightseeing stopover at Mount Vernon. The cruise itself takes an hour each way. The Mount Vernon cruises run from the end of March until mid-October, but check on departure times. Call (202) 554–8000.

NEARBY ATTRACTIONS

Maryland

Adventure Theater. These delightful plays for children are presented year-round at a small theater (air-conditioned in summer) located in Glen Echo Park, MacArthur Blvd. and Goldsboro Rd., Glen Echo, Md. Call 320–5331 for reservations for weekend performances at 1:30 P.M. and 3:30 P.M.

Great Falls of the Potomac. Spectacular cataract of the river. Walk along C&O Canal towpath and see the locks and Canal Museum. At western end of MacArthur Blvd. Call (202) 299–3613.

Trolley Museum. Restored trolleys from the U.S. and Europe, rides available through countryside. Nominal fare. Saturday–Sunday, noon–5 P.M. North on Georgia Ave. from Capital Beltway Layhill Rd.; turn right, go two miles to Bonifant Rd.; turn right to the museum. Call (301) 384–9797.

Fort Washington. Massive ramparts of an 1814 fort where a shot was never fired. Fun to climb around, but there are some sheer drops that bear watching. Play area and picnic tables. Great view of the Potomac. Capital Beltway, exit Indian Head Highway south, 4½ miles to sign on right. Fort open 7:30 A.M.–5 P.M. wintertime, to 6 in summer.; park open 7:30 A.M.–dark daily. Call (301) 763–4600. Free.

Cabin John Regional Park. A favorite with small children who love its Noah's Ark zoo, the extensive playground, and train ride (75 cents). Ice skating in winter for a small fee. The rest is free. Picnic tables. From Capitol Beltway take Old Georgetown Rd. north for about 1½ miles. Turn left at Tuckerman Lane; about one mile on the left is the entrance to the playgrounds. Open year-round. Call (301) 299–4555 for information.

Oxon Hill Farm. A working farm of the early 1900s, with daily and seasonal farm activities—tobacco and corn planting and harvesting, lambing, sheep shearing, cider pressing, spinning. Capital Beltway exit Indian Head Highway south; right on Oxon Hill Rd. at end of ramp, and immediate right to farm. Open daily 8:30 A.M.–5 P.M., closed winter holidays. Free. Call (301) 839–1177.

National Colonial Farm. Authentic 18th-Century agricultural and historical museum in action. Farm animals, herb garden, and Colonial kitchen where bread is baked, and produce preserved. Across Potomac from Mount Vernon. Capital Beltway, exit Indian Head Highway south, 10 miles to Bryan Point Rd., turn right, 4 miles to farm. Open daily 10 A.M.–5 P.M. except Monday and winter holidays. Adults $1, children under 12 free. Call (301) 283–2113.

Virginia

Arlington Children's Theater. Musicals and plays geared to children's tastes and performed by children at Lubber Run Amphitheater in summer; other performing arts centers in spring and fall with small admission fee. Summer performances free. Call (703) 739–2900 for program information and directions.

The Claude Moore Colonial Farm. An intimate look at everyday life of a poor Colonial family, their one-room cabin, livestock, wild turkeys, garden, and chores. The "family," in period costume, goes about their business while visitors watch. Capital Beltway, exit Route 193 east, 2½ miles on 193 to left turn into farm. Open April–December, Wednesday–Sunday 10 A.M.–4:30 P.M.; $1.00 for adults, 50 cents for children. Call (703) 442–7557.

Gulf Branch Nature Center. Focus is on understanding and appreciating nature. There are nature trails, a museum exhibiting local animal and plant life, a restored 17th-Century log house and blacksmith shop and forge. Close to Washington, but getting there is complicated. Call (703) 558–2340 for directions. Open Tuesday–Saturday, 9 A.M.–5 P.M.; Sunday, 1–4. Closed Monday and holidays. Free.

Woodlawn Plantation. Charming mansion to tour, and Touch and Try room where children can play with Colonial toys. Open daily 9:30 A.M.–4:30 P.M., closed winter holidays. Adults $4, children and full-time students $3. George Washington Parkway past National Airport and through city of Alexandria, to Mount Vernon, right on 135, three miles to Woodlawn. Call (703) 780–4000.

Wolf Trap Farm Park for the Performing Arts. Only national park of its kind. Woods and lawns to picnic on; performing arts programs—drama, dance, song, mime, puppetry—in which children participate; International Children's Festival over the Labor Day weekend featuring folk music and colorful costumes from around the world; bang-up Fourth of July celebration with all-day picnic, military bands, and fireworks; some free performances by resident artists; paid performances by top professionals; and something exciting going on, especially for children, Monday–Friday in July and August. Most of it free. Performing arts program from late spring to early fall. Park open year-round. For information write to Wolf Trap, 1624 Trap Rd., Vienna, Va. 22180. Or call (703) 255–1916.

THE NATIONAL ZOO. The Zoo—who can resist it?—is within Rock Creek Park. Wave at the bears, some of which wave back, and watch the elephants, wildebeests, big and little cats, and timid mousedeer, among hundreds of other species. Don't forget the new Smokey the Bear, and the Chinese pandas (usually asleep, but check out the lesser pandas, which are more fun). Be sure and see the spectacular walk-in Great Flight Cage, which you and the birds can occupy together. New attractions are constantly being added. Zoolab is a learning center, where all sorts of zoological hands-on things are available, plus books and art materials for sketching or painting the animals. Limited hours. Check first. The Zoo is at Adams Mill Rd. and Beach Dr., with another entrance in the 3000 block of Connecticut Ave., N.W. Buildings are open daily except Christmas, September 16–April 30, 9 A.M.–4:30 P.M.; May 1–September 15, 9 A.M.–6 P.M. The zoo grounds are open 8 A.M.–6 P.M., September to May; 8 A.M.–8 P.M., June–August. Paid parking on the grounds, with space at a premium ($3 per car). Go early on weekends. The Zoo is free. There are two Metrorail stops for the Zoo; Woodley Park-Zoo, southside, and Cleveland Park, northside, both on the Red Line. Connecticut Ave. buses also serve the Zoo. Call 673–4800 for information.

THE GREAT OUTDOORS. Rock Creek Park, that miraculously preserved wilderness in the middle of Washington, has 15 miles of trails, a bicycle path, bridle path, picnic groves, playgrounds, and a boulder-strewn creek that is its reason for being (do not drink or swim in the water, alas). The **Nature Center,** south of Military Rd. on Glover Rd., is the foremost attraction for children. A child can spend hours seeing, touching, smelling, even tasting the nature exhibits, which are a good preparation for a nature walk with a Park Service guide. The **Planetarium** at the center presents the wonders of the night sky at different times of the year. And there are many special programs for children, listed in the printed monthly calendar of events, available with maps and other park information from the Park Manager, Rock Creek Headquarters, 5000 Glover Rd., N.W., Washington, D.C. 20015. Or call (202) 426–6834. **Peirce Mill,** also in the Park, is of interest to children because of its old waterwheel. The 1820 mill has been fully restored. It is situated at the waterfall, where Park Rd. crosses Beach Dr. and becomes Tilden St.

Theodore Roosevelt Island is in the middle of the Potomac, between Georgetown and Northern Virginia. There are 3½ miles of footpaths through woods and meadows, explorable with a Park Service guide or independently, and a memorial to Theodore Roosevelt. Accessible only on Virginia side via a footbridge. Cross Theodore Roosevelt Bridge at west end of Constitution Ave., N.W., to George Washington Memorial Parkway north. Follow signs. Parking lot. Free. Call 285–2600 for information.

East Potomac Park, and **Hains Point** at the tip end, provide a beautiful oasis for weary sightseers. Children can be turned loose in the playground while you find a picnic table under the trees, preferably one on the south side, facing that busy National Airport across the river. Explore the new sculpture, *The Awakening,* near the tip of the peninsula—a gigantic figure of a man, seemingly emerging from the earth. Approach the park via Maine Ave., S.W., heading west; or Independence Ave., heading east past the Tidal Basin. Follow signs and lanes carefully to East Potomac Park. Within these 328 acres are a driving range, one 18-hole and two 9-hole golf courses, miniature golf (spring and summer), and a swimming pool. (If you missed the cherry blossoms at the Tidal Basin, catch the double blossoms here a week or so later.)

Glen Echo Park. This small park was once the site of the Chautauqua Assembly built in 1891. The National Park Service offers space here to artists, sculptors, weavers, and writers to conduct classes. The Glen Echo Gallery shows the work of these artists and their students at exhibits held monthly in the stone tower, the last remaining building left complete from the Chautauqua period. During the summer the Spanish Ballroom provides the setting for dancers to swing to big-band music. The small *Adventure Theater* offers live theater to the toddler set weekends, year-round (320–5331). Call 492–6282 for more information. The antique carousel is open Wednesday and Saturday afternoons. Goldsboro Rd. and MacArthur Blvd. (about a 20-minute car ride from downtown Washington).

SUMMER SPORTS. Golf. If you'd rather play than watch, there are two public golf courses open year-round from sunrise to sunset—East Potomac Park, (202) 863–9007, and Rock Creek Park, (202) 723–9832—with rental bags and clubs. There are scores of others in the suburbs.

Land and water vehicles. Rowboats, swan boat rides, canoes, and paddle boats are for hire at the north end of the Tidal Basin. Both Thompson's Boat Center, at Rock Creek Parkway and Virginia Ave., N.W., (202) 333–4861, and Fletcher's Boat House, 4940 Canal Rd., (202) 244–0461, on the C&O Canal Tow Path, will rent you a canoe, rowboat, or bicycle. Other bicycle rental centers are listed in the Yellow Pages telephone directory.

Horseback riding. Washington's only horse riding facility is the Rock Creek Park Horse Center, Military and Glover rds., N.W., (202) 362–0117. It offers guided trail riding in the upper areas of Rock Creek Park year-round, except Monday, for $11 an hour.

WINTER SPORTS. Skating. For a list of ice-skating rinks in and around the city, consult the Yellow Pages. Once every few years the C&O Canal freezes over, and the scene is one from an old Dutch painting. There are occasions when the public is allowed to skate on the Reflecting Pool at the base of the Washington Monument. A delightful new spot for skaters is The Sculpture Garden Rink, at 7th and Constitution Ave., N.W., on the Mall, (202) 289–7560, where there are skates for rent, a warming area, music, and inspiring vistas of museums and government buildings. Just a stone's throw from the White House is the new ice rink at Pershing Park, Pennsylvania Ave., N.W. between 14th and 15th sts.

SPECTATOR SPORTS. Football. During the fall season the Washington Redskins play at R.F.K. Stadium at 1:30 P.M. Season tickets to these football games are snatched up by the fans the minute they go on sale, but just in case . . . call their office at (202) 546–2222. If you're here in

August, and don't mind sweltering, attend a Redskin pre-season exhibition game, when getting a ticket is no problem.

Racing. Fans may enjoy horse racing almost year-round within easy driving distance of Washington. Laurel, Md. (18 miles), Bowie (20 miles), and Pimlico (40 miles—near Baltimore) boast thoroughbred horse racing in spring and fall, and a harness racing season is held at Freestate and Rosecroft. Two West Virginia tracks, Charles Town and Shenandoah, about 60 miles from Washington, operate during much of the summer and winter.

Tennis. Several professional tennis tournaments are held in the city throughout the year: the Virginia Slim's (part of the women's professional tennis circuit) in late January at George Washington University's Smith Center; and the men's D.C. National Bank Tennis classic in late July, at the 16th and Kennedy Sts., N.W., Rock Creek Park tennis courts.

Boating. The President's Cup Regatta, inaugurated in 1926, is held in early June off Hains Point. This event, comparable to the Indianapolis "500," attracts the world's fastest and most expensive speedboats, which compete for the coveted President's Cup. Other events of the regatta include rowing and canoe races.

Other sports. Washington's professional **basketball** team, the Bullets, and its **ice hockey** team, the Capitals, play at the Capital Center, Capital Beltway and Central Ave., Landover, Md., from October–April.

For the immediate future, Washington is without its own baseball team.

Polo games are played at different locations in the summer and fall, usually at 2 P.M. on Sunday. Call (202) 972–7288 for where to go and when. **Cricket** enthusiasts may attend games played by members of the British Commonwealth.

HISTORIC SITES. Arlington National Cemetery. Arlington, Virginia, at the west end of Memorial Bridge, (703) 692–0931. This military cemetery serves as the final resting place for men who fought in one or more American conflicts. Visitors will want to see the grave of President John F. Kennedy, the Tomb of the Unknowns, and Arlington House, the home of General Robert E. Lee. As private cars are not allowed in the cemetery the most convenient way to cover the considerable distances between the principal points of interest is to hop aboard a Tourmobile at the visitor's center. Tickets for a narrated Arlington tour cost $2.25 for adults and $1 for children. (The complete Washington/Arlington route costs $7 for adults and $3.50 for children.) About two hours should be allowed. Call (202) 554–7950 for information. The watch is changed at the Tomb of the Unknowns every hour on the hour from October through March and every half hour from April through September—be sure to see it. The cemetery is open daily, October through March, 8 A.M.–5 P.M.; April through September, 8 A.M.–7 P.M.

The Capitol. Capitol Hill, at the east end of the Mall, 224–3121. If your schedule permits only one stop, head for the Capitol, the most important building in the city and in the nation. It stands on the most prominent hill, making it visible from most places in downtown Washington. The original design of the building was the result of a competition won in 1793 by Dr. William Thornton, a physician and amateur architect. George Washington laid the cornerstone on September 18, 1793. The first part of the Capitol was completed in 1800, a square two-story section just to the north of the rotunda. The Senate and House held their first joint session there on November 22, 1800. Many great architects have contributed their talents to the evolution of the building, including Benjamin Latrobe, Charles Bulfinch, and Thomas U. Walter, whose dome (finished in 1863) took nine million pounds of iron. The most recent "improvement" was completed in 1962 when the East Central front was extended 32½ feet. It is best to join a guided tour for an in-depth look at the Capitol's interior. The tour takes about 30 minutes and is free. Tours leave from the Rotunda at frequent intervals. You will be able to observe the Senate or House in action (if it is in session). from the Visitor's Gallery, but if you wish to return for a longer period of time, ask for a pass from your Senator or Representative's office.

You are allowed to tour on your own, but if you decide to do so, the chances of you getting hopelessly lost are high, and you will be deprived of a vast amount of Capitol lore. Your do-it-yourself tour should cover the following: the Rotunda with its marvelous paintings by the "artist of the Revolution," John Trumbull; the "Apotheosis of Washington" by Brumidi, an Italian immigrant, in the eye of the Dome; Statuary Hall (the original House of Representatives); the original Senate Chamber; the old Supreme Court Chamber; the crypt (ground floor, directly beneath the Rotunda); and the colorful frescoes on the walls and ceilings of the corridors on the Senate side of the building. For the best view of the city walk around to the West Front of the Capitol—the view is spectacular. Open daily, 9 A.M.–4:30 P.M.; 9 A.M.–8 P.M. in summer. Closed Christmas, Thanksgiving, and New Year's.

The J. Edgar Hoover FBI Building. 10th St. and Pennsylvania Ave., N.W., 324–3447. Many harsh words have been directed toward the somewhat pretentious and overbearing new FBI building, but the tours remain as popular as ever. As many as 5,000 visitors a day are taken to see dramatic presentations of some of the FBI's most famous cases. Other exhibits illustrate the FBI's investigative activities in organized crime, bank robbery, espionage, and extortion. The tour takes about an hour, but plan to spend some time waiting in line unless you are with a group of 15 or more with a confirmed reservation. The marksmanship demonstration at the end may well be the highpoint of a child's visit to Washington. Open Monday–Friday, 8:45 A.M.–4:15 P.M. Free.

Ford's Theatre. 511 10th St., N.W., 426–6927. Tucked away on a side street in a rather shoddy part of downtown Washington is Ford's Theatre. It reopened in February 1968, almost 103 years after President Lincoln was shot while sitting in his box on the night of April 14, 1865. On the lower level is a museum filled with Lincoln memorabilia and an exhibit containing John Wilkes Booth's diary as well as one of his boots. Performances of musicals, reviews, and presentations of Americana are given in the 740-seat theater. To see the Petersen House where Lincoln was carried after being shot by John Wilkes Booth, walk across the street to 516 Tenth St. The small and simple house has been restored to the way it was when Lincoln died in the bedroom at the rear of the house on the morning of April 15, 1865. Both the theater and the Petersen House are open daily, 9 A.M.–5 P.M. On days of matinees and rehearsals, check hours for viewing the theater.

The Iwo Jima Memorial (also called the Marine Corps Memorial). On the Virginia side of Memorial Bridge between the entrance to Arlington

Cemetery and Arlington Boulevard (Route 50), (202) 485–9666. When viewed from a distance the Marine Corps War Memorial appears dramatic, especially when lit up at night, with the flag flying perpetually from a 60-foot flagpole. Up close it is overwhelming. Felix de Weldon sculpted the massive statue depicting the moment when five Marines and a Navy hospital corpsman raised the American flag on Mount Suribachi on the island of Iwo Jima in 1945. Joe Rosenthal took the photograph that inspired the statue. Open daily.

Jefferson Memorial. On the south bank of the Tidal Basin, West Potomac Park, 426–6821. John Russell Pope designed this memorial to Thomas Jefferson, which was dedicated in 1943, 200 years after his birth. The graceful, domed building features architectural motifs favored by Jefferson, an amateur architect, in buildings he designed—his home, Monticello, and the rotunda of the University of Virginia. The heroic 19-foot bronze statue of Jefferson by Rudolph Evans weighs five tons and stands on a black granite pedestal six feet high. The four interior walls set forth excerpts from Jefferson's writings. The site of the Memorial and the surrounding land have been entirely reclaimed from the Potomac. Jefferson died on July 4, 1826, aged 83. He is buried near his Virginia home. Always open. Very beautiful at night. If you are here during the summer, try to attend a Service band concert on the plaza in front of the Memorial.

Library of Congress. First St. and Independence Ave., S.E., 287–5000. This florid Italian Renaissance building, named for Thomas Jefferson, was considered to be "the most beautiful building in the world" when it opened in 1897. Today it is part of the largest national library in the world with more than 83 million items in its collections—from maps and charts to musical instruments and scores of letters, papers and, of course, books—in 470 languages on 532 miles of shelves. You will see the Great Hall featuring carved balustrades, huge columns, multi-colored marble floors, statues, and mosaic murals. From the Visitor's Gallery above the second floor, you will look down on the Main Reading Room, the heart of the Library and one of the most impressive interior spaces in Washington. Among the Library's many treasures are Alexander Graham Bell's first sketch of the telephone and the contents of Abraham Lincoln's pockets the night he was assassinated. The Library of Congress long ago outgrew its original building and in 1930 The John Adams Annex opened (2nd St. and Independence Ave., S.E.). It is one of the finest examples of Beaux Arts architecture in the country. In 1980, the James Madison Memorial Building opened (101 Independence Ave., S.E.). It has a lovely view from its top-floor cafeteria where visitors to the Library are welcome. (The Library also includes the National Library Service for the Blind and Physically Handicapped, located elsewhere in the City.) An 18-minute slide presentation about the Library's history and function is shown every hour, followed by a guided tour (weekdays, 8:45 A.M.–8:45 P.M., and on weekends and holidays 8:45 A.M.–5:45 P.M.). Free guided tours leave from the Visitor Services Center hourly, 9 A.M.–4 P.M. weekdays.

Lincoln Memorial. West end of Mall, 426–6895. To most visitors the Lincoln Memorial is Washington's most impressive and inspiring building. Henry Bacon, the architect, chose a classic Greek temple of purest white marble for the Memorial; it was completed in 1922. Daniel Chester French was the sculptor of the seated Lincoln, which is 19 feet high and required 28 blocks of marble and four years of carving. The view of the

Mall with the reflecting pool mirroring the Washington Monument and the sight of the Capitol two miles away is magnificent. However, you should take a few more minutes to walk to the Potomac side of the Memorial where you will enjoy the view of Robert E. Lee's home on a hill above Arlington Cemetery. Try to see the Memorial both by day and by night. Open 24 hours a day.

For an added dimension enter the Memorial through the small door at the end of the sidewalk to the left of the Memorial's staircase. You will see the gigantic underpinnings which hold up the huge marble edifice. An elevator will take you up to view the seated Lincoln.

Call 426–6842 (6 weeks in advance) to arrange a tour of the stalactites and stalagmites in the caves beneath the Lincoln Memorial. Tours are conducted from August to November and from March to June.

The Kennedy Center for the Performing Arts. New Hampshire Ave. and Rock Creek Pkwy., N.W., 254–3600. Since the Kennedy Center opened on September 8, 1971, the nation's capital has been able to attract the best national and international dance, theater, and music companies to perform in its four theaters. The well-known architect Edward Durell Stone designed the imposing building, which is faced with Carrara marble and measures 630 feet in length. Plan to attend a performance, tour on your own, eat at one of its three restaurants, or take the excellent guided tour offered daily between 10 A.M. and 1:15 P.M. The Center's location on the banks of the Potomac River is dramatic, as is the red-carpeted Grand Foyer lit by 18 crystal chandeliers. A 7-foot-high bronze bust of John F. Kennedy by sculptor Robert Berks dominates the center of the foyer. The two entrances from the plaza lead to the Hall of States and the Hall of Nations, where appropriate flags add a festive note to the lengthy corridors. Open daily from 10 A.M. to late evening. Free tours. Parking underneath the building or at the nearby Watergate.

Mount Vernon. See the description of George Washington's plantation under *Historic Homes*.

National Archives. 8th St. and Constitution Ave., N.W. (schedule information, 523–3000; research information, 523–3220; tours, 523–3183). This handsome building serves as a permanent depository for the nation's most precious documents—the original copies of the Declaration of Independence, the Constitution, and the Bill of Rights. Research facilities are available to anyone interested in the nation's heritage, and in genealogical research. The classical building, completed in 1934, was designed by John Russell Pope, who was the architect for the National Gallery of Art and the Jefferson Memorial. Open daily, 10 A.M.–5:30 P.M. Extended summer hours are determined annually.

Supreme Court of the United States. At the corner of First and East Capitol sts., 479–3000. You will want to tie in your visit to the Supreme Court with your tour of the Capitol, the Library of Congress, and the Folger Shakespeare Library, as they are all within walking distance of one another. This stunning building, suggestive of ancient Greek temples, was designed by Cass Gilbert, constructed of the whitest Vermont marble, and completed in 1935. Until then the Court had held session for 135 years in seven different locations in the Capitol building. If you are lucky you will see the Court in action. Its yearly schedule begins on the first Monday of October and continues through June; cases are usually heard between 10:00 A.M. and 3:00 P.M., Monday through Wednesday during the first two weeks of the month. For the following two weeks the Justices deliberate the cases they have heard, and one of them writes the majority opinion. When the Court is not in session, a staff member talks informally every half-hour, explaining how the Court operates. Monday is the best day to attend a session, as that's when the decisions are usually handed down. A "3-minute line" for tourists allows visitors to enter the courtroom, have a quick look-around, and leave promptly. Another line is for those who wish to hear cases presented to the Court, and operate on a first-come basis. Once seated, you may stay as long as you wish. Security measures are strict. Umbrellas, briefcases, coats, cameras, etc., must be checked before entering the courtroom. Open weekdays, 9 A.M.–4:30 P.M.

Vietnam Veterans Memorial. Constitution Gardens at 23rd St. and Constitution Ave., 634–1568. The V-shaped black granite memorial, designed by Maya Lin and dedicated in November 1982. Listing the names of 58,132 Americans who died or were lost in Vietnam, the sobering monument has become one of Washington's most visited.

Washington Monument. Center of Mall, Constitution Ave. at 15th St., N.W., 426–6839. The 555-foot high marble obelisk designed by Robert Mills as a memorial to our first president bears a tell-tale line about a third of the way up, marking the place where construction stopped for 26 years between 1854 and 1880. Lack of funds, political squabbling, and the Civil War were responsible for the long delay; the shaft was completed in 1888. The top may be reached only by elevator, and the view from the top will not disappoint (except on a foggy day). Open daily, 8 A.M.–midnight, April–Labor Day; 9 A.M.–5 P.M., September–March. Free.

The White House. 1600 Pennsylvania Ave., N.W., 456–7041. This magnificent mansion has been home to every President with the exception of George Washington, who died before construction was completed. The design for the "President's Palace" (as Pierre L'Enfant called it) was chosen from those submitted in answer to a national design competition: the winner was James Hoban, an Irish architect who based his plan on Leinster Hall in Dublin. Over the years many structural changes have taken place as Presidents have added to, redecorated, or embellished the mansion. Because the White House is such a stellar attraction (on an average day more than 7,000 people see the state rooms) it is necessary to proceed as follows to obtain your tour ticket between the end of May and Labor Day. Visitors must pick up their tickets at booths on the Ellipse (the 52-acre park just south of the White House) on a first-come, first-served basis. Tickets are free; they cannot be reserved, nor can a representative pick up a block of tickets for a group. Each ticket shows the approximate time your tour will form on the Ellipse; wait for the park ranger to escort you to the East Gate of the White House. Do not go there on your own. The ticket booths are open from 8 A.M. to noon, Tuesday through Saturday; the White House is open 10 A.M. until noon. If all the tickets for a particular day are distributed before noon, the booths may close earlier. No tickets are required the rest of the year. Visitors should wait in the line which forms outside the East Gate.

On rare occasions, because of an official White House function, visitors may not tour the mansion. There is no guided tour—you literally walk through—and the line moves swiftly. Once inside you will see the great East Room, the Green Room, the Blue Room, the Red Room, and the

State Dining Room. Special early morning tours may be arranged by writing to your Congressman well in advance of your trip to Washington.

ARCHITECTURE. Washington is a wonderful place to study many different styles of architecture, from Egyptian to Modern. Listed below are a few representative styles and buildings of unusual interest or quality:

Egyptian. *Washington Monument,* center of Mall. Robert Mills, architect. Completed in 1884 and opened to the public in 1888.

Federal. *Cox's Row,* 3327–3339 N St., N.W., in Georgetown (north side of street). Built about 1790.

French Second Empire. *The Old Executive Office Building,* formerly the State, War and Navy Building, S.E. corner of 17th St. and Penn. Ave., N.W. Alfred B. Mullett, architect. 1871–88.

Georgian. *Gunston Hall,* Lorton, Va., on the Potomac River southwest of Mount Vernon. Built 1755–58.

Lloyd House, 220 North Washington St., Alexandria, Va. John Wise, architect. Built in 1793.

Woodlawn Plantation, three miles south of Mount Vernon. Dr. William Thornton, architect. Built 1800–15.

Gothic. *Washington Cathedral,* Mount St. Alban, Wisconsin Ave. and Woodley Rd., N.W. Dr. George Bodley of London and Henry Vaughan of Boston, architects. Started in 1907; nearly completed.

Greek. *Lincoln Memorial,* west end of Mall. Henry Bacon, architect. Completed in 1922.

Supreme Court Building, Capitol Hill, East Capitol and 1st St., N.E. Cass Gilbert, architect. Completed in 1935.

Greek Revival. *Arlington House* (formerly called the Custis-Lee Mansion), in Arlington National Cemetery. George Hadfield, architect. Built 1802–17. One of the earliest and most notable of the houses of the Greek Revival period.

Islamic. *Islamic Center* (Mosque), 2551 Massachusetts Ave., N.W. Completed in 1949.

Italian Renaissance. *Library of Congress,* Capitol Hill, 1st St. and Independence Ave., S.E. Smithmeyer and Pelz, architects. Built 1886–97.

Modern. *East Building* of the National Gallery of Art, 4th St. and Constitution Ave., N.W. I.M. Pei, architect. Completed in 1978.

National Geographic Society Building, 17th and M Sts., N.W. Edward Durell Stone, architect. Completed 1964.

Kennedy Center for the Performing Arts, Rock Creek Parkway at New Hampshire Ave., N.W. Edward Durell Stone, architect. Completed in 1971.

Dulles International Airport, (Building) Chantilly, Va. Eero Saarinen, architect. Completed in 1962.

Roman. *Union Station.* Massachusetts and Delaware Aves., N.E. Daniel H. Burnham, architect. The main waiting room is a copy of the central hall of the Baths of Diocletian in Rome. Completed in 1908.

Spanish. *Pan American Union Building* (OAS), 17th St. and Constitution Ave., N.W. Albert Kelsey and Paul Cret, architects. Completed in 1910.

Victorian. *Smithsonian Institution Building,* "The Castle," the Mall at 10th St. James Renwick, architect. Romantic Revival style. Completed in 1852.

Architecture buffs will also enjoy walks through Georgetown (houses in Georgian, Federal, Victorian, and Classical Revival styles); Capitol Hill (houses dating back to pre-Civil War days); Lafayette Square (town houses from early 19th century); and Alexandria (many buildings, houses, churches, and stores from the late 18th and early 19th centuries, when the town was a tobacco port).

Mount Vernon and *Gunston Hall* are excellent examples of 18th-century Virginia plantations. In a more modern vein two "new towns," Columbia, Md. (near Baltimore) and Reston, Va. (near Dulles airport) may be visited as good examples of successful planned communities. Both of them were developed in the 1960s and are still growing.

FAMOUS LIBRARIES. The Library of Congress, 1st St. and Independence Ave., S.E., ranks among the great libraries of the world. On permanent exhibition are a three-volume 1455 edition of the Gutenberg Bible, and Thomas Jefferson's "rough draft" of the Declaration of Independence. Among other things, it houses the world's largest collection of comic books. For more detailed information, see *Historic Sites.* For information on concerts held from Oct. to April, see *Music.*

The Folger Shakespeare Library, 201 East Capitol St., S.W., (202) 544–4600, houses the world's largest collection of Shakespeareana and an extraordinary collection of material in English dealing with the 17th and 18th centuries. The *Exhibition Hall* reproduces the great hall of an Elizabethan palace. The *Shakespearean Theater* is a full-size replica of a public playhouse of Shakespeare's day, except that it does not open to the sky. Plays are presented throughout the year by the *Folger Theater Group.* Open Monday–Saturday 10 A.M.–4 P.M. (See *Theater.*)

NOTABLE CHURCHES. The original L'Enfant plan for Washington specified one location for a sort of "national pantheon or church" that would have a role in the new Federal City like that of Westminster Abbey in London or Notre Dame in pre-Revolutionary Paris. A Greek Revival temple finally arose on the site, between 7th and 9th, F and G Sts., N.W., but before completion in 1867 it was pressed into service as a Civil War hospital, then became the Patent Office. It now houses the National Portrait Gallery and the National Museum of American Art.

The **National Cathedral,** atop Mount St. Alban at Massachusetts and Wisconsin Ave. is under the governance of the Episcopal church, but is a truly interdenominational place of worship. Formally named the Cathedral Church of St. Peter and St. Paul, this has been called "the last of the great cathedrals," because it is being built stone by stone in the centuries-old traditional manner without the use of steel or any shortcuts. The cornerstone was laid in 1907 and it is nearly completed. There are conducted tours Monday through Saturday, 10 A.M.–noon and 1–3:15 P.M.; Sunday 1 and 2 P.M. The attractive grounds include a *Bishop's Garden* and *Herb Cottage.* There are frequent carillon and organ recitals and occasionally there is a full symphonic and choral concert such as the Berlioz Requiem.

The **National Shrine of the Immaculate Conception,** Michigan Ave. at Fourth St., N.E., is the largest Roman Catholic church in the U.S. and one of the largest in the world. It is said to be the only Catholic church building in America to which every parish in the country contributed funds. Authorized in 1914, it was dedicated in 1959. Of Romanesque and

Byzantine style, a bell tower built beside the shrine reminds many of that of St. Mark's in Venice. It contains a 56-bell carillon. Tours start in *Memorial Hall* every half-hour 9 A.M.–4 P.M. from Monday–Saturday, 1:30–4 P.M. on Sunday. Major symphonic and choral concerts are also presented here.

Near the National Shrine and the Catholic University of America is another long-popular visitation center, the **Franciscan Monastery and Gardens,** 14th and Quincy sts., N.E. Within it are reproductions of such Holy Land shrines as the Grotto of Bethlehem and the Holy Sepulcher and underneath is a version of the Roman catacombs. Lovingly tended gardens include roses that often are in bloom at Christmas time.

Many Washington churches are mostly known for their associations with presidents, and that may even be true of **St. Matthew's Cathedral,** the seat of Washington's Catholic archbishop. Just off busy Connecticut Ave. on Rhode Island Ave., N.W., this Renaissance-style church was long a focus of Washington's "Easter Parade." It's now famous as a church in which John F. Kennedy frequently worshipped and where his funeral mass was held.

St. John's Episcopal Church, directly across from the White House on Lafayette Square, is often called "Church of the Presidents" because almost every Chief Executive has attended at least one service there. Gerald Ford went to the church for private worship before his announcement of a pardon for Richard Nixon.

Richard Nixon, although reared a Quaker, preferred attending family services conducted in the White House by such visiting clerics as the Rev. Billy Graham. Herbert Hoover, however, regularly attended the **Friends Meeting House** at 2111 Florida Ave., N.W.

Both Harry Truman and Jimmy Carter frequently worshipped at the **First Baptist Church,** a brief walk from the White House up 16th St. to O St. It's a comparatively new (1950s) pseudo-Gothic structure.

Faithful to the church of his fathers (Dutch Reformed), Theodore Roosevelt regularly attended **Grace Reform Church,** 15th and O Sts., N.W., while his wife and family went to nearby **St. John's Episcopal.** The church, whose cornerstone "Teddy" laid, maintains a collection of Roosevelt memorabilia.

The **National Covenant Presbyterian Church** attended by President and Mamie Eisenhower stood for decades at the corner of Connecticut and N Sts., N.W., its rough-hewn tower looking like a perfect crossbowman's redoubt. It, however, has given way to an office building and the church has moved to 4101 Nebraska Ave., N.W., near American University. Serving as the national church for Presbyterians, the new structure contains a Chapel of Presidents, with stained-glass windows depicting modern man and Biblical themes.

Some churches are worth visiting for their special meanings to ethnic groups. The **Metropolitan African Methodist Episcopal Church,** 1518 M St., N.W., was the church of Frederick Douglass. The land for it was bought in 1850. The congregation of slaves and free blacks worked for 30 years to build it, laboriously scraping old bricks for reuse. It has been called the National Cathedral of African Methodism.

Old Adas Israel Synagogue, now at Third and G Sts., N.W., was the first building constructed as a synagogue in Washington and was dedicated in 1876 with President Grant attending. Saved from demolition for subway construction, it was moved to its present site and restored as a museum.

The **Islamic Mosque and Cultural Center,** 2551 Massachusetts Ave., N.W., (202) 332–8343, could hardly be mistaken for anything else. From its 160-foot-high minaret the Moslem faithful are called to their prayers five times daily. Very much in the news within recent years, the center welcomes visitors, who are asked to remove their shoes as in any other of the world's mosques. It is open daily from 10 A.M.–5 P.M.

Anyone who rounds the Capital Beltway near Kensington, Md., can't miss the gleaming white towers (one of them topped by the golden angel, Moroni) of the **Washington Temple of the Church of Latter-Day Saints,** otherwise known as the Mormons. The $15-million marble temple is closed to non-Mormons, but there's a visitors center on the grounds at 9900 Stoney Brook Dr., Kensington. There's a multimedia presentation and tours of the grounds offered daily 10 A.M.–9:30 P.M. (301) 587–0144.

The Masonic Order, while not exactly a religion, does contain a religious element combined with a special sort of veneration (hence the name) for the great builders of antiquity. Two Washington-area Masonic shrines worth at least a quick look are based on the designs of two of the Seven Wonders of the Ancient World. They are the **Scottish Rite Temple** at 1733 16th St., N.W., patterned after the Mausoleum of Halicarnassus, and the **George Washington Masonic National Memorial** in Alexandria, modeled after the ancient lighthouse at Alexandria, Egypt. The room devoted to Washington memorabilia merits a visit. On display is the trowel used by the President in laying the cornerstone of the Capitol in 1793, and the clock from his bedroom at Mount Vernon, stopped at the moment of his death. Open daily, 9 A.M.–5 P.M.

Two cemeteries often visited for various reasons are **Oak Hill** in Georgetown and **Rock Creek,** off North Capital St. Rock Creek Cemetery, the oldest in the city, is strangely not at all near Rock Creek, while Oak Hill overlooks it. Oak Hill is at the top of 28th and 29th Sts. next to Montrose Park. It was given and endowed by W.W. Corcoran, the banker who also founded the Corcoran Gallery of Art. Although it contains the graves of many notables, it is most visited because of the jewel-like Renwick Chapel, designed and built in 1850 by James Renwick, who also did the fanciful Smithsonian "castle." Rock Creek Cemetery, at Rock Creek Rd. and Webster St., N.W., contains **St. Paul's,** the District of Columbia's oldest church, established in 1719. It is most noted for what is generally believed to be the most distinguished and moving sculpture in the city, the memorial Henry Adams commissioned from Augustus Saint-Gaudens for his wife who had committed suicide. It is commonly but mistakenly called "Grief," from a remark by Mark Twain that the figure embodied all of human grief. No inscription appears on the monument itself, but Saint-Gaudens had called it "The Mystery of the Hereafter" and "The Peace of God That Passeth Understanding."

MUSEUMS AND GALLERIES. Washington has become one of the world's great museum centers. Fortunately for the visitor, entrance to most of the museums is free of charge, and many of the attractions are within walking distance of one another on the Mall. The National Gallery of Art and its new East Building should be on everyone's list, and plan to visit as many of the others mentioned below as time and energy will allow.

The following telephone numbers may be helpful: Dial a Phenomenon, 357–2000; Dial a Museum, 357–2020; Visitor Information, 357–2700.

See the end of this section for information about Smithsonian museums.

B'nai B'rith Klutznick Museum. 1640 Rhode Island Ave., N.W., 857–6583. Displays show the contribution Jews have made in the development of our democracy. The museum also includes one of the largest collections of Jewish ceremonial objects and folklore material in the United States. Open Sunday–Friday, 10 A.M.–5 P.M.; closed legal and Jewish holidays.

Capital Children's Museum. 800 3rd St., N.E., near H St., 543–8600. This is a wonderful "hands-on" place for children to learn by doing. They can even make tortillas at the Mexican exhibition. (See Children's Activities.) Open 10 A.M.–5 P.M. daily. Admission $4 per person; children under 2, free. Special group discounts.

Corcoran Gallery of Art. 17th St. and New York Ave., N.W., 638–3211. The Corcoran is the capital's oldest art gallery and is distinguished for its outstanding collection of American art. The museum bears the name of William Wilson Corcoran whose original collection was housed in the present Renwick Gallery. Works by the first great American protraitists, including John Copley, Gilbert Stuart, Rembrandt Peale, and other members of the gifted Peale family. The Hudson River School is well represented as is the late 19th-Century American impressionist school. A small but excellent selection of works by European masters, including Rubens, Degas, and Rembrandt, may also be enjoyed. The Biennial Exhibition of contemporary American painting held for six weeks attracts nationwide attention. In recent years the museum has featured exhibitions of fine photography and works by artists from the Washington area. The Corcoran School of Art adjacent to the museum is one of the oldest art schools in the nation. The Gallery Shop offers an excellent variety of books pertaining to art, as well as posters, reproductions, and gift items. Open Tuesday–Sunday, 10 A.M.–4:30 P.M.; Thursday until 9 P.M. Free. Free tours at 12:30 P.M. Tuesday through Sunday.

Daughters of the American Revolution National Society Headquarters. 1776 D St., N.W., 628–1776. The headquarters of the Daughters of the American Revolution (DAR) are housed in three separate buildings of classic style. Until the Kennedy Center was built *Constitution Hall* served as the capital's only suitable auditorium for concerts, recitals, and lectures (entrance on 18th St.). *DAR Memorial Continental Hall* houses the third largest genealogical library in the U.S. It is open for use by the public for a fee. The *DAR Museum* features 29 period rooms ranging from a formal sitting room to an attic filled with children's toys. The collection of Revolutionary War period artifacts, including silver made by Paul Revere, is outstanding. Open Monday–Friday, 8:30 A.M.–4 P.M.; Sunday 1–5 P.M. Tours are offered between 10 A.M. and 2:30 P.M.

Dumbarton Oaks Collection. 1703 32nd St., N.W., 338–8278. The small museum housing the unparalleled collections of Byzantine and pre-Columbian art is perfection itself—small, intimate, original in design, with a series of uncrowded miniature galleries. Designed by architect Philip Johnson, it was added to the magnificent Georgian mansion, one of Georgetown's most distinguished buildings. The conference that led to the formation of the Charter of the United Nations was held in the music room. Mr. and Mrs. Robert Woods Bliss left Dumbarton Oaks and its magnificent gardens to Harvard University in 1940 to be used as a research center. Open Tuesday–Sunday, 2–5 P.M.

Interior Department Museum. C St. between 18th and 19th Sts., N.W., on first floor, 343–2743. In this somewhat old-fashioned museum the visitor may enjoy lifelike dioramas depicting subjects such as George Washington meeting the Marquis de Lafayette in 1780 and an Indian trading post at Fort Union in 1835. Top quality Indian crafts and souvenirs are for sale in Room 1023 across the hall. Open Monday–Friday, 8 A.M.–4 P.M. Closed weekends and holidays.

National Building Museum. Judiciary Sq., N.W.; 272–2448. Formerly the Pension Building, this remarkable edifice has been completely renovated. The great interior space of this pre–Civil War building is an unforgettable sight. Open Monday–Friday 10 A.M.–4 P.M.; weekends noon–4 P.M. Tours Tuesday–Friday at 12:30 P.M., weekends at 1 P.M. Free.

National Gallery of Art. 6th St. and Constitution Ave., N.W., on the Mall, 737–4215. In order to save confusion for the visitor we shall refer to the older, original gallery as the *West Building,* and the new addition as the *East Building.*

The *West Building,* designed by John Russell Pope, opened in March, 1941. It was made possible by a gift from Andrew W. Mellon, financier and Secretary of the Treasury during the Hoover administration, who donated 126 pictures from his private collection and $15 million for the construction of the building. Here is the most comprehensive survey of Italian painting and sculpture in the western hemisphere, as well as the only painting by Leonardo da Vinci outside Europe. A daily schedule of events appears on bulletin boards at both the Constitution Ave. and Mall entrances. If time permits, the introductory tour of the gallery is recommended. There is a fine restaurant located in the connecting passageway between the old and new museums. A free concert each Sunday at 7 P.M. is given in the East Garden Court between late September and early June, but seating is limited and guaranteed only to early arrivals. Gift shops at several locations offer outstanding reproductions of the museum's masterpieces, as well as books, postcards, and gift items. The Garden Café is on the ground floor.

The East Building was opened in June, 1978, and has already proven to be one of the city's most popular attractions. The well-known Chinese-American architect I.M. Pei is credited with this imaginative design. The building is divided into two interlocking triangles in order to fit into the peculiar trapezoid-shaped piece of land. The pinkish Tennessee marble matches that of the original gallery built 35 years earlier. The building serves not only as a showplace for paintings and sculpture but also as an office building that houses an art library, the gallery staff, and the new National Gallery Center for Advanced Studies in the Visual Arts. At the entrance to the building is Henry Moore's huge sculpture composed of two bronze sections, each $17\frac{1}{2}$ feet high. Inside the stunning court hangs Alexander Calder's 920-pound mobile with its balanced rods and red, blue, and black floating pods that move with the air currents. After marveling at the light-filled court with its ever-changing effects the visitor should mount the steps to enjoy a new view from the bridge, and seek out the many galleries, including several hidden away in towers. The workmanship throughout the building is magnificent. Although some of the paintings are shown on a semipermanent basis, many of the galleries are used for special exhibits. The Café/Buffet on the Concourse level, as well as cafés on the Tower level and in the West Building, are delightful places for a light meal.

Both the West and East buildings are open daily 10 A.M. to 5 P.M.; Sunday, noon–9 P.M. Closed Christmas and New Year's Day. The $94.4-million gallery was a gift to the nation by Paul Mellon, the late Ailsa Mellon Bruce, and the Andrew W. Mellon Foundation.

National Geographic Explorer's Hall. (See *Children's Activities* section.)

National Museum of Women in the Arts. 1250 New York Ave., N.W.; 783–5000. Opened in April of 1987, the National Museum of Women in the Arts is dedicated to the celebration of women's contributions to all art forms. The permanent collection of over 500 works, ranging from the Renaissance to the present, includes paintings, sculpture, prints, drawings, and photography, and features works by Georgia O'Keeffe, Mary Cassatt, Vigee Le Brun, and Judy Chicago. This is all, ironically, housed in a renovated 1907 building that used to be a Masonic (men's) temple.

The museum also features changing exhibits. Two slated for 1988 include Olga Mills, a Swedish artist (spring), and Camile Claudel, a gifted sculptor and Rodin's lover (summer). Incidentally, experts in some art circles are now questioning the authorship of some of Rodin's pieces and are attributing them to Claudel. In addition to special exhibits, the museum has also set up a group of "state committees" which generate exhibits focusing on woman's art in a particular state. In 1988, for example, the State Gallery will show exhibits from North Carolina, Colorado, and Texas. Open Tuesday–Saturday, 10 A.M.–5 P.M.; Sunday, noon–5 P.M., closed Monday. Suggested donation: $2 adults, $1 children and senior citizens.

The Octagon House. 1799 New York Ave., N.W., 638–3105. How fortunate was the Octagon House to be the recipient of the knowledge, know-how, and tender-loving care of the American Institute of Architects who own it and are responsible for its fine restoration. Dr. William Thornton, architect of the Capitol, designed it originally in 1800 for the Tayloe family. Despite its name there are only six, not eight, sides. During the War of 1812 it served as temporary quarters for the French ambassador. The French tricolor flying from its roof may have saved it when the British marched on Washington in August, 1814, setting fire to both the Capitol and the White House. Driven from the Presidential Palace by the burning, President and Dolley Madison moved into the Octagon for nine months while their residence was rebuilt. President Madison signed the Treaty of Ghent that ended the War of 1812 on a table in a second floor room on February 17, 1815. The AIA has built its modern headquarters behind the house. A tour of the mansion begins when you enter. Open Tuesday–Friday, 10 A.M.–4 P.M. Saturday and Sunday, noon–4 P.M. Closed Mondays and major holidays. Free, but donations are appreciated. (Call in advance for group tours.)

Phillips Collection. 1600 21st St., N.W., one block west from the Dupont Circle Metro, and just off Massachusetts Ave., 387–0961. A prominent Washington art critic speaks of the Phillips as "a place of quiet harmonies." Those who prefer to savor rather than gulp the masterpieces, which hang on the walls and the stairways of Mr. and Mrs. Duncan Phillips' former home, can do so in an unhurried fashion and even sit down when shoes pinch and concentration lags. Open to the public in 1918, this collection was the first museum of modern art. Mr. Phillips believed in living artists and he bought their pictures enthusiastically; Bonnard, Klee, John Marin, and Rothko were among his favorites. The paintings of many French Impressionists and Post-Impressionists hang in his gallery, including Degas, Monet, Manet, Van Gogh, and Cezanne. Renoir's *Luncheon of the Boating Party* is probably the best-known picture in the collection. This charming small museum has just undergone a giant renovation. Open Tuesday–Saturday, 10 A.M.–5 P.M.; Sunday, 2–7 P.M. Closed Monday. Free, but contributions are suggested.

Textile Museum. 2320 S St., N.W., 667–0441. George Hewitt Myers founded this unusual museum in 1925 to share with the public his extensive collection of textiles and oriental rugs, and to provide a center to carry on technical studies in the textile field. His stately red-brick home designed by the well-known architect John Russell Pope, and the adjoining building, designed by Waddy Wood, have been adapted to form the museum we visit today. There are more than 10,000 textiles and 1,100 rugs in the collection. The changing exhibitions are of a high order, as is the museum shop which features publications relating to rugs, textiles and crafts, as well as yarns, textiles, jewelry, and other gift items. Open Tuesday–Saturday, 10 A.M.–5 P.M.; Sunday, 1–5 P.M. Closed Monday and public holidays. Donations: $3 for adults; 50 cents for children.

Smithsonian Museums

Extended spring and summer hours for the Smithsonian museums on the Mall are determined annually. During the summer of 1987 only the Air and Space Museum and the National Gallery of Art were open evenings, until 9 P.M.

Arts and Industries Building. Jefferson Dr. and Independence Ave. at 9th St., S.W. on the Mall, 357–1300, 357–2700. This red-brick building constructed in 1879 was restored for the Bicentennial to house exhibits from the Philadelphia Exposition of 1876. It is a delightful "period piece" and a favorite with tourists who revel in Victoriana. Many of the displays include objects actually shown in the original exhibits—ornate silver and furniture, horse-drawn vehicles, and unusual objets d'art from this exuberant period. A fine gift shop offers all manner of temptations, from books to a studio where families may sit in borrowed costumes for a daguerreotype portrait. Open daily, 10 A.M.–5:30 P.M.

Freer Gallery of Art. 12th St. and Independence Ave., S.W., on the Mall, 357–2700. This museum houses one of the finest collections of Far and Near Eastern art outside the Orient. The layout of the gallery is most attractive, with the exhibition halls built around a central courtyard. The donor of this magnificent collection was Charles L. Freer, a Detroit industrialist, who retired in 1900 to devote the rest of his life to collecting Oriental art. He died in 1919. Even the uninitiated will gain tremendous pleasure from viewing the Oriental porcelains, Japanese screens, Persian miniatures, Chinese paintings and bronzes, and Egyptian gold pieces. Mr. Freer was also a patron and close friend of James McNeill Whistler. Not to be missed is the *Peacock Room* (gallery XII), Whistler's only surviving attempt at interior decoration. It was originally the dining room of a London town house owned by Frederick R. Leyland. Open daily, 10 A.M.–5:30 P.M. Free tours.

The Joseph H. Hirshhorn Museum and Sculpture Garden. Independence Ave. at 8th St., S.W., on the Mall, 357–2700. This superb collection of more than 6,000 19th- and 20th-century paintings and sculptures was donated to the nation in 1966 by Joseph H. Hirshhorn, a self-made millionaire, financier, and industrialist. His gift was estimated to be worth $50 million. Mr. Hirshhorn died in 1981. American painters such as Thomas Eakins, Jackson Pollock, Mark Rothko, Frank Stella, and Willem de Kooning are well represented, although the collection is international in scope. Opened in 1974, the museum is irreverantly nicknamed "the Doughnut on the Mall." The sunken Sculpture Garden, located north of the museum on Jefferson Dr., includes *Balzac* and *The Burghers of Calais* by Auguste Rodin and *Backs* by Henri Matisse. An outdoor terrace cafeteria is open in the summertime. Open daily, 10 A.M.–5:30 P.M.

National Museum of African Art. 950 Independence Ave., S.W., 357–2700. This museum, reopened in September of 1987 in a striking new building, shows the heritage of African art through displays of sculpture, musical instruments and jewelry. It was founded by former Foreign Service Officer Warren Robbins in 1964. In 1979, through Congressional legislation, the museum was merged with the Smithsonian Institution. Open daily 10 A.M.–5:30 P.M.

National Air and Space Museum. Jefferson Dr. and Independence Ave. betweeen 6th and 7th Sts., S.W., on the Mall, 357–2700. Opened on July 1, 1976, in celebration of the Nation's Bicentennial, this gigantic museum is a celebration of flight as well as a showcase for the evolution of aviation and space technology. The visitor enters the Milestones of Flight Gallery on the ground floor where Lindbergh's *Spirit of St. Louis* hangs from the ceiling. In this small plane he made the first solo nonstop flight across the Atlantic Ocean on May 20–21, 1927. It took 33 1/3 hours. Other attractions are the full-size walk-through model of the *Skylab* orbital workshop, the *X-1,* the first airplane to break the sound barrier, and a simulated World War 1 airstrip. Tickets are sold on the ground floor for the five movies, "The Dream is Alive," "Flyers," "To Fly," "Living Planet," and "On the Wing." We suggest that you head for the ticket office as soon as you enter the museum, then tour on your own until the designated time for your show. (Fee.) If time permits see, too, the presentations in the Albert Einstein Spacearium on the second floor. Open daily, 10 A.M.–5:30 P.M. Summer hours determined annually.

National Museum of American Art and National Portrait Gallery. 8th and G Sts., N.W. and 8th and F Sts., N.W., 357–2700. These two distinguished Smithsonian museums share the old Patent Office Building, a superb example of Greek Revival architecture. The architect was Robert Mills, whose Washington Monument and Treasury Building are better known. His masterpiece was completed in 1867; at that time it was the largest building in the United States. Until 1932, the Patent Office occupied the building. Had it not been for the intervention of Commissioner of Fine Arts, David Finley, in 1953, the building might well have been razed for a parking lot. He brought the matter to the attention of President Eisenhower, who is credited with having saved it from the wrecker's ball.

The *Museum of American Art* houses more than 23,000 items and provides more than 25 exhibitions a year. Works by Benjamin West, Gilbert Stuart, George Catlin (famous for his Indian paintings), Albert Pinkham Ryder are displayed as well as a major portion of the original plasters of the noted sculptor, Hiram Powers. The Lincoln Gallery should be visited, for it was here that Lincoln's second inaugural ball and banquet took place on March 7, 1865.

The *Portrait Gallery* serves as a treasure house of American history, with portraits of Americans who have made significant contributions in many different fields. They include such diverse notables as Pocahontas, Horace Greeley, and Edwin Booth. In the Presidential Corridor is a portrait of each of our presidents. Not to be overlooked is the recently renovated Gallery in the third floor hall. Closed for almost a century, it is an outstanding example of America's Victorian Reniassance architecture. Open daily, 10 A.M.–5:30 P.M.

National Museum of American History. Between 12th and 14th Sts., N.W. on Constitution Ave., N.W., 357–2700. This huge museum, built in 1960, is as conspicuous for its lack of exterior adornment as some of its neighbors are for their columns, pediments, and other monumental manifestations of importance. A favorite among the Smithsonian museums, it is a treasure house of some of America's most important inventions. They include Eli Whitney's cotton gin, Elias Howe's sewing machines, and Thomas Edison's phonograph. The tattered flag that flew over Fort McHenry, Baltimore, during an attack by the British fleet in 1814 is dramatically displayed on the ground floor near the Mall entrance. Not to be missed is the exhibit of First Ladies and Presidential hostesses gowns on mannequins standing in authentic reproductions of rooms in the White House. A steam locomotive built in 1926 for the Southern Railway, a Conestoga freight wagon, and a 1913 Model T Ford that cost $325 when new are other popular attractions. Even George Washington's false teeth command an audience. There is a large cafeteria on the lower level. Open daily, 10 A.M.–5:30 P.M.

National Museum of Natural History. 10th St. and Constitution Ave., N.W., 357–2700. The giant Fenkovi African bush elephant greets all comers in the octagonal rotunda of this museum that tells the story of man and his natural surroundings. Shot in Angola in 1955, he stands 13 feet 2 inches at the shoulder, weighed eight tons when he was alive, and is thought to be the largest elephant ever recorded. The Hall of Gems displays the Hope Diamond, which was smuggled out of India in the 17th century, and which has brought tragedy to many of its owners. At 45.5 carats it is the largest blue diamond in the world. In the Hall of Mammals you will see hundreds of animals in settings reflecting their normal surroundings. The 92-foot life-size model of a blue whale took two years to construct. In the Dinosaur Hall, you can study creatures that became extinct 63 million years ago. There is a 12-minute movie and skeletons of several of more than 250 kinds of dinosaurs that scientists have identified. The gift shop is first rate and members of the Smithsonian Associates may dine in their own restaurant on the ground floor. Open daily, 10 A.M.–5:30 P.M.

Renwick Gallery. 17th St. and Pennsylvania Ave., N.W., 357–2700. James Renwick, who designed the Smithsonian "castle" as well as St. Patrick's Cathedral in New York, was responsible for this distinctive building in the Second Empire style. Commissioned in 1858 by the wealthy banker and art collector William Wilson Corcoran, the building was soon turned over to the Quartermaster Corps during the Civil War. After the War Corcoran's collection outgrew this building and was moved to its present location on 17th St. Saved from demolition in 1958, the Renwick Gallery came under the jurisdiction of the Smithsonian Institution. Since 1965 it has served as a gallery for the display of American design, crafts, and decorative arts. Its shows have ranged from exhibitions of Shaker furniture to the industrial designs of Raymond Loewy. The impressive main staircase leads to a second-floor gallery that re-creates a formal parlor of the 1880s, with overstuffed furniture, potted palms, and some of Mr. Corcoran's oil paintings. Concerts and lectures are sometimes held here. The gift shop is well worth visiting, with outstanding handcrafted objects for sale, as well as books, posters, and reproductions. Open daily, 10 A.M.–5:30 P.M.

Arthur M. Sackler Gallery, 1050 Independence Ave., S.W., 357-2700. This new museum, opened in 1987, houses nearly 1,000 masterpieces of Asian and Near Eastern art and complements the collections in the adjacent Freer Gallery. It also includes the Vever collection, an outstanding collection of ancient Persian miniatures, books, illustrations and textiles. Open daily, 10 A.M.–5:30 P.M.

Smithsonian Institution "Castle." Jefferson Dr. between 9th and 12th Sts., S.W., 357–2700. This charming and romantic red-brick building, designed by James Renwick, symbolizes to many the versatility and orginality of the many museums mentioned in this chapter that are under the Smithsonian's jurisdiction. Built in 1855, it houses the administrative offices of the Smithsonian. Near the entrance is the tomb of James Smithson, an Englishman who in his 1826 will provided that his entire fortune of $541,379 should go to the United States to found an institution bearing his name. A remarkable fact is that he had never spent a day in this country. Many visitors find it helpful to study the layouts of the city, past and present, which are part of the permanent exhibit called "Federal City: Dreams and Realities," on the main floor. Open daily, 10 A.M.–5:30 P.M.

Barney Studio House. 2306 Massachusetts Ave., N.W., 357–3111. This unusual home and studio once belonged to the arts patron Alice Pike Barney, a wealthy and talented artist in her own right. Her Sheridan Circle mansion (built in 1902) was described as "the meeting place for wit and wisdom, genius and talent." Plays were presented in her living room, which was complete with a musician's gallery. Studio House is now under the wing of the Smithsonian Institution. There are guided tours Wednesday and Thursday at 11 A.M., and 1 P.M. as well as the 2nd and 4th Sundays of the month at 1 P.M. Reservations required. Free.

HISTORIC HOMES. A visit to some of the historic homes in Washington and the surrounding area will give the visitor an insight into the way many notable Americans lived. All are open to the public except for the Blair-Lee Houses.

Blair-Lee Houses. 1651–53 Pennsylvania Ave., N.W. These graceful mansions date back to the 1820s. However, only official guests of the President are invited inside. Blair House was named after its second owner, Francis Preston Blair, who purchased it in 1836 for $6,500. The adjoining Lee House was built for the Blairs' only daughter just before the Civil War. Over the years six cabinet members lived in the House. President Truman occupied the House following President Roosevelt's death, and during the 1948–52 renovation of the White House.

Arlington House. In Arlington National Cemetery, atop the bluff due west of Memorial Bridge. The distinctive Greek Revival plantation home of Robert E. Lee is visible from the west front of the Lincoln Memorial and from Memorial Bridge. It was designed by George Hadfield, a young Englishman who came to this country in 1795 to supervise work on the Capitol. Work on the house was started in 1802, but it was not completed until 1817. Just in front of the mansion's portico is the grave of Pierre L'Enfant, who laid out the original plans for the capital at George Washington's request. Open daily 9:30 A.M.–6 P.M. April through September; 9:30 A.M.–4:30 P.M. October through March. Call 557–0613.

Decatur House. 748 Jackson Place, N.W., 673–4030. This handsome red-brick house, built in 1819, was the first private home erected on Lafayette Square and the last to be privately occupied. Its architect was Benjamin H. Latrobe, who also designed St. John's Church, just a block away. Stephen Decatur, a dashing Naval hero of the Barbary Wars, commissioned Latrobe to design the house. Decatur and his wife lived in it for only one brief season; he was killed by Commodore James Barron in a duel in Bladensburg. Decatur House is now operated by the National Trust for Historic Preservation. The first floor is furnished in 18th-century style, as it was when Commodore Decatur lived there; the second floor, furnished in the Victorian style, looks as it did when a later owner, General Edward F. Beale, occupied the house. Open Tuesday–Friday, 10 A.M.–2 P.M.; weekends and holidays, 12–4 P.M. Admission: $2.50, adults; $1.25 students and senior citizens.

Dumbarton House. 2715 Q St., N.W., in Georgetown, 337-2288. This fine early Federal house serves as headquarters for the National Society of Colonial Dames of America. On display are authentic pieces of furniture from 1780 to 1815 as well as a noteworthy collection of china and silver. At one time the house sat in the middle of what is now Q St.; when the street was cut through (in 1915) the house was moved up the hill to its present location. Open Monday–Saturday, 9 A.M.–12:30 P.M.; closed Sunday, holidays, and the month of August. Donations accepted.

Dumbarton Oaks. 3101 R St., N.W., 388-8278. This magnificent estate was originally part of a Queen Anne land grant to Ninian Beall in 1702. The original house was built in 1801. Career Diplomat Robert Woods Bliss and Mrs. Bliss bought the estate in 1920, completely restored the house, and developed the magnificent gardens, yet only resided there seven years between overseas posts. It was given to Harvard in 1940. (See *Dumbarton Oaks Collection* under *Museums.*) Gardens open daily, 2–5 P.M. November–March; 2–6 P.M. April–October. Admission: April–October, $2, adults; $1, seniors and children; free November–March.

The Frederick Douglass Home. (Cedar Hill) 1411 W St., S.E., 426-5961. This was the home of the noted black abolitionist Frederick Douglass, who lived here from 1877 to his death in 1895. He was born a slave in 1817, escaped bondage in 1838, and later became an eloquent leader of the abolitionist movement. The house has a fine view of the old Federal City, and is maintained as a museum in Douglass' memory. You will see many artifacts of his life and many of his personal effects. Open daily mid-May to Labor Day, 9 A.M.–5 P.M.; rest of year, 9 A.M.–4 P.M. Free.

Gunston Hall. Route 242, 4 miles east of Route 1, Lorton, Va., (703) 550-9220. If you go to Alexandria and Mount Vernon, plan to spend another few hours visiting Gunston Hall Plantation. Construction of this compact, red-brick Georgian mansion began in 1755. The interior is among the finest to be seen in America, particularly for the beauty of the carving done by William Buckland, an indentured servant. George Mason, whom Thomas Jefferson called "the wisest man of his generation" developed the plantation, which now consists of 550 acres of gardens and woodlands. Mason wrote the Fairfax Resolves and the Virginia Bill of Rights. The boxwood gardens are extensive and a restored kitchen and schoolhouse merit a visit. Delightful museum and gift shop. Open daily 9:30 A.M.–5 P.M. Tours. Admission: adults $3; senior citizens, $2.50; children, $1.

The Octagon House. (See under *Museums.*)

The Old Stone House. 3051 M St., N.W., in Georgetown, 426-6851. Purported to be the oldest surviving building in the District of Columbia, the Old Stone House was completed in 1764, 14 years after Georgetown was founded. It typifies the substantial homes built by the early settlers in this area. Subsequent tenants enlarged and remodeled the house. The house is furnished with items typical of the period from 1765 to 1810. The gardens, in season, are delightful. Spinning demonstrations are presented. Open Wednesday–Sunday, 9:30 A.M.–5 P.M. Free. Group tours by appointment.

The Society of the Cincinnati or **Anderson House.** 2118 Massachusetts Ave., N.W., 785-0540. This enormous and palatial house was once the private residence of Ambassador and Mrs. Larz Anderson, who lived here between 1905 and 1937. Today it serves as headquarters of the Society of the Cincinnati, an organization composed of lineal male descendants of commissioned officers who served in the regular American Army or Navy during the Revolutionary War. Present membership is about 3,200. The first floor houses an outstanding collection of relics of the Revolution as well as a 10,000-volume reference library on the war. The magnificent formal rooms on the second floor are furnished in much the same way as they were when the Andersons lived there. Even today official Washington uses the House for formal receptions. Open July 1–Labor Day, Tuesday–Friday, 1–4 P.M.; rest of year, Tuesday–Saturday, 1–4 P.M. Library open Monday–Friday 10 A.M.–4 P.M. Free. (For groups of 20 or more a guided tour can be arranged.)

The Woodrow Wilson House. 2340 S St., N.W., 673-4034. This large Georgian-style brick house, located on one of Washington's prettiest streets, served as President Wilson's retirement home after his second term as President. He and his second wife, Edith Bolling Galt Wilson, moved here in 1921; he died on February 3, 1924, and is buried in the Washington Cathedral. At her death in 1961 the house was left to the National Trust for Historic Preservation as a memorial to the 28th President. On display are memorabilia from the Wilson era, including the brass shell that held the first shot fired by the American troops in World War I. Open Tuesday–Sunday, 10 A.M.–4 P.M. Admission: adults, $3.50; children, $2; National Trust members, free.

Mount Vernon. 16 miles south of Washington on George Washington Memorial Pkwy. in Virginia, (703) 780-2000. Despite its distance from the city, a visit to Mount Vernon, George Washington's plantation on the Potomac, is strongly recommended. An early arrival, whether by boat, car, or bus, is also recommended, as Mount Vernon may well be the most visited national shrine in America—10,000 visitors during the "season" is not at all unusual. Washington acquired the estate from the widow of his half-brother, Lawrence, in 1754 and over a period of years increased its size from 5,000 to 8,000 acres. It was divided into five farms, each with its own overseer and workers. About 125 slaves worked the farms; near the gift shop you may see one of the reconstructed slaves' quarters. Washington married Martha Custis, a widow with two children, in 1759. They lived the good life of Southern plantation owners here until 1775, when he left to assume command of the Continental Army. Until his death in 1799 he spent his happiest years at Mount Vernon, although many years were spent away from his home while serving as General and as President. There is much to be seen at Mount Vernon—the Bowling Green, laid out by Washington in 1785, the mansion itself, the many outbuildings, a delightful 18th-century formal garden, a museum, the kitchen, the vegetable garden, the carriage house, and, down the hill toward the boat landing, the tomb of George and Martha Washington. Today the estate looks very much as it did when the Washingtons lived there. In fine weather you may want to take a few minutes to sit in one of the Windsor chairs lined up on the portico and enjoy much the same view up and down the Potomac that the Washingtons enjoyed. In order to keep the view intact much of the valuable land across the river has been bought by the Federal government; other land has been donated by private individuals. Allow at least an hour and a half for your visit—then plan to travel south a few miles to see Woodlawn Plantation, Pohick Church, and Gunston Hall. Open daily 9 A.M.–5 P.M., March–October; 9 A.M.–4 P.M., November–February. Admission: adults, $5; senior citizens, $4; children, $2. This is a Tourmobile stop from June 1 to September 15.

Woodlawn Plantation. On Route 1, 13 miles south of Washington, and three miles south of Mount Vernon in Virginia. Those who visit Mount Vernon without driving the additional three miles south to Woodlawn Plantation deprive themselves of an unusual treat. From an architectural standpoint the house is noteworthy. Dr. William Thornton, who designed the original plans for the Capitol, was its architect. It was built for Washington's step-granddaughter, Nellie Custis, who married his favorite nephew Lawrence Lewis, on land that was originally part of the Mount Vernon estate. Even today you can see Washington's home from the house. Nellie Custis and her husband moved into a wing of the house in 1802; building was not completed until 1805. By 1839 her husband and six of her eight children had died, and she moved to her son's plantation in Clarke County, Virginia. Today the National Trust for Historic Preservation administers Woodlawn. If you are lucky you will be here at a time when one of three outstanding yearly events takes place at Woodlawn: needlework exhibit for several weeks in March; caroling by candlelight sometime in December; and a special outdoor evening in July for music, picnicking, and dancing. For details, call 780–4000. Admission: adults $4; children and senior citizens, $3. Open daily, 9:30 A.M.–4:30 P.M. Also on the grounds is the Pope-Leighey House, designed by Frank Lloyd Wright.

MOVIES. One of the handicaps to a revival of Washington's old downtown shopping area, as far as tourists are concerned, is that it doesn't have a single movie house, except the kind that plays X-rated films. The old Capitol, Palace, and RKO-Keith's, with their massive auditoriums and mighty pipe organs, are long gone.

There are still, however, a sizable number of thriving, smaller houses in peripheral areas frequented by tourists. In Georgetown are the **K-B Cerberus,** a three-screen house with first-run popular features; the **Biograph,** which frequently runs festivals of foreign films and classic films; and the four-screen **Key,** which also specializes in foreign movies.

The **Circle,** a longtime repertory tradition on Pennsylvania Avenue, has been demolished, but the nearby **Circle West End** theaters—four at 23rd and L Sts., N.W. and another three screens at 23rd and M—run a lot of arty and foreign first-runs.

In the Dupont Circle, 19th St. "Corridor" area, an ever-popular nightlife section, are the **K-B Janus,** a three-screen establishment with a penchant for imports; and the **K-B Fine Arts,** generally showing good U.S. films.

Mecca for film fans who regard the media as a serious art form is the **American Film Institute** at Kennedy Center. Almost everything shown here is part of a "festival." For example, you may find a Roman Polanski Festival followed by a Ginger Rogers-Fred Astaire Festival.

One of the more curious city film houses is the not-so-aptly named **American Theatre** in the L'Enfant Plaza complex. It shows nothing but Oriental, mostly Chinese, movies in the original language.

As in most American cities, most movie-going is now done in the suburbs, and most movie houses are part of shopping centers.

The chic White Flint shopping center in Bethesda, Md., for example, has a five-screen house with a variety of films chosen to appeal to widely different tastes.

Recently opened are movie theaters in The Mazza Gallerie (the shopping center at Wisconsin and Western Aves., N.W.); in the Foundry, on Thomas Jefferson St. in Georgetown, next to the Canal; and the Cineplex Odeon on Wisconsin Avenue. Theaters recently enlarged and/or refurbished include the *West End,* the *MacArthur* in the Palisades area, and the *Avalon,* uptown.

Both Washington newspapers carry complete listings of the area's movies, including show times and telephone numbers.

MUSIC. The best source of information for what's going on during your visit is the local newspapers. A tabloid, "Weekend," published with Friday's *Washington Post* is especially helpful.

A wealth of music is performed during the year in Washington and surrounding areas. Many concerts are free.

Cut-rate tickets may be obtained for theatrical and music performances on the day of the event at *Ticketplace,* 12th and F Sts., N.W., TIC–KETS, open Monday noon–2 P.M., Tuesday–Saturday, 11 A.M.–6 P.M. *Ticketron,* a computerized ticket service, handles a variety of Washington, Baltimore, and New York attractions. Their main office is at 1101 17th St., N.W., open Monday–Friday; 659–2601.

The John F. Kennedy Center for the Performing Arts opened in 1971 and since then the cultural life of the city has blossomed. In five halls, the *Opera House,* the *Concert Hall,* the *Eisenhower Theater,* the *Terrace Theater,* and the *American Film Institute Theater,* a tremendous variety of cultural events takes place in every season. Some nights all five houses are playing simultaneously to capacity audiences, but with staggered hours for the performances. Traffic and parking are handled with the minimum amount of confusion. For what is playing when, consult the *Washington Post* or *The Washington Times.* In most cases you can reserve tickets over the telephone and charge them on any one of several credit cards. Parking in garage under the Kennedy Center or at the nearby Watergate. For general information, call 254–3600.

The National Symphony Orchestra, conducted by Mstislav Rostropovich, performs a regular series of concerts from October through April at the Kennedy Center Concert Hall. A special Fourth of July concert before the firework display is presented each year on the plaza below the West Front of the Capitol. Free. For information, call 785–8100.

The D.A.R. Constitution Hall, 18th and D Sts., N.W., still is host to many concerts and recitals. Vladimir Horowitz, the great pianist, for example, prefers to play here. Watch the newspapers for announcements. For information, call 638–2661.

The Washington Performing Arts Society, for more than a generation under the leadership of Patrick Hayes, has booked the world's outstanding artists into Washington concert halls for a season extending from September through May, usually in the Kennedy Center theaters. For a current schedule write: WPAS, 1029 Vermont Ave., N.W., Suite 1100, Washington D.C. 20005, or call (202) 393–3600. Tickets to performances often may be picked up without advance reservations by arriving at the box office an hour before the show.

The Phillips Collection, 1600 21st St., N.W., presents free concerts and recitals Sundays at 5 P.M., mid-September–May in the living room of this small but choice gallery. No reservations, and only 120 seats (free), so come early. For information, call 387–0961.

The National Gallery of Art, 6th St. and Constitution Ave., N.W., offers free concerts Sundays at 7 P.M. in the East Garden Court. No reservations are necessary, but seating is limited. Starting in October and going on through most of June, you may combine an evening of art and music, and enjoy a snack in the cafeteria. For information, call 737–4215.

The Opera Society of Washington, in its 31st season, presented eight operas in 76 performances in the Kennedy Center's Opera House and more intimate Terrace Theater. The opera season runs from the end of October to the beginning of March. Call 822–4757 for details. For a brochure and booking instructions write: The Washington Opera, John F. Kennedy Center, Washington, D.C. 20566.

The Library of Congress, 1st St. and Independence Ave., S.E., presents chamber music concerts by the *Juilliard String Quartet* and others from September through April, one or two nights a week (usually Thursday and Friday). Reserve free tickets by calling 287–5502.

The Corcoran Gallery of Art presents a *Contemporary Music Forum* at 8 P.M. on the third Monday of each month from September–May. Music ranges from John Cage and Charles Ives to works by composers such as Sotireos Viahopoulos and Alti Heimir Sxeinsson. More information from The Corcoran Gallery of Art, 17th St. and New York Ave., N.W., Washington, D.C., 20006 (638–3211).

Wolf Trap Farm Park (the Filene Center), a half-hour drive from downtown off the Dulles Airport Access Highway in Vienna, Virginia, is the first national park dedicated to the performing arts. A magnificent red cedarwood amphitheater burned down in the spring of 1982 but has been rebuilt and was reopened in June 1984. Plan to take a picnic supper and enjoy it in this lovely setting before attending a program of ballet, opera, jazz, or dance. The rest of the year, the Barns at Wolf Trap offers an impressive schedule of nationally-known folk and acoustic acts in an intimate and appropriately rustic 350-seat indoor hall. For information, call 255–1860.

Merriweather Post Pavilion, Columbia, Md., presents a full schedule of musical entertainment during the summer months. Allow 50 minutes to get there from downtown Washington. For information, call 982–1800.

Band Concerts featuring the Army, Navy, and Marine Bands, and the Air Force Symphony Orchestra, are held during the summer months almost every night, June–August. See newspaper for which band is playing where. No tickets are required and seating is on a first-come, first-served basis. Free.

The service bands also perform several evenings a week at 8 P.M. on the Capitol steps—a memorable setting; free.

The Carter Barron Amphitheatre, 16th St. and Colorado Ave., N.W., in Rock Creek Park, 485–9666, sponsors a summer musical festival from June–August. Popular singers and entertainers, jazz and soul music are featured. This lovely out-of-doors theater in the heart of the park provides a fine natural setting for these performances. Saturday and Sunday nights only. Be sure to call for information and schedule. Plenty of free parking at 16th and Kennedy Sts. in the park.

The Smithsonian's Division of Performing Arts presents concerts in museums. For information, call "What is Going on at the Smithsonian?" (202) 357–1300.

STAGE AND REVUES.

The theaters on the following list are usually open during the entire year. However, it is wise to check the schedule of performances in a newspaper or by phone, as some productions are held over longer or are closed earlier than previously planned.

For notes on the *John F. Kennedy Center for the Performing Arts* and obtaining tickets through Ticketron and Ticketplace, see *Music.*

Operating at the same location since 1835, the **National Theater,** at 1321 E St., N.W., has played host to every president in office since then, with the exception of President Eisenhower. It presents pre- and post-Broadway plays. The Theater, closed for several years while undergoing a thorough facelift, opened in the fall of 1983 with the musical *42nd Street.* Now under the management of the Schuberts, it boasts a smashing new décor. For information, call 554–1900 or 628–6161.

The **Warner Theater,** 13th and E St., N.W., a former movie and vaudeville palace, now houses pop and jazz concerts, musicals and other entertainment. For information, call 626–1050.

The **Arena Stage** (theater-in-the-round) and its stepbrother, the **Kreeger Theater,** 6th and M sts., S.W., have excellent resident companies which present both new and established productions about eight times during the season. In the **Old Vat Room,** you may enjoy cabaret-style theater (most nights it's the longest- running one-man show in town, Stephen Wade's *Banjo Dancing*) while having drinks and snacks at your table. Usually closed late July–August, but check. Tickets may be reserved by telephone and picked up one half-hour before curtain time. For information on all three Arena stages, call 488–3300.

The **Folger Theater Group,** 201 East Capitol St., S.E., a professional theater group, presents both new plays and innovative productions of Shakespeare's plays. For information, call 546–4000.

Ford's Theater, 511 10th St., N.W., has been restored to the way it appeared the night Lincoln was shot in the presidential box, April 14, 1865. Plays with family appeal are emphasized. For information, call 347–4833.

Hartke Theater, Harewood Rd., N.E., on the grounds of Catholic University. Showcase of a distinguished university drama school. For information, call 635–5367.

At the **Sylvan Theater** on the grounds of the Washington Monument, big-band, military and pop-rock concerts are held during the summer, from early June through late August. The schedule changes, so see the newspapers for days and times. Lawn seating. 485–9666.

Olney Theater, Olney, Maryland—a 50-minute ride from downtown, presents traditional summer-theater fare in a pleasant converted barn located in this delightful, typical Maryland country town. For information, call 924–3400.

Washington also has a growing corps of scrappy and independent avant garde theater groups, including: **Source Theater** (with two stages, the Main Stage and the Warehouse Rep, at 1809 14th Street N.W.; 462–1073); **Horizons Theater** (with performances at Georgetown's Grace Episcopal Church, 1041 Wisconsin Ave. N.W.; 342–7706); and **Woolly Mammoth,** 1401 Church St., N.W.; 393–3939).

SHOPPING. Before Washington became a cosmopolitan city, less than a generation ago, Washingtonians went downtown to shop. Downtown meant seven short blocks of F St., N.W., between Seventh and 14th, and three blocks of Seventh St., from Pennsylvania Ave. to F. The shops and department stores in that L-shaped corridor offered all the practical necessities.

For those who had the necessities but wanted a little more—and could afford it—exclusive jewelry, fur, and leather goods shops dotted lower Connecticut Ave. They formed an elegant setting for the Easter Parade.

The more affluent took off for New York in search of high fashion. Bargain hunters drove to Baltimore.

Now, *haute couture* has moved to Washington. Designer fashions abound. Mexican wedding gowns, saris, dashikis, and Aran sweaters are also available, along with camel saddles, hookah, Waterford crystal, and Appalachian apple dolls.

The city has acquired branches of Saks Fifth Avenue, Lord & Taylor, and even Texas's Neiman-Marcus. Import shops and boutiques offer goods that range from the exotic to the bizarre, with prices to match.

In general, prices and quality rise east to west in the city. New shopping centers cluster around current or proposed Metro rail (subway) stops, just as wildly proliferating suburban malls hug the Capital Beltway.

Note: Washington, D.C. sales tax is 6 percent on general merchandise, 8 percent on food.

Downtown F Street

The old downtown shopping section is anchored by a brand new **Hecht Company** at 12th and G streets, plus a **Garfinckel's** at 14th St. and **Woodward & Lothrop's,** or "Woodies," as it is affectionately known to Washingtonians, occupying practically the entire block between F, G, 10th and 11th, with an annex across G St. accessible underground. (Deeper underground is Metro Center, the transfer point for all subway lines. Escalators rise to the store's center.)

Woodies has a wide range of merchandise, from designer fashions to budget items, furniture, bakery goods, and computers. They also provide services. There are now 16 Woodward & Lothrop satellite stores throughout the greater metropolitan Washington area. Hecht's new flagship store, one of few freestanding department stores built in any American downtown area in a decade, offers a similar mix of merchandise as Woodies. There are 15 Hecht's outlets around the metropolitan area.

Hecht's, offers as wide a range of goods and services as Woodies but caters to less traditional tastes. Some of its departments have taken on a disco air in the last few years.

At the far end of F St., N.W. at the corner of 14th St. stands **Garfinckel's,** a distinctive specialty store largely for women, but with a small selection of men's wear. Garfinckel's is proud of its carriage trade, and attempts to treat each customer "like a guest." This grand old lady of F St. was founded in 1902.

The rest of the six-block stretch of F St. has specialty shops—clothing, records, food, jewelry. A good many are on the tacky side, but some old favorites retain their quality. Prices are generally moderate. **Rich's Shoe Store,** a family-run business in the downtown area for 113 years, is across the street at 1321. **Reeves Bakery & Restaurant** at 1209 is the place to stop for coffee and a piece of their famous strawberry pie or devil's food cake, when you want to take a break from shopping.

Two new tourist attractions are the group of shops located in *The Pavilion* at the Old Post Office, 1100 Pennsylvania Ave., N.W. and *The Shops at National Place,* in the sprawling new complex between F, G, 13th and 14th streets which also houses the J.W. Marriott and the National Press Building. At both these pleasant and bustling mini-malls, you will find clothing boutiques, toy, stationery, candy, jewelry and hat shops, and others. Having exhausted yourself shopping, have a snack or a meal at one of the attractive restaurants.

Lower Connecticut Avenue

Connecticut Avenue has class. The tone is set at the start of this broad thoroughfare by the elegant Mayflower Hotel, just north of L Street, with its own branch of **Cartier.**

Most of the wall-to-wall-carpeted shops look, feel, and smell—and are—expensive, and the aristocrats of the trade. This rarefied atmosphere lasts for less than three blocks, and then the boutiques and stores tend to become trendy and more colorful, up to Florida Ave.

Within these exclusive precincts on the avenue's east side, **Camalier & Buckley,** north of De Sales at 1141, offers leather goods and a number of non-leather gift items, all top-notch.

At 1147 Connecticut Ave., N.W., **Wellington Jewels,** displayed in an elegant setting, has flagrantly fake "gems." They are presented with a fine flair and look expensive, but compared to the real thing, are not. Proof positive is a look at the real, real thing at the **Tiny Jewel Box,** at 1143. In the next block, at 1213, **Pampillonia** offers fine jewelry and does custom design.

Should you feel the need of a quick grooming before entering these hallowed walls, **Elizabeth Arden** is waiting at 1147 Connecticut Ave., N.W.

(an address shared with Wellington). After beautification, she also provides costume jewelry and couture fashions. Next door is the veddy British **Burberry's,** with raincoats and woollens for men and women, and there's a new **Jaeger** shop for women on the northeast corner of Connecticut and M.

Other upscale clothing stores in the area include **Claire Dratch** at 1009 Connecticut and **Rizik** at 1260, offering designer clothes for women. Ralph Lauren's **Polo Shop** for men and women is at 1220, and **Britches,** at 1219, carries spiffy clothes for the man about town. Its **Britches for Women** shop on the northwest corner of Connecticut and M does the same for stylish career women. And for kids, there's **The Kid's Closet** at 1226.

The tone changes as Connecticut goes north and dips under Dupont Circle. There are numerous restaurants along here, and some shops of interest—notably **Trocadero Asian Art** at 1501. **Uzzolo** at 1718 has trendy Italian furnishings, and **Ginza** at 1721 has all manner of fine things Japanese.

For those who hunger and thirst after pâté, a little quiche, a split of wine, and intellectual stimulation, try **Kramer Books and Afterwords,** 1517 Connecticut—browsy bookstore in front, a casual café in rear.

Metrorail serves both ends of this shopping area: Blue Line, Farragut West stop (walk one block north to Connecticut and K); Red Line, Farragut North stop for lower Connecticut, Dupont Circle stop for northern end.

Georgetown

The trouble with Georgetown is that it charms you into thinking you actually *need* a hand-carved hummingbird feeder, and a matched pair of fish poachers ($70, marked down from $150), and a Mexican tin mask, and genuine leather cowboy boots, and carry-out croquembouche.

Georgetown has created a world unto itself, and a seductive world it is. Its shops and its shoppers have the mixed-culture, multinational look of a port city, which it was, of course, when the nation's capital was a dismal swamp.

On its crowded, narrow streets, St. Laurent suits stroll next to cutoffs and sexplicit T-shirts; saris brush against dashikis; British pith helmets pass beaded cornrows. Nobody stares. And everybody is eating—ice cream, cookies, Napoleons, madeleines. Georgetown shoppers eat constantly, and no wonder: It has the best gourmet food in the entire city. Much of it is carry-out.

The two main shopping corridors are M St. from 28th to 35th, and Wisconsin Ave. north to about R St. Shops spill over into many of the side streets, especially between M and the river to the south. Sometimes one small doorway opens into a whole complex of shops, or a narrow stairway leads to unexpected riches. Georgetown is full of surprises. Explore. Enjoy.

Parking in Georgetown's narrow, heavily traveled streets is difficult, but not impossible. Note that there's no parking allowed on Georgetown's main streets Saturday nights. Police are vigilant and speedy with the tickets. To help shoppers, the free Georgetown "Trolley" runs (on rubber wheels) along M St. and Wisconsin Ave., covering the area described here about every half hour between 10:30 A.M. and 3:30 P.M. Tuesday–Saturday.

Watch for the green and white signs and listen for the clanging bell. It looks like a San Francisco cable car, and is great fun to ride. Its terminals are 24th & M to the east and the Rosslyn stop over the river in Virginia. There are no Metro stops in Georgetown proper. The two nearest stops are in Rosslyn, Virginia, and Foggy Bottom, 23rd and I St., N.W. (a 10-minute walk from Georgetown).

Georgetown's shopkeepers generally stay home on Mondays, and come in on weekdays after 10 A.M.

Especially Recommended on M St.

Junior League Shop, 3037. First-rate clothing for women and children at secondhand prices. Cast-offs of the wealthy. No credit cards.

In the Bag, 3106. Every conceivable kind of carryall, from totes to backpacks.

The Kite Site, 3106 upstairs. Every kind of kite imaginable, and more.

Earl Allen, 3109. Exquisite classic suits, sweaters, dresses for the young and not-so-young professional woman, in all natural fibers.

The Door Store, 3140 (fabric store at 3146). A do-it-yourself furniture store. Kits for bookcases, chairs, etc. Custom-built butcher-block tables a specialty.

Georgetown Pipe and Tobacco, 3144. Heady aroma of fine tobacco, great pipe selection. Has what this country needs: A good five-cent cigar (if damaged). Others up to $4 apiece.

Laura Ashley, 3213. English fabrics, wallpaper, home furnishings, ladies garments, all natural fibers, all very British and beautiful.

Outstanding Shops on Wisconsin Ave.

Conran's, at foot of Wisconsin, via wooden ramp over the Canal; entrance also on Grace Street. Brightly colored contemporary accents for the home—drapes, bedspreads, lamps, huge array of kitchen needs and furniture.

Bowl and Board, 1066. Butcher blocks, birdhouses, salad bowls, toys, in wood.

Red Balloon, 1073. Imaginative toys and some children's clothing.

Britches Great Outdoors, 1225. Boots, cowboy hats, and britches, of course, for the Marlboro Man. (A more urban man's Britches of Georgetown is at 1247 Wisconsin.)

Georgetown Coffee, Tea and Spice, 1330. A very special little store that makes you want to believe that the aromatic coffees, teas, and spices are just off the boat from exotic places—and some actually are. Imported goodies from all over the world line the shelves and spill out of the open bins. Also coffee grinders, fish poachers, copper bowls, and other kitchen luxuries. A chalk-written sign on a small blackboard out front announces each day's latest delectable arrival. Shoppers seeking Christmas stocking stuffers look no further. This is the place.

Francis-Reilly, 1361. An elegant, rather English-accented children's clothing and toy shop.

Peter's Flowerland. 1365. Open late (like everyplace hereabouts). Stop and smell the eucalyptus, at least.

Appalachian Spring. 1415. Folk art, crafts, pottery, quilts, and jewelry.

Little Caledonia, 1419. A miracle of merchandising good taste and quality, with a staggering variety of items—china, *objets d'art,* cooking wares, toys, cards, stationery, lamps, fabrics, outdoor furniture. All manage to keep their dignity and class in a space no larger than the ground floor of a long town house.

Commander Salamander. 1420. Everything for Madonna wanna-be's: crinolines, punk hair pieces, colored hairspray, wild T-shirts, and funky cheap jewelry.

The Phoenix, 1514. The best offerings from Mexico in candelabra, tin masks and other handwork, serapes, rugs, and brilliant fabrics. Women's clothing ranging from white, hand-tucked, demure wedding gowns to flamboyant explosions of color in Mexican cotton. A first-class shop.

Other Georgetown Finds

Distinctive shopping centers are rising like French bread, especially along Georgetown's historic C & O Canal, just south of M Street. Each of the malls has a parking garage. The most spectacular addition is **Georgetown Park,** with 120 elegant shops and restaurants opening onto two balconied levels and the ground-floor promenade—all under a glass dome, and decorated with 1890s-style ironwork "aged" with a lovely green patina. It is located on the south side of M St., between 32nd and 33rd, and reaches out to *Conran's* by bridge over the Canal in the rear. A new wing adds 40 shops on two levels overlooking fountains and cherub-topped pillars. Notable shops include: *The White House,* all-white clothing and accessories for women; *The Sharper Image,* high-tech gadgets; and *Schoofs Belgian Chocolates* and coffee bar.

Georgetown Court, a half block west of Wisconsin Ave., between Prospect and N, has 25 shops, restaurants, and galleries, and a courtyard where you can rent croquet mallets and play a game on an Astroturf lawn. *Robin Weir & Co.,* hairdressers to the rich and powerful (including Nancy Reagan) is here, along with the *Galerie des Parfums, Jaeger,* and *The Mineral Kingdom,* selling semiprecious stones in elegant settings. *Au Croissant Chaud* at the N Street entrance has early-morning coffee and croissants, which you can eat at an outdoor table.

Other notable shops in Georgetown include:

Booked Up, at 1209 31st St., just north of M St., is a favorite. It has the look of an Edwardian library, clutter and all. Rare books only. No credit cards.

Across the street, at 1220 31st, is the **Old Print Gallery,** featuring original 18th- and 19th-century American prints. Also framing.

Hats in the Belfry, at 1237 Wisconsin, sells funny, elegant, weird, or conservative hats for all occasions and seasons.

Martins, at 1304 Wisconsin, is where Washington brides register for the finest in crystal, china, and silver.

Urban Outfitters, at 3111 M St., is a collection of boutiques in a former Woolworth's. Funky young clothes, T-shirts, jewelry, novelties. Stays open late, and it's fun to browse and watch the crowd.

Museum Shops

The museum shops offer some of the best buys in the city. They sell quality items that are unquestionably what they are claimed to be, and are charming, in addition. Think ahead to Christmas.

The **National Museum of American History** entrances on Constitution Ave. and the Mall, between 12th and 14th Sts., N.W., has a children's toyshop, bookshop, and handicraft shop. All feature things related to exhibits in the museum, with emphasis on handcrafts, such as folk toys, needlepoint kits, signed and dated pottery, Russian hand-painted boxes, and hobby kits. Mostly American.

The **National Museum of Natural History,** entrances on Constitution Ave. and the Mall, at 10th St., N.W., also offers a great deal of handcrafted work—Japanese porcelain, African wood carving, Mexican textiles, Chinese painted straw items, plus rocks and minerals and jewelry. Also books on natural history.

The **National Air and Space Museum,** entrances on Independence Ave. and the Mall, at 7th St., S.W., naturally presents articles related to rockets, winged craft, and outer space. Some spectacular posters, and a whole kite section. Don't miss the Astronaut freeze-dried ice cream.

The **Arts and Industries Museum,** next door to the Castle, on the Mall, has a shop that features action toys, antique reproduction toys and books, kites, gyroscopes, and model kits, plus lively books on American history.

The new **Museum of African Art** and the **Arthur M. Sackler Gallery of Asian and Oriental Art** both have shops featuring gifts and reproductions reflecting their subject areas.

The **Hirshhorn Museum and Sculpture Garden** on the Mall, with an entrance to the building at Independence Ave. at 7th, S.W., specializes in 20th-century art related to the Hirshhorn's exhibits.

The **Freer Gallery,** entrance on the Mall only—at the west side of the Castle—has a small shop focusing on Oriental *objets d'art.*

The **National Gallery of Art,** Constitution Ave. at 6th, N.W., entrances on the Mall and 5th St., offers shoppers two golden opportunities: one in the main building, the other in the underground passage leading to the East Building. The former is unsurpassed for reproductions of the Gallery's masterpieces, from postcards to posters. It also has a few reproductions of sculpture, and a number of art books. The shop in the passageway is less extensive, and reflects the modern art of the East Building. Exhibition catalogs are also on sale at other locations.

The **Renwick Gallery,** 1661 Pennsylvania Ave., N.W., has a small but inviting shop featuring folk arts and crafts.

The **National Portrait Gallery,** 8th and F Sts., N.W., and **National Museum of American Art** feature a shop for each. The latter specializes in American fine arts books and related children's books. The Portrait Gallery shop has pewter, silver, glassware and portraits.

The **Indian Craft Shop,** located in the Interior Department Building, 1801 C St., N.W., is devoted to presenting the best in American Indian arts and crafts—jewelry, carvings, pottery, baskets, sand paintings, Kachinas, and a choice selection of Navajo rugs.

National Geographic Society, 17th and M Sts., N.W., has, as everyone knows, the best maps available. They are for sale on regular or heavy chart paper, in addition to globes, National Geographic books and records with an international flavor.

Folger Shakespeare Library, 201 East Capitol St., has a collection of whimsical, Bard-related greeting cards that would delight the heart of any Shakespeare buff. It also offers books, maps, and other reminders of the Elizabethan Age, plus T-shirts with funny quotes from the plays, such as "Tush, tush! Fear Boys with BUGS!"

Library of Congress, First and East Capital St., has a fabulous collection of recordings for sale—unknown to most visitors or even natives. The Recorded Sound Division will let you look over its catalogue of Folk Recordings and Spoken Recordings to make selections. Oral history, poetry, speeches, and music from America and foreign countries.

Organization of American States' Pan American Gift Shop, 17th and Constitution Ave., N.W., overflows with colorful and beautiful gifts and clothing accessories handmade in Latin America.

Commercial Galleries

There seems to be a limitless number of commercial art galleries in Washington, each changing exhibits every few weeks, and many changing their addresses every few months. Consequently, we have selected only those highly respected (and firmly entrenched) galleries considered by experts to be the most representative of the Washington art world.

Franz Bader Inc., 1701 Pennsylvania Avenue, N.W., 659–5515, is one of the oldest commercial galleries in the Washington area. Bader represents a number of established Washington artists. There are frequent exhibits of paintings, drawings, or sculpture, plus portfolios and racks of art work. Some artists associated with the gallery are: Peter Milton, Lee Weiss, Robert Marx, and Herman Maril. The gallery also has a fine collection of Canadian Eskimo carvings and prints. Tuesday–Saturday, 10 A.M.–6 P.M.

Middendorf, 2009 Columbia Rd., N.W., 462–2009, specializes in 20th-Century American paintings, sculpture, and prints. The gallery represents such Washington artists as Sam Gilliam, William Christenberry, Otto Natzler, and Leon Berkowitz, and exhibits the work of other contemporary American artists. Tuesday–Friday, 11 A.M.–6 P.M.; Saturday, 11 A.M.–5 P.M. By appointment only in August.

Fendrick Gallery, 3059 M St., N.W., 338–4544, focuses on important contemporary American art—prints, sculpture, and eclectic works, including such exhibits as: Furniture as Art, by Wendell Castle; Iron as Art, by Albert Paley; and Art to Wear, by Sao. Tuesday–Saturday, 9:30 A.M.–5:30 P.M. (Closed weekends in July and August.)

Gallery K, 2010 R St., N.W., 234–0339, features paintings and drawings by talented young artists from all over the world, many of them surrealists. Also exhibits established American artists of the '50s, such as Robert Motherwell, Jackson Pollock, Richard Lindner, and Edward Dugmore. Tuesday–Saturday, 11 A.M.–6 P.M.

Jane Haslem Gallery, 406 7th St., N.W., 638–6162, shows American works from 1900 to the present, with a focus on graphics. Some of the artists represented include Mauricio Lasansky, Gabor Peterdi, and Mark Tobey. Haslem also offers a unique collection of original political cartoons and comic strips. Tuesday–Saturday, 10:30 A.M.–5:30 P.M.

Hom Gallery, 2103 O St., N.W., 466–4076, specializes in fine prints and works on paper from the late 15th to the 20th century. Jem Hom is one of the most knowledgeable dealers in the country. Open Tuesday–Friday, 10 A.M.–5 P.M.; Saturday, 10 A.M.–2 P.M.

Seventh St., between Pennsylvania Ave. and F St., N.W. is being reborn as a mecca for the arts. **Washington Project for the Arts** at 434 7th St., N.W., now has art galleries, a small theater, and moveable feasts of dance, painting, sculpture, photography, and other related exhibitions, including a book store for and about artists. There are also other small galleries up and down 7th St., N.W.

Choice, Out-of-the-Way Shops

Some of these are very old Washington institutions. Some are spanking new. All are choice.

Washington Cathedral's Herb Cottage, Gift and Book Shop, London Brass Rubbing Center, and Greenhouse, Wisconsin and Massachusetts Ave., N.W., 537–6267, within the Cathedral Close. The *Herb Cottage,* nestled next to the Bishop's Garden across the driveway from the Cathedral, smells of lavender and cinnamon and rosemary, and looks like a Beatrix Potter creation. Gifts, cards, toys, candles, tea, tea sets, tea cozies, and every kind of herb and spice. The *Gift and Book Shop,* in the Cathedral's undercroft, has a fine collection of cathedral glass bowls, pitchers, and window hangings at reasonable prices; religious items in good taste; Christmas cards, records, and books on the finest in medieval and contemporary religious art and music. Within the *Gift Shop,* there is a very popular brass-rubbing section where, for a nominal fee, you can do your own rubbings of Elizabethan and medieval brasses. The *Greenhouse,* east of the Cathedral, sells potted plants and shrubs and English ivy. All open 7 days a week, except the Herb Cottage, which is closed Sunday.

Eastern Market, Seventh St. at North Carolina Ave., S.E., is another old Washington institution, where produce and meat stands offer such delicacies as pheasant and quail, as well as farm eggs and Potomac oysters in season. On Saturdays, farmers set up stalls and globe-trotting merchants set up their wares from Peru, China, and Africa, along with local craftspeople. At Christmas, the Market is green with wreaths and holly for sale. Across from the market, on Seventh St., and south on Eighth below Pennsylvania Ave., new shops are opening that cater to the new sophistication of the old Capitol Hill area.

Fish Market, at Maine Ave., S.W., just west of the 14th St. Bridge, brings in freshly caught seafood from the lower Potomac River and Chesapeake Bay, and sells it right off the boat. The seafood is incomparable; the stench unbearable on a hot, calm day. But most shoppers find it worth the sacrifice.

The Connecticut Connection, at Connecticut Ave. and L St., N.W., is a new complex for the "lunch crowd," centered around the Red Line Metrorail stop at Farragut North. On several levels, it includes restaurants, a health food shop, cookie and candy shops, a produce stand, a bakery, a newsstand, and a few clothing stores. All are small, resembling the shops in Montreal's underground complexes. And across the street is the new **Washington Square,** a glass-fronted complex with shops such as *Bally of Switzerland, Victoria's Secret, Pappagallo,* and *Chocolate Chocolate.*

Hotel Shops

A few of the first-class hotels have clusters of prestigious boutiques and specialty shops offering designer items and imports of the highest quality.

The largest is at **Watergate,** Virginia and New Hampshire Aves., N.W., just east of Kennedy Center. In fact, Watergate has two shopping complexes—*Les Champs,* featuring furs, crystal, antiques, jewels, graphics, and designer fashions in awesomely elegant boutiques; and *Water Gate Mall,* on the lower level of the Watergate apartment building, with some shops facing Virginia Ave. *The Mall* has specialty shops and all the necessities for daily living.

L'Enfant Plaza Hotel, 480 L'Enfant Plaza East (off Independence Ave., S.W., south of the Smithsonian Castle) is in the midst of a plaza that includes a large shopping complex on the lower level—clothes, restaurants, records, books, stationery, food, and jewelry.

Willard Hotel, Pennsylvania Ave. and 14th St., N.W. This restored grand hotel also offers an upscale shopping complex with an outdoor fountain and lush landscaping. There's *Neuchatel* for Belgian chocolates, *Mondi* for women's wear, and *MCM* for top-of-the-line imported leather luggage. And there's *Jackie Chalkley* for American designer jewelry and clothing, the patriotic *Wicker & Hicks,* the *American Store,* for American-made natural-fiber clothes, pottery, and linens.

Sidewalk Stands

Shops without walls are mushrooming throughout Washington. After a threat to close them down, which was quickly withdrawn, they are spreading across the city, adding a bohemiam—and often colorfully ethnic—touch to the usually dignified city.

The streets around the reflecting pool at the foot of Capitol Hill are lined with open-sided vending trucks offering a remarkably similar line of tourist "attractions": Washington T-shirts, film, fast food, drinks, and the usual gimmicky souvenirs.

Open-air stands of the card-table variety abound in Georgetown, along Wisconsin Ave., setting up shop on the spur of the moment, and leaving just as unpredictably. The usual fare is the ubiquitous T-shirt with a message, or ethnic clothing, jewelry, hats, art work, and crafts.

F St., N.W., just west of Seventh, has a spurt of such stands from time to time. And they also cluster at the corner of 17th and K, Connecticut and L and 19th and M Sts. The food vendors here are a little more exotic than those on Capitol Hill—they sell Chinese egg rolls, shish kebab, and yogurt. Also, popcorn has become a big item among the health-conscious downtown professional community.

Despite their precarious position in the world of merchandising, they seem to make more sales in an hour than the name-brand stores make in a month. Different strokes for different folks.

Chevy Chase

Washington's newest center for shopping clusters around Wisconsin and Western Aves., on the D.C.-Maryland line, in the area known as Friendship Heights. The top retail giants have brought their stores and prestige into a roughly three-block triangle, convenient to the more affluent uptown citizens and the close-in suburbanites. The triangle now has its own Metro stop, also.

Woodward & Lothrop's (Chevy Chase branch of downtown Woodies) is at the northwest corner of Wisconsin and Western; **Lord & Taylor's** is up a block on Western; **Saks Fifth Avenue** is a block north on Wisconsin; and **Neiman-Marcus** is in the sparkling new Mazza Gallerie on Wisconsin between Jennifer and Western.

Mazza Gallerie is a shopping complex on four levels, with status shops ringing tiers of balconies surrounding an open concourse. In addition to *Neiman-Marcus* and *Raleigh's* for clothing, it offers specialty shops such as the *Tennis Lady* for court clothes, the *Tinder Box* for tobacco, *Saville of London* for impeccable tailoring, *Pierre Deux* for charming French prints by-the-yard, *Williams-Sonoma* for unusual kitchen items, *F.A.O. Schwarz* for imaginative toys, and *Swensen's Ice Cream Factory* for calories. For the really spectacular in chocolates, there is *Kron Chocolatier,* from which you may purchase a lifesize chocolate leg (female) with garter, that costs an arm and a leg but is fun. Their chocolate-covered fruits are devilishly expensive, divinely delicious.

At 4400 Jennifer St., the **Jennifer Mall** features *Crown (discount) Books* and *Nettle Creek* custom decorating. In the next block, toward Wisconsin Ave., at 4350 Jennifer, *Herman's World of Sporting Goods* flexes its muscles and caters to joggers, canoers, campers, and other outdoor types.

Occupying a large area of the northeast corner of Wisconsin and Western, **Chevy Chase Center** stores seem unperturbed by the newcomers. They were the pioneers in this part of town. The Center consists of individual specialty shops—clothing, jewelry, shoes, leather, fabrics, hardware—that are, for the most part, satellites of original, long-established downtown stores.

The same holds true for several of the shops that stretch out along approximately two blocks on the west side of Wisconsin. Starting with **The Gap** at 5430 Wisconsin Ave. (if you are "into" jeans and casual wear), you may run the gamut all the way up to the rarefied atmosphere of **Brooks Brothers,** 5500 Wisconsin Ave., for men, and **Saint Laurent Rive Gauche** at 5510 Wisconsin Ave., for the ultimate in brand-name dropping. In addition, **Saks-Jandel** furs and Saks-Jandel ladies apparel are both there to serve you, a few doors apart at 5512 and 5514. Gucci's is at 5504.

Abundant parking is available; abundant cash or proper credit cards advisable. Dedicated shoppers, however, can pick up remarkable bargains of highest quality merchandise at fine clothing stores by watching for end-of-season sales, especially between Christmas and New Year's, when these exclusive shops take on the look of a Woolworth's on an average Saturday.

Betweeen sales, go anyway—to browse, to dream, perchance to buy. The quality of their merchandise, is, after all, what made the name for the name-brands.

NIGHTLIFE AND BARS. When twilight falls over the nation's capital, the city continues to hum—an art opening at the Corcoran, dinner dances along Embassy Row, a celebrity gala at the Kennedy Center, a book-signing party in Georgetown. And though the sounds and motions may not be as bright and frenzied as, say, those of Broadway, Washington is certainly no longer the sleepy Southern town it was several decades back.

The fact is that both the city and the people drawn to it have changed dramatically over the last 30 years. Washingtonians often play as hard as they work—whether their office is in the White House, a federal agency, a local university, or a downtown law firm. And many times the "play" is nothing more than an extension of work—drinks and a show with clients or handling delicate negotiations over a glass of riesling at a wine bar. But when Washingtonians do leave the pressure and intense competition behind, there are plenty of diversions from which to choose—dancing cheek-to-cheek to the Big Band sounds, joining a sing-along at an Irish pub, doing the two-step to the twang of country music, or attending an avant-garde dinner theater.

The after-work crowd generally heads to one of three areas of the city where nightspots cluster—Georgetown, Capitol Hill, or that portion of the downtown business district, known as "the 19th Street Corridor," the rough parameters being 19th Street from Pennsylvania Ave. north to Dupont Circle. The Happy Hour action is particularly intense in this last area, as young professionals flee their offices to wind their way through various bars and to take advantage of reduced price drinks and free hors d'oeuvres. Georgetown has been beset by some teenage rowdiness, but the police patrol the area heavily—and on weekend nights have instituted a parking bar in the area around the Wisconsin and M crossroads to relieve congestion.

Elsewhere around the city and its suburbs, there are magic acts and bluegrass bands and comedy revues and superior jazz clubs to suit almost anyone's fancy. Though not a comprehensive guide to all of Washington's nightspots, the following are recognized favorites.

Take Note: Beer, wine, and liquor (by the drink) are available in the District of Columbia bars, cafés, and restaurants Sunday–Thursday until 2 A.M., Friday and Saturday until 3 A.M. Virginia and Maryland hours vary, so check by telephone if necessary. The newly instituted drinking age is 21, but those under-21s born before September 30, 1968, can consume beer and wine.

Jackets for men are required—or suggested—in most hotels and restaurants. Dress code in bars is usually a management "policy," for the most part, informal and casual. In this era of "dress jeans," you're on your own. There is ample parking late at night in some downtown locations in the District; however, you may have to resort to a parking garage in some congested areas. Many of the places mentioned may be reached by the Metro subway system (although the trains stop at midnight).

Beware of hookers and pickpocket artists on the 14th St. "strip" between H St., N.W., and Thomas Circle, also around the bus station. Incidentally, a few of the "ladies" are in drag.

Drinks in hotels are on the pricey side; that goes for many bars, too. In some cases, there is a drink minimum. Check it out or look for a table "tent."

To determine what performers are in town, consult the "City Lights" listing in the *Washingtonian* magazine, the "Weekend" section that appears on Friday in the *Washington Post* or in the free weekly alternative tabloid, *City Paper.*

19th Street Corridor Area Bars

The Bottom Line. 1716 I St., N.W.; 298–8488. A resident deejay draws a young crowd with oldies and top 40 tunes, guest bartender nights, dance contests, and trivia quizzes that have made The Bottom Line is a popular after-work spot downtown. Local sports personalities can often be spotted. After 5 festivities, 5–7:30 P.M., with reduced price drinks, hors d'oeuvres. Open Monday–Thursday, 11 A.M.–2 A.M.; Friday–Saturday, 11–3 A.M.; closed Sunday. AE, CB, DC, MC, V.

Deja Vu. 2119 M St., N.W.; 452–1966. The many rooms of this cavern-ous "Big Chill"-era dance club are often full, even a decade after opening adjacent to Blackie's House of Beef. The dance floor is very large, and very crowded, and the deejay loves to take requests—especially if the song was popular in 1969. AE, DC, MC, V.

Ha'Penny Lion. 1101 L St., N.W.; 296–8075. Happy hour brings out swarms of office workers for the free eats at this downtown bar and restau-rant. And when the crowd thins out, there's room for dancing. AE, MC, V.

Rumors. 1900 M St., N.W.; 466–7378. Brass bar railing, hanging plants, and an eager crowd of professionals make Rumors the quintessential 19th St. singles bar. In fact, this nightspot has not only spilled over into one enclosed sidewalk café, but the café has spawned a smaller open-air patio. A deejay spins oldies, top 40 hits, soul, and other sounds nightly. Free hors d'oeuvres Monday–Thursday during Happy Hour. Dancing every night—there's usually a band on Monday nights—and patrons are casual-ly dressed. Light menu of steaks, sandwiches, and salads available. AE, MC, V.

Sign of the Whale. 1825 M St., N.W.; 223–4152. Sign of the Whale has rapidly become the "in" place for young professionals. In fact, the bar seems to have more lawyers or paralegals per square inch than a copy of *Martindale Hubble*—not surprising considering it's plunked down right in the middle of Washington's legal ghetto. The music is taped, the crowd can get noisy, and the hors d'oeuvres are free at Happy Hour. Has won *Washingtonian* magazine's "best hamburger in town" award four years running. The Whale is also one of the latest to open a suburban branch in Northern Virginia, a la Deja Vu, Rumors, Bullfeathers, and Mr. Smith's. Mainly business attire during the week; the management encour-ages sports jackets on the weekends. AE, CB, DC, MC, V.

Georgetown Bars

Champions. 1206 Wisconsin Ave. N.W.; 965–4005. A museum's worth of sports paraphernalia—real retired Bullets and Capitals jerseys, bats, cleats, and more baseball and football cards than you can shake that hock-ey stick at—makes veteran Georgetown pub owner Mike O'Harro's ven-ture worth a sidetrip down the alley in the heart of Georgetown. And that's not even mentioning the decidedly upscale but fun-loving crowd. AE, DC, MC, V.

Clyde's. 3236 M Street, NW; 333–0294. Ask anyone—no matter if he is a native or an out-of-towner—about the quintessential Georgetown bar, and without exception the answer will be "Clyde's!" Certainly this restau-rant-cum-bar has spawned hundreds of imitators all across the country with its handsome atrium, highly polished brass, and tonier-than-thou crowd of college students, young professionals, and Washington notables. There is no entertainment *per se,* but the omelettes and the chance to min-gle at the two attractive bars are sufficient enticements. The dress is casual but runs decidedly to Polo shirts; in fact, Britches—the swank men's cloth-iers—purveys Clyde's chili along with Giorgio Armani suits. Between 4 P.M. and 7 P.M. it's "afternoon delights"—reduced price hors d'oeuvres. Among other enterprises, this Georgetown landmark opened a $5.2 mil-lion Virginia branch to the rave reviews of interior designers. *Clyde's at*

Tysons Corner (8332 Leesburg Pike, Vienna, Va.; 703–734–1901), with its leaded and stained glass partitions, mahogany and oak bars, and extensive collection of artwork has attracted such notables as Elizabeth Taylor and Senator John Warner when they were still a pair. AE, CB, DC, MC, V.

F. Scott's. 1232 36th St., N.W.; 965–1789. One of Washington's most stunning bars, F. Scott's transports its older, well-heeled clientele back in time with its elegant Art Deco design and dancing and music from the 30s and 40s. A favorite spot with Hollywood notables like Warren Beatty, Donald Sutherland, and Meryl Streep. Sports coats for men required; the crowd is chic and so is the dress. Valet parking a boon in crowded Georgetown. Recently purchased and renovated by Clyde's, along with the adjacent French restaurant **1789** and Georgetown student hangout, **The Tombs.** AE, CB, DC, MC, V.

J. Paul's. 3218 M St. N.W.; 333–3450. A place to see and be seen, J. Paul's is mostly an update on the upwardly mobile Clyde's look, with a slightly more ambitious menu and a better view from the bar of the passing show out on M Street (and vice versa). AE, CB, DC, MC, V.

Paul Mall. 3235 M St. N.W.; 965–5353. The quintessential Georgetown college bar, with live top-40 bands on stage every night. On weekends there's almost always a line formed in front of the big guys at the door. AE, DC, MC, V. Similar to the likewise long-standing **Crazy Horse,** just up the block at 3259 M St. N.W., but not quite as loud and a little less casual.

Capitol Hill Bars

Bullfeathers. 410 1st St., S.E.; 543–5005. This Capitol Hill restaurant and watering hole was voted the city's most popular new bar by the *Washingtonian* magazine, and for good reason. Its handsome dark woodwork and etched glass partitions make it a perfect spot to unwind from those long Senate subcommittee meetings. What's more, the atmosphere is lively and nonpartisan, and Bullfeathers is packed on weekends, with the overflow seated at the sidewalk café. AE, DC, MC, V.

The Hawk 'n Dove. 329 Pennsylvania Ave., S.E. 543–3300. A friendly watering hole in the shadow of the U.S. Capitol dome, frequented by legislative aides, Capitol Hill residents, and members of the press, but don't be surprised if you see an occasional Congressman. Basic pub food is served, and prices are reasonable. AE, CB, DC, MC, V.

Jenkins Hill. 223 Pennsylvania Ave., S.E.; 544–6600. When the city fathers started casting around for a spot on which to build the Capitol, they turned to Jenkins Hill from which this immensely popular pub takes its name. The bar is a favorite with the Hill crowd, old *Washington Star* reporters, and media types. Saturday night music is provided by Nards, starting at 9 P.M. when a deejay spins tunes from the 50s, 60s, and 70s. There's dancing—even on the tables—and a youngish crowd decked out in alligator shirts lines up outside the door to join in the fun. Lobster night, Thursday, $8.95, 6 P.M. until the lobsters go. AE, MC, V.

Tune Inn. 331½ Pennsylvania Ave., S.E.; 543–2725. A fern-and-blondwood singles' bar this isn't. In fact, the Tune Inn fits more easily into the hole-in-the-wall category. Nonetheless, this unpretentious bar is a favorite with Capitol Hill residents, newspaper people, and such visiting celebrities as Robert Redford. A country-music jukebox provides the music, the friendly crowd provides the entertainment, and the kitchen serves up a mean—and inexpensive—cheeseburger. No credit cards.

Tunnicliff's Tavern. 222 7th St., S.E.; 546–3663. Handsome and friendly bar and restaurant across from Eastern Market and famous for its mesquite grill. Outdoor cafe. AE, CB, DC, MC, V.

Irish Pubs

The Dubliner. 520 North Capitol St., N.E.; 737–3773. Located across from Union Station, the Dubliner is without a doubt the most attractive Irish bar in town, with its muted green walls, handsome woodwork, and two bars. Capitol Hill toilers in business attire pile in for Guinness on tap after work; many of the 20- to 60-year-old crowd join in the singing when the live entertainment starts every night around 9 P.M. and goes on until closing. On Sunday, the music begins early—at 3 P.M. Good, substantial pub food like Beef O'Flaherty and fish-and-chips is served. AE, DC, MC, V.

Gallagher's Pub. 3319 Connecticut Ave., N.W.; 686–9189. It may have Harp on tap and bill itself as an Irish bar, but Gallagher's also offers a variety of live entertainment, from bluegrass to rock 'n roll. Monday the Washington Folklore Society holds traditional open mike, with various members performing. Sunday, Wednesday, and Thursday, folk and blues can be heard. On Friday and Saturday, there are local folk and pop groups. No cover and no drink minimum. The bar's informal, laid-back atmosphere attracts a diverse group of patrons, most of whom are in their '20s and '30s. AE, DC, MC, V.

Ireland's Four Provinces. 3412 Connecticut Ave., N.W.; 244–0860. This neighborhood Irish bar, with its daily selection of live entertainment, draws everyone from families with small children to singles. Performers kick off the music at 9 P.M., swinging from ballads to lively jigs and encouraging the crowd to join in the singing. There is also a video game room and two dart lanes, plus Guinness Stout and Harp on tap. Typical Irish fare—lamb chops and fish-and-chips—is served. AE, MC, V.

Ireland's Own. 132 North Royal St., Alexandria; 549–4535. Old Town Alexandria may have been founded by Scottish settlers, but today it boasts two Irish bars. Ireland's Own is popular with a youngish after-work crowd as well as the neighborhood regulars. Local Irish performers play Tuesday through Saturday starting at 9 P.M., and Sunday and Monday at 9 P.M. Among the regular performers is the exceedingly entertaining Seamus Kennedy whose rendition of "Bang the Drum Slowly" is "soulful enough to make you weak," according to *Washingtonian* magazine. There is no cover or drink minimum. Full menu served. Weekday Happy Hour features reduced-price drinks and free hors d'ouevres. AE, DC, MC, V.

Matt Kane's Bit 'OJ Ireland. 1118 13th St., N.W.; 638–8058. To say this working-class Irish bar is a Washington fixture is an understatement. For years it's attracted a loyal following that includes Marines on leave from Quantico (the bus station is close by) to House Speaker Tip O'Neill, who officially opened the stone-clad upstairs pub back in 1963. Closed Sunday. No credit cards.

Murphy's. 713 King St., Old Town Alexandria; 548–1717. One of the liveliest nightspots in Old Town, Murphy's packs in a boisterous, fun-loving crowd of neighborhood regulars and young professionals. Local

Irish bands like The Irish Breakdown perform Tuesday through Saturday starting at 9 P.M. There's another performer upstairs on Friday and Saturday; otherwise the upstairs is open just for regular dart tournaments. The patrons sing along, occasionally pounding the tables in time to the music. There is Irish beer and whiskey plus a few native dishes—stew and mixed grill—on the mostly American menu. Open 11–2 A.M. seven days a week. AE, DC, MC, V.

Gay Bars

D.C. Eagle. 639 New York Ave., N.W.; 347–6025. This gay bar runs heavily to the leather-and-Levi's set. There is no live entertainment, but taped music and reduced-price drinks during the weekdays Happy Hour ensure its popularity with the 21- to 35-year-old patrons. AE, MC. V.

The Fraternity House. 2122 P St., N.W. (Rear); 223–4917. This gay hangout, with its four bars and game rooms, attracts a young, collegiate crowd, many of whom come to make new friends. There are two cruise bars and a disco downstairs (which starts at 9 P.M.), and upstairs two other bars offer full-length films, pinball and video games, and pool tables. Soup and light meals are served. The mostly male crowd, a number of whom are dressed in Western garb, range in age from 21 to 35. Those in business attire will feel uncomfortable here. No credit cards.

The Lost and Found. 56 L St., S.E.; 488–1200. This secluded, very attractive bar draws a preppily dressed crowd of young gay professionals who come to dine, mingle, and dance. The dance floor, with a deejay spinning disco and operating a light show, is a popular attraction. In addition to a restaurant, there is an attic game room and an outdoor deck where food and drinks are served. AE, MC, V.

Tracks D.C. 1111 First St., S.E.; 488–3320. A predominantly gay dance bar that attracts partygoers from New York to North Carolina. The funky music and live entertainment also attract the straight crowd. Dancing till 2 A.M. during the week, till 6 A.M. on Friday and Saturday. Cover ranges from $3 to $8. No credit cards.

Jazz

Blues Alley. At the rear of 1073 Wisconsin Ave., N.W.; 337–4141. It's finally official: Blues Alley, long regarded as one of the premier jazz clubs in the country, is now a bonafide street—or rather alley—in Georgetown. Come here expecting to encounter the likes of Mel Torme, Shirley Horn, Dexter Gordon, and Stephan Grappelli. The crowd packing the 140 seats runs the gamut from Georgetown University students to diplomats. There are Friday and Saturday shows—8:30 P.M., 10:30 P.M. and 12:15 A.M.—and cover charges vary from $10 to $30. Reservations are a must, and those eating dinner (the flavor runs heavily to Creole cooking) get preferential seating. There is a one-drink minimum. Open every night 7 P.M.–2 A.M. AE, CB, DC, MC, V.

Garden Terrace Lounge. In the J. W. Marriott Hotel, 14th and Pennsylvania Ave., N.W.; 393–2000. A plush Japanese garden setting—with trees, marble-top tables, and colorful Oriental artifacts—serves as the backdrop for some fine music. A pianist entertains daily from 4:30 P.M. to 8:30 P.M. While the focus is on contemporary jazz, there's also a sprinkling of traditional sounds, and the dance floor can get to hopping. Most of the crowd is rather conservatively dressed with jacket and tie for the men the norm, but a few hotel guests in slacks and even shorts wander in from time to time. AE, CB, DC, MC, V.

Henry Africa's. 607 King St., Old Town Alexandria, Va.; 549–4010. Despite its name, don't expect to see masks and spears decorating the walls of this supper club. Instead, the food is French, the atmosphere sophisticated, and the jazz some of the best around. Lunch is served Tuesday–Saturday, 11:30 A.M.–2:30 P.M.; dinner, 6–10:30 P.M. Tuesday–Thursday, until 11 P.M. Friday and Saturday. On Sunday, there's brunch, 11 A.M.–3 P.M.; dinner, 5:30–9:30 P.M. No cover is charged to listen to combos turn out sounds as classy and cool as the setting. The crowd is largely in their thirties and forties; men are required to wear a jacket. AE, CB, DC, MC, V.

Mr. Henry's Adams Morgan. 1836 Columbia Rd., N.W.; 797–8882. The last, and best, of several saloons operated by popular Henry Yaffe since 1966. Regulars from the Adams Morgan neighborhood cheer on local favorite Julia Nixon. After flirting with Broadway in *Dream Girls,* she returned home to belt out a combination of jazz and gospel. Some nights, popular jazz musicians perform. There's a $7.50 cover charge Friday and Saturday for each of two shows (9:30 P.M. and 11 P.M.) by Julia and Company. Tuesday and Wednesday nights are open mike for local musicians. DC, MC, V.

One Step Down. 2517 Pennsylvania Ave., N.W.; 331–8863. Located between downtown and Georgetown, this small, friendly and determinedly low-key jazz spot continues to attract groups like the Pepper Adams Quartet and other local and out-of-town talents. There are no reservations, so be sure to come early. Cover $8 Friday-Saturday; $5 the rest of the week. Three sets nightly beginning at 10 P.M. When the live performances stop, there is an all-jazz jukebox to fill in the gaps. Light menu of burgers, pizzas, deli sandwiches, and salads. AE, CB, DC, MC, V.

219's Basin Street Lounge. 219 King St., Alexandria, Va.; 549–1141. One of the most popular nightclubs in Old Town, featuring live entertainment every night by some of the area's best jazz trios and quartets. There is a $1–$2 cover during performances, which is similar to the charge down the street at the 219's sister restaurant, the Wharf (119 King St.; 549–1141). The nightly bands in the Wharf's darker and more intimate Quarterdeck Lounge lean more toward rock and pop. AE, MC, V.

Cabaret/Piano Bars

Fairfax Piano Bar. 2100 Massachusetts Ave., N.W.; 293–2100. Located in the elegant Ritz-Carlton Hotel, the Fairfax is an extremely attractive, cozy lounge with one of the most popular piano bars in Washington. Locals come to hear top-name pianists and area favorites play jazz and contemporary tunes Tuesday–Saturday evenings. Music runs from around 9:30 P.M. to 1 A.M., and the lounge draws a well-dressed group in their 30s to 50s. Jackets requested. No cover or drink minimum. There is a light menu available after 11 P.M. AE, CB, DC, MC, V.

Marquee Lounge. In the Shoreham Hotel, 2500 Calvert St., N.W.; 234–0700. Mrs. Foggybottom and Friends present satirical songs and skits, Thursday through Saturday at this Deco nightclub. Funny lady Joan

Cushing provides the mirth at the expense of well-known Washingtonians. $16 cover Thursdays, $19 weekends; no minimum. AE, CB, DC, MC, V.

Four Seasons Garden Terrace. (The Four Seasons Hotel in back of lobby). 2800 Pennsylvania Ave., N.W.; 342–0444. The piano bar and the setting overlooking Rock Creek Park on the edge of Georgetown draw Washingtonians and visitors alike to the lounge of this handsome hotel. Louis Sherr plays piano 4:30 P.M.–12:30 A.M.; Tuesday, Wednesday, and Thursday, 4 P.M.–12:30 A.M.; and Sherr and Dennis Kaspar take turns at the piano Friday, 4 P.M.–1:30 A.M.; Saturday, 10–1:30 A.M.; and Sunday, 3 P.M.–12:30 A.M. Light Continental fare is served—open-faced sandwiches, cold cheese and meat platters, and French pastries. No cover or drink minimum. And there's champagne by the glass. Most of the patrons are elegantly dressed. AE, CB, DC, MC, V.

Rock 'n Roll/Rhythm & Blues

The Bayou. 3135 K St., N.W.; 333–2897. Located under the Whitehurst Freeway at the foot of Georgetown, the Bayou attracts an 18- to 30-year-old clientele by booking such diverse local and national performers as John Prine, Hall & Oates, Graham Parker, Steve Goodman, and Southside Johnny. Cover charge varies from $2 to $10 depending on the entertainment. There are no reservations, so arrive before 9 P.M. when the action picks up. There's room to dance. The dress is casual, and sandwiches and pizza are served. No credit cards.

Roxy. 1214 18th St., N.W., at Connecticut Ave.; 296–9292. National acts, often with a country-rock or sixties flavor; some local bands; and a lot of reggae. Call for schedules and cover. Live music three to four nights a week. $6 cover weekends. AE, MC, V.

Bluegrass

Birchmere. 3901 Mt. Vernon Ave., Alexandria, Va.; 549–5919. An unassuming shopping center off an Alexandria side street houses what is unquestionably the best folk, and acoustic music club in the Washington area. The management consistently books some of the finest performers in the business—The Country Gentlemen, Arlo Guthrie, Tony Rice, and the D.C. area's own Jonathan Edwards and Thursday night regulars the Seldom Scene. Unlike some of the rowdy bars of this genre, the Birchmere draws an attentive group of young, casually dressed fans who take the music seriously. Acts run from 9 P.M. until 12 or 1 A.M. Cover ranges from $6 to $14, no drink minimum. Beer only, plus hot sandwich menu. No credit cards. Closed most Sundays and Mondays.

Avant-Garde/New Wave

Cities. 2424 18th St., N.W.; 328–7194. A chic restaurant in urban-renewed Adams Morgan decorated as a picturesque urban ruin, with a busy bar and dancing in the upstairs lounge Wednesday–Saturday, 10 P.M.–the wee hours. Cover is $7 weekends, $5 weekdays. AE, DC, MC, V.

Dakota. 1777 Columbia Rd., N.W.; 265–6600. Another trendy Adams Morgan addition to the night scene. Dinner and dancing with videos, light show, and a mix of young and not-so-young. Slick and sophisticated.

Music begins at 9:30 P.M. Tuesday–Sunday. Weekend cover is $7; Thursday $4; no cover Tuesday and Wednesday. AE, MC, V.

d.c. space. 443 7th St., N.W.; 347–4960. This avant-garde restaurant-cum-nightspot is a showcase for national as well as local entertainment. On Thursday, Friday, and Saturday nights there is a dinner theater with music afterwards, which may run from jazz to reggae to punk rock. Recitals, poetry readings, and art shows are scheduled on a random basis. As might be expected, the mix of patrons is eclectic—from bureaucrats and artists who work in the neighborhood to young rockers. The kitchen serves an innovative selection of light fare from chili to plum tarts. Cover ranges from $5 to $8 for musical entertainment. Music usually starts at 10 P.M. Theater tickets are $5–$8.50, with a food minimum of $5. AE, MC, V.

East Side. 1824 Half St. S.W.; 488–1205. East Side's recent new ownership has turned the place into a cavernous spot where all are welcome to linger, preferably in fashionable new duds, and to dance beneath a state-of-the-art laser lightshow downstairs, or upstairs in front of a large stage, populated most weekends by local and some nationally known new-music bands. Cover ranges from $5 to $10. Open Thursday–Sunday only. No credit cards.

Fifth Column. 915 F St., N.W.; 393–3632. An arty, upscale disco in a renovated bank with a huge dance floor and changing art installations. Open Wednesday–Saturday; $7 admission on weekends. AE, MC, V.

Nightclub 9:30. 930 F St., N.W.; 393–0930. Modeled after the New York punk clubs, 9:30 is located in the old downtown section that's become an arts center of sorts. The young patrons—who turn out in green mohawks, leather mini's, and high-top sneakers—drink and slam-dance to the frenetic beat of new-wave tapes while a screen over the bar shows clips of crowds, strippers, and other assorted non-sequitur footage. The club books nationally known live acts several nights a week. Covers range from $5 to $11. Though Nightclub 9:30 is not the place for three-piece business suits, many non-New Wave fans drop in to watch the goings-on. The action picks up around midnight. Light sandwich and pizza menu served. No credit cards.

River Club. 3223 K St., N.W.; 333–8118. The new in-place for Washington high-flyers and visiting celebrities. In Georgetown, it's a glitzy art-deco restaurant with a small dance floor—the perfect place to dress up à la Ginger Rogers, sip champagne, and kick up your heels to big band music. Music starts at 9 nightly. No cover. AE, CB, DC, MC, V.

Comedy

Comedy Café. 1520 K St., 638–5112. Located above an exotic dance emporium, Comedy Café is the city's most centrally located comedy club. Thursday is Open Mike night when aspiring comedians can try out their acts; cover is $3.49. On Friday, three comedians take the stage for two shows, at 8:30 P.M. and 10:30 P.M.; Saturday there are three shows at 7:30, 9:30 and 11:30 P.M. There is a $7 cover on weekends, and dinner specials are available at $14.95, including the show. Casually dressed young crowd. Closed Sundays. AE, DC, MC, V.

Garvin's Comedy Club. L St. between 13th and 14th Sts. N.W.; 726–1334. Up-and-coming comedians try to make you laugh Friday at 8:30 and 10:30 P.M.; Saturday at 7:30, 9:30, and 11:30 P.M. Tuesday is open mike, Wednesday is improvisation, and Thursday it's local joke-els. Cover on weekends is $7. AE, MC, V.

Special Places

The Astor. 1813 M St., N.W.; 331–7994. Located in the heart of the downtown business district, this Greek restaurant and nightspot features the best belly dancers and bouzouki bands in town. Performances start at 8:30 P.M. upstairs and run until 2 A.M. There is no cover, and food is served in the performance area until 1:30 A.M. The Greek entrees and appetizers are good and reasonably priced, making the Astor one of the city's best bargains. AE, CB, DC, MC, V.

Brickskeller. 1523 22nd St., N.W.; 293–1885. Quite simply, the Brickskeller is a beer lover's paradise: The bar stocks over 500 varieties of domestic and imported beers, ales and lagers, and the accommodating bartender will even open cans on the bottom for beer-can collectors. Upstairs, a game room with dart lanes and video games plus a jukebox provides diversion from all the suds. Basic pub fare is served. Dress is casual. AE, CB, DC, MC, V.

Kramer Books & Afterwords Café. 1517 Connecticut Ave., N.W.; 387–1462. A very popular neighborhood hangout, this unusual Dupont Circle bookstore offers food, drink, and weekend entertainment. You can browse through the front stacks for an interesting title, then take your purchase to the rear of the store where a dining area, bar, and outdoor café offer exotic bar concoctions and a limited menu in addition to espresso and cappucino. Live music Thursday–Saturday. The casually dressed patrons tend toward the 25- to 35-age group, with young, artsy professionals mixing with foreign visitors. AE, MC, V.

WINE BARS. La Colline. 400 North Capitol St., N.W.; 737–0400. $2.75–$3.50 a glass. Open Monday–Friday, 11:30 A.M.–10 P.M.; Saturday, 6–10 P.M. AE, CB, DC, MC, V.

Flutes. 1025 Thomas Jefferson St., N.W.; 333–7333. A plush, romantic nightspot in Georgetown, more properly called a champagne bar; there's champagne by the glass or bottle from a selection of 110 brands of bubbly. Contemporary jazz and light rock set the rhythm on the intimate dance floor. Open 5 P.M. till 2 A.M. weeknights; till 3 A.M. weekends. AE, CB, DC, MC, V.

Suzanne's. 1735 Connecticut Ave., N.W.; 483–4633. $2.75–$4.75 a glass. Open Monday–Thursday, 11:30 A.M.–11 P.M.; Friday and Saturday, 11:30–1 A.M.; closed Sunday. MC, V.

INDEX

Index

Adas Israel Synagogue, 148
Adventure Theater, 137
AFL-CIO headquarters, 51
Agriculture, Department of, 69
Air & Space Museum. *See*
    National Air & Space
    Museum
Air travel. *See* Planes
Alexandria, 81, 83, 84–88, 147
    hotels, 100
    map, 86
    restaurants, 100
    seasonal events, 130
    transportation to & in, 127
American Chemical Society
    (building of), 51
American Film Institute, 160
American Film Institute of
    Architects, 70–71
American Red Cross Building,
    70
Anderson House. *See* Society
    of the Cincinnati
Aquariums, 135
Arboretum, 128, 132
Architectural styles, 146–147
Arena Stage, 18, 162
Arlington, 88–89
    hotels, 100–101
    map, 82
    restaurants, 100–101

seasonal events, 130
    transportation to & in, 127
Arlington Children's Theater,
    138
Arlington House, 60, 88, 146,
    156–157
Arlington Memorial Bridge, 60
Arlington National Cemetery,
    60, 81, 88–89, 129, 141
Art galleries. *See* Galleries
Arts and Industries Building,
    18, 68, 153
Atheneum Gallery (Alexandria),
    87
Automobiles. *See* Car travel
Avant-Garde/New Wave Music,
    179–180

Ballet, 18
Baltimore-Washington
    International Airport, 4
Band concerts, 162
Barney Studio House, 156
Bars. *See* Nightlife
Bartholdi Fountain, 67
Baseball, 9
Basketball, 9, 141
Bed and breakfast, 7
Bethesda
    hotels, 103
Bicycle rentals, 140

Blair House, 62, 156
Bluegrass music, 179
B'nai B'rith Museum, 132, 150
Boats, 140
    children and, 137
    cruises, 125
    Mount Vernon, 83
    rentals, 140
Bodisco House, 74
Bolivar, Simon, statue of, 70
Botanic Gardens, 67, 128, 132
"Bridges of Sighs," 69
British Embassy, 75
British visitors, 2
Budget tips, 2
Buffalo Bridge, 75
Bureau of Engraving and
    Printing, 69, 131
    children and, 133
Business hours, 8
Bus travel
    in Washington, 125, 127
    to Washington, 4
    tipping, 8

Cabaret/Piano Bars, 178–179
Cabin John Regional Park, 138
Camping, 7–8
Canal Square, 74
Capital Children's Museum,
    135, 150
Capitol, 22, 28–30, 64–66, 141–142
    bars on, 175–176
    children and, 134
Capitol Hill, 16–17, 64–67,
    141–142, 147
Captain's Row (Alexandria), 87
Carlyle House, 84
Carter Barron Amphitheatre,
    129, 162
Car travel, 5
    in Washington, 125
    to Washington, 5
    parking, hotels and motels,
    5–6
    rentals, 5

"Castle," The (Smithsonian
    Institution), 68, 156
Cemeteries, 149
    Arlington National Cemetery
Central Intelligence Agency,
    80–81
Chamber of Commerce, U.S.
    (building of), 62
Cherry Blossom Festival, 60,
    128
Chesapeake & Ohio (C&O)
    Canal, 71, 72, 74, 140
    Clipper, 137
Chevy Chase, shopping in,
    171–172
Children's activities, 133–139
    in Maryland, Virginia,
    137–139
    monuments, 133–134
    museums, 134–136
Christ Church (Alexandria), 85
Christmas events, 130
Churches (notable), 147–149
Climate (weather), 3–4
Claude Moore Colonial Farm,
    138
Columbia Island, 81
Colvin Run Mill Park, 90
Comedy shows, 180–181
Commerce Department
    Building, 62
Comsat, 68
Confederate Monument, 81
Constitution, the, 63, 144
Constitution Gardens, 56, 60
Constitution Hall, 70, 161
Corcoran Gallery of Art, 70,
    150
    concerts in, 70, 161
Costs, 2
Cox Row, 74, 146
Cricket, 141
Crystal City, 81
Custis-Lee Mansion. *See*
    Arlington House
Custom House, 72

Daughters of the American
Revolution (D.A.R)
(headquarters), 70
concerts in, 161
museum, 150
Children's Attic, 136
Decatur House, 62, 157
Declaration of Independence,
63, 144
District Building, 62
District of Columbia War
Memorial, 56
Dodge Center, 74
Doll's House and Toy Museum
of Washington, 136
Douglass, Frederick, House,
157
Drinking laws, 9
Dulany House (Alexandria), 87
Dulles International Airport, 80,
146
hotels, 102
Dumbarton House, 72, 75, 157
Dumbarton Oaks, 72, 75, 128,
150, 157
Gardens, 132
Dupont Circle, 76

East Potomac Park, 60, 140
Education Department, 67
Embassy Row, 75–76
Emergencies, 11
Energy, Department of. *See*
Forrestal Building
Engraving and Printing, Bureau
of, 69, 131
children and, 133
Entertainment
movie houses, 159–160
music, 160–162
nightlife, 172–173
sports, 140–141
theater, 162–163
Evermay (house), 75
Executive Office Building, 69,
146

Facts and figures, 1
Fairfax, Lord (house of), 85
Federal Trade Commission
(building of), 63
Federal Triangle, 35, 63, 77–78
map, 61
First Baptist Church, 148
"Flounders" (Alexandria
houses), 87
Foggy Bottom, 71
Folger Shakespeare Library, 66,
147
Folger Theater Group, 162
Football, 9, 129, 140–141
Ford's Theater, 142, 163
Forrestal Building, 68
Fort Belvoir, 91
Fort Hunt, 83
Fort Stevens, 33, 38
Fort Washington, 137
Foundry, The, 74
Franciscan Monastery and
Gardens, 148
Freer Gallery of Art, 18, 68, 153
Free events, 130
"Friendship" (house), 74
"Friendship" Fire Company
(Alexandria), 87
Friends Meeting House, 148

Gadsby's Tavern (museum and
restaurant), 85
Galleries, 75–76, 149–156. *See
also specific galleries*
commercial, 169–170
Gardens, 132–133. *See also
specific gardens*
Gay nightlife, 177
Gentry's Row (Alexandria), 87
Georgetown, 37, 71–75, 147
map, 73
movie houses, 159–160
nightlife, 174–175
shopping, 165–166
Georgetown Park, 74
Georgetown University, 74

Glen Echo Park, 140
Golf, 140
Government, 21–26
Grace Reform Church, 148
Grant Memorial, 64
Great Falls of the Potomac, 90, 137
Greek Embassy, 75
Gulf Branch Nature Center, 138
Gunston Hall, 84, 146, 147, 157–158

Hains Point, 60, 128, 139–140
Handicapped travelers, 9–10
Hartke Theater, 163
Hay-Adams Hotel, 51, 94
Health and Human Services Department, 19, 67
H.E.W. Building, 67
Hillwood (estate & gardens), 133
Hirshhorn, Joseph, H., Museum and Sculpture Garden, 18, 67, 153–154
Historic homes, 156–159. *See also specific homes*
Historic sites, 141–146. *See also specific sites*
History, 27–39
Hockey, 9
Holidays, 8–9, 128–130
Hoover, J. Edgar, F.B.I. Building, 63, 77, 142
Horizons Theater, 163
Horseback riding, 140
Horse-racing, 130, 141
Hotels and motels, 5–7, 93–103
  categories of, 93
  costs and, 93
  shops in, 170–171
  tipping and, 8
Hours of business, 8–9
House Office Buildings, 22–23, 66
House of the Americas, 70, 146

Ice hockey, 141

Ice-skating, 140
Information sources, 1–2, 51, 127–128
  Alexandria, 84
Interior Department Building, 70
  Museum, 70, 151
Internal Revenue Service (building of), 63
International Visitors Information Service (IVIS), 127
Introduction to Washington, 15–20
Irish Embassy, 75
Irish pubs, 176–177
Islamic Mosque and Cultural Center, 75, 146, 149

Jackson, Andrew, statue of, 50
Jackson Place, 60, 62
Jamestown (Virginia), 91
Japanese Chancery, 75
Jazz, 177–178
Jefferson Memorial, 60, 129, 143
  children and, 134
Jogging, 9
Johnson, Lady Bird, Park, 81
Johnson, Lyndon B. (memorial), 81
Jones, John Paul, (statue of), 56
Justice Department (building of), 63

Kenilworth Aquatic Gardens, 132
Kennedy, John F., Center for the Performing Arts, 18, 38, 76, 129, 144, 146, 160
Kenyan Embassy, 75
Korean Embassy, 75
Kreeger Theater, 162

Labor Department (building of), 63
Lafayette House (Alexandria), 87

Lafayette Square (Lafayette
    Park), 50, 60, 69, 147
Lee House, 156
Lee-Fendall House, 85
Lee, Robert E., boyhood home,
    85
Leesburg, 90
L'Enfant Plaza, 68–69, 130
Libraries, 147
Library of Congress, 19, 66,
    143, 146, 147
  concerts at, 161
Life-styles, 40–45
Lincoln Memorial, 56, 60, 128,
    143–144, 146
  children and, 134
Lisner Auditorium, 71
Lloyd House, 85, 146
London Brass Rubbing Center,
    136
Lyceum (Alexandria), 87

Mall, the, 56
Manassas National Battlefield
    Park, 91
Maps and plans
  Alexandria, 86
  Arlington area, 82
  Federal Triangle, 61
  Georgetown, 73
  Mall/Capitol Hill area, 61
  Metro subway, 126
  Washington, D.C. area, viii–ix
  Washington, D.C. city plan,
    52–53, 57–58
Marine Corps War Memorial
    (Iwo Jima Memorial), 89,
    129, 142–143
Maryland
  children's activities, 137–138
  hotels and restaurants,
    103–104
Mason Neck Wildlife Refuge, 84
Masonic National Memorial,
    George Washington, 81, 88,
    149
Memorial Continental Hall, 70

Metro Center, 76–77
Metropolitan African Methodist
    Episcopal Church, 148
Metro subway (Metrorail), 50,
    51, 76–77, 127
  children and, 136
  map, 126
Military Bands, 129
Monuments, 57–78. *See also*
    specific monuments
  children and, 133–134
Morven Park, 90
Mosque and Islamic Center, 75,
    146, 149
Mount Vernon, 83–84, 128, 147,
    158–159
Movies, 159–160
M Street, 71
Murder Bay, 78
Museum of American History.
    See National Museum of
    American History
Museum of History and
    Technology. *See* National
    Museum of American
    History
Museum of Modern Art of
    Latin America, 70
Museum of Natural History, 18,
    63, 155
  children and, 134, 135
Museums, 63–64, 75–76,
    149–156
  for children, 134–136
  shops in, 167–169
Music, 160–162. *See also*
    Nightlife

National Aeronautics and Space
    Administration Buildings,
    67
National Air and Space
    Museum, 18, 67, 129, 154
  children and, 134
National Aquarium, 135
National Arboretum, 128, 132
National Archives, 63, 144

National Building Museum
(Pension Bldg.), 131, 151
National Cathedral, 129, 146,
147
shopping, 170
National Collection of Fine
Arts. *See* National Museum
of American Art
National Colonial Farm, 138
National Covenant Presbyterian
Church, 148
National Education Association
(building of), 51
National Fine Arts Associates,
130
National Gallery of Art, 18,
63–64, 146, 151–152
children and, 134
concerts at, 161
National Geographic Society,
51, 130, 146
children and, 136
National Housing Center, 131
National Institute of Health, 19
National Museum. *See* Museum
of Natural History
National Museum of African
Art, 18, 68, 154
children and, 135
National Museum of American
Art (National Collection of
Fine Arts), 63, 154
National Museum of American
History, 18, 63, 154
children and, 135
National Museum of Women in
the Arts, 152
National Park Service, 127
National Portrait Gallery, 63,
154
National Rifle Association, 131
National Shrine of the
Immaculate Conception,
147–148
National Symphony Orchestra,
161

National Theater, 162
National Zoological Park (Zoo),
68, 139
Nature Center, 139
Naval Observatory, 75, 131–132
Navy and Marine Memorial, 81
Navy Memorial Museum, 131
children at, 135–136
Navy Yard, 129, 135–136
Netherlands Carillon Tower, 89,
129
Nightlife, 172–181
19th Street "Corridor" (bars),
173–174

Oak Hill Cemetery, 75–149
Oatlands Estate, 90
Octagon House, 70, 152
Old Presbyterian Meeting
House (Alexandria), 87
Old Stone House, 72, 158
Old Vat Room, 162
Olney Theater, 163
Opera Society of Washington,
161
Organization of American
States, 70, 132
Oxon Hill Farm, 138

Package tours
tipping and, 8
Paddle boats, 137, 140
Pan American Union Building.
See House of Americas
Parking. *See* Car travel
Parks, 139–140. *See also*
specific parks
Peirce Mill, 139
Pennsylvania Avenue, 77–78
Pentagon, 89
Pershing Square, 77
Petersen House, 142
Philatelic Sales Center, 68
Phillips Collection, 18, 75–76,
152–153
concerts at, 161

Places of worship, 147–149
Planes
children and, 136
to Washington, 4
Planetarium, 139
Pohick Church, 84
Polo, 9, 141
Pope-Leighey House, 84
Population, 1, 16
Postal Service, U.S., 69
Post, Merriweather, Pavilion,
129, 162
Post Office Department
Buildings, 62–63
Potomac River, 1, 69, 76
tours, 136
Prospect House, 74

Quality Hill, 74
Quantico, 91

Railroads. *See* Trains
Ramsay, William, House, 84
Rawlins Square, 70–71
Rayburn, Sam, House Office
Building, 22, 66
Reading list, 11
Red Cross Museum, 70
Reflecting Pool, 56
Religious sites, 147–149
Renwick Chapel, 75, 149
Renwick Gallery, 62, 155–156
Restaurants, 103–124
Afghan, 104–105
American International,
105–108
Austrian, 114
British, 108
cafeterias, 108–109
categories of, 103–104
Chinese, 109–110
Continental, 111
costs and, 104
Ethiopian, 111
Filipino, 112
French, 112–114

German, 114
Greek, 114–115
Hungarian, 115
Indian-Pakistani-Nepalese,
115–116
Italian, 116–117
Japanese, 117–118
Latin American, 118
Mexican, 118–119
Middle Eastern, 114–115
pizza, 119
Polynesian, 112
seafood, 119–121
Spanish, 121
steak houses, 121–122
Swiss, 122
Thai, 122–123
tipping and, 8
vegetarian, 123
Vietnamese-Asian, 123
for view, 124
Reston, 80
Roaches Run Sanctuary, 82
Rock and Blues music, 179
Rock Creek Cemetery, 149
Rock Creek Park, 75, 76, 139
children and, 139
Romanian Embassy, 75
Roosevelt, Theodore, Island,
80, 139
Rosslyn, 80
Row of Four Houses, 74

Sackler, Arthur M., Gallery, 68,
156
children and, 135
St. John's Church (Church of
the Presidents), 51, 148
St. John's Episcopal Church,
74, 148
St. Matthew's Cathedral, 76,
148
St. Paul's Church, 149
Scott-Grant House, 74–75
Scottish Rite Temple, 149
Sculpture Garden Rink, 140

Seasonal events, 4, 128–130.
See also specific events
Alexandria & Arlington, 130
Security, 10
Senate office buildings, 22
Senior citizens, discounts for, 8
Shenandoah Mountains, 91
Sheridan Circle, 75
Shopping, 163–172
in Chevy Chase, 171–172
choice, out-of-the-way shops,
170
commercial galleries, 169
downtown F Street, 163–164
in Georgetown, 165–167
hotel shops, 170–171
on Lower Connecticut
Avenue, 164–165
museum shops, 167–169
sidewalk stands, 171
Silver Spring
hotels, 103
Smithsonian Institution, 18, 19,
67–68, 129, 146, 153–156
children and, 134–135
concerts at, 162
Society of Colonial Dames of
America Headquarters, 72
Society of the Cincinnati, 158
Source Theater, 163
Soviet Embassy, 51
Special nightspots, 181
Spirit of Mount Vernon (ship),
83
Spirit of Washington (ship), 125,
137
Sports, 9, 140–141
Stabler-Leadbeater Apothecary
Shop, (Alexandria), 87
State Department Building, 71
Diplomatic Reception Rooms,
131
Statuary Hall (Capitol), 65
Students, discounts for, 8
Studio House. *See* Barney
Studio House
Subway. *See* Metro subway

Supreme Court, 24, 66–67,
144–145, 146
Sylvan Theater, 56, 129, 163

Taxis, 125
tipping and, 8
Telephone Service, 10–11
emergency, 11
Tennis, 9, 141
Textile Museum, 153
Theater, 162–163. *See also
specific theaters*
Theatre Guide, 128
Tidal Basin, 60, 128, 137, 140
Time, local, 8
Tipping, 8
Tomb of the Unknowns, 88–89,
129
Tomb of the Unknown Soldier
of the American
Revolution, 87
Torpedo Factory, 85
Tourist information services,
1–2, 51, 127–128
Alexandria, 84
Tourmobile, 125
Tours, 130–131
House, Garden and Embassy,
129
Mount Vernon, 83–84
special interest, 131–132
Towpath Row, 74
Trailers, 7
Trains (railroads)
to Washington, 4
tipping and, 8
Transportation. *See also
specific types*
tipping and, 8
in Washington, 124–125, 127
to Washington, 4–5
Transportation, Department of,
67
Traveler's checks, 10
Treasury Building, 62
Trolley Museum, 137
Turkish Embassy, 75

Tyson's Corner, 90
  hotels, 102

Union Station, 64, 146
University Club, 51

Veterans Administration
    (building of), 51
Vietnam Veterans Memorial, 56,
    60, 145
Virginia, 79–92
  children's activities, 138–139
  hotels, 100–102
  restaurants, 100–102
Virginia Beach, 91
Voice of America, 67, 131

Warner Theater, 162
Washington, George, home of.
    See also Mount Vernon
  town house (Alexandria), 85
Washington Cathedral. *See*
    National Cathedral
Washington Circle, 71
Washington, D.C., Convention
    and Visitors Association,
    51, 127, 128
Washington, D.C., Convention
    Center, 77
Washington, D.C., maps
  area, vii–ix
  downtown, 52–53
  orientation, 57–58
Washingtonian, (magazine), 19,
    72, 128
Washington (George) Masonic
    National Memorial, 82, 88,
    149
Washington (George) Memorial
    Parkway, 80–81
Washington Monument, 55–56,
    128, 129, 145, 146
  children and, 133
Washington National Airport,
    81
  children and, 136
Washington Performing Arts
    Society, 161
Washington Post, 127
Washington Temple of the
    Church of Latter-Day
    Saints, 149
Washington Times, 127
Washington (George)
    University, 71
Washington Visitor Information
    Center, 127
Watergate Complex, 76
Weather (climate), 3–4
Western Plaza, 77
West Potomac Park, 60
White House, 24, 28, 51, 54–55,
    145–146
  children and, 134
Willard Hotel, 77
Williamsburg (Virginia), 91
Wilson, Woodrow, House, 158
Wine bars, 181
Wisconsin Avenue, 74
  shopping, 166–167
Wolf Trap Farm Park for the
    Performing Arts, 18, 80,
    129, 161–162
  children and, 138–139
Woodlawn Plantation, 84, 138,
    146, 159
Wooly Mammoth Theater, 163

Yorktown (Virginia), 91
Youth hostels, 7

Zoo, 68, 139

Fodor's Travel Guides

U.S. Guides

Alaska
American Cities
The American South
Arizona
Atlantic City & the
  New Jersey Shore
Boston
California
Cape Cod
Carolinas & the
  Georgia Coast
Chesapeake
Chicago
Colorado
Dallas & Fort Worth
Disney World & the
  Orlando Area

The Far West
Florida
Greater Miami,
  Fort Lauderdale,
  Palm Beach
Hawaii
Hawaii (Great Travel
  Values)
Houston & Galveston
I-10: California to
  Florida
I-55: Chicago to New
  Orleans
I-75: Michigan to
  Florida
I-80: San Francisco to
  New York

I-95: Maine to Miami
Las Vegas
Los Angeles, Orange
  County, Palm Springs
Maui
New England
New Mexico
New Orleans
New Orleans (Pocket
  Guide)
New York City
New York City (Pocket
  Guide)
New York State
Pacific North Coast
Philadelphia
Puerto Rico (Fun in)

Rockies
San Diego
San Francisco
San Francisco (Pocket
  Guide)
Texas
United States of
  America
Virgin Islands
  (U.S. & British)
Virginia
Waikiki
Washington, DC
Williamsburg,
  Jamestown &
  Yorktown

Foreign Guides

Acapulco
Amsterdam
Australia, New Zealand
  & the South Pacific
Austria
The Bahamas
The Bahamas (Pocket
  Guide)
Barbados (Fun in)
Beijing, Guangzhou &
  Shanghai
Belgium & Luxembourg
Bermuda
Brazil
Britain (Great Travel
  Values)
Canada
Canada (Great Travel
  Values)
Canada's Maritime
  Provinces
Cancún, Cozumel,
  Mérida, The
  Yucatán
Caribbean
Caribbean (Great
  Travel Values)

Central America
Copenhagen,
  Stockholm, Oslo,
  Helsinki, Reykjavik
Eastern Europe
Egypt
Europe
Europe (Budget)
Florence & Venice
France
France (Great Travel
  Values)
Germany
Germany (Great Travel
  Values)
Great Britain
Greece
Holland
Hong Kong & Macau
Hungary
India
Ireland
Israel
Italy
Italy (Great Travel
  Values)
Jamaica (Fun in)

Japan
Japan (Great Travel
  Values)
Jordan & the Holy Land
Kenya
Korea
Lisbon
Loire Valley
London
London (Pocket Guide)
London (Great Travel
  Values)
Madrid
Mexico
Mexico (Great Travel
  Values)
Mexico City & Acapulco
Mexico's Baja & Puerto
  Vallarta, Mazatlán,
  Manzanillo, Copper
  Canyon
Montreal
Munich
New Zealand
North Africa
Paris
Paris (Pocket Guide)

People's Republic of
  China
Portugal
Province of Quebec
Rio de Janeiro
The Riviera (Fun on)
Rome
St. Martin/St. Maarten
Scandinavia
Scotland
Singapore
South America
South Pacific
Southeast Asia
Soviet Union
Spain
Spain (Great Travel
  Values)
Sweden
Switzerland
Sydney
Tokyo
Toronto
Turkey
Vienna
Yugoslavia

Special-Interest Guides

Bed & Breakfast
  Guide: North America
  1936...On the
  Continent

Royalty Watching
Selected Hotels of
  Europe

Selected Resorts
  and Hotels of the U.S.
Ski Resorts of North
  America

Views to Dine by
  around the World